CULTURE & TACTICS

SUNY SERIES, PRAXIS: THEORY IN ACTION

Nancy A. Naples, editor

CULTURE

& TACTICS

Gramsci, Race,
and the Politics of Practice

Robert F. Carley

SUNY
PRESS

Published by State University of New York Press, Albany

For information, contact State University of New York Press, Albany, NY
www.sunypress.edu

Library of Congress Cataloging-in-Publication Data

Names: Carley, Robert F., 1973- author.
Title: Culture and tactics : Gramsci, race, and the politics of practice /
    Robert F. Carley.
Description: New York : State University of New York Press, [2019] | Series:
    SUNY series, Praxis: theory in action | Includes bibliographical refer-
ences and index.
Identifiers: LCCN 2018053985 | ISBN 9781438476438 (hardcover)
    | ISBN 9781438476445 (e-book) | ISBN 9781438476421 (pbk.) Subjects:
        LCSH: Social movements—Political aspects. | State, The. | Ideology. |
    Race. | Gramsci, Antonio, 1891–1937—Political and social views.
Classification: LCC HM881 .C3657 2019 | DDC 303.48/4—dc23
LC record available at https://lccn.loc.gov/2018053985

10 9 8 7 6 5 4 3 2 1

CONTENTS

ACKNOWLEDGMENTS

A good deal of the impetus for writing this book is connected to the conversations that happened between myself and many others who are often connected to the scholarly meetings that I attended between 2011 and 2018. Many of these conversations, especially in the case of people affiliated with cultural studies, were based on reimagining, rethinking, and disrupting the link between culture and discourse (or rhetoric and communication) when thinking about resistance. My intervention is to think about the connection between culture and protest tactics. Although none of the people mentioned in these acknowledgments bear any responsibility for the limitations of this book, I owe a debt of gratitude, in some cases deep, to the following people and organizations for the following reasons.

To begin, fragments of *Culture and Tactics* were presented at several academic meetings. Principle among these was the Union for Democratic Communications (UDC). My work found its home here and also with some of the Gramsciani from the United States, Canada, the United Kingdom, and Brazil who organized and participated in panels and special seminars at the National Communication Association (NCA), the Cultural Studies Association (CSA), Rethinking Marxism, and the American Association of Geographers Socialist and Critical Geography Knowledge Community or Socialist Geographers Circle, and the International Social Theory Consortium.

At the NCA and in the Union for Democratic Communications, I wish to thank the following people. First, I want to thank the organizers of Revolutionary Voices: Marxism, Communication, and Social Change preconference seminar at the 2011 meeting of the NCA in New Orleans, where I presented portions of what would become the second chapter of this book: Stephen H. Macek, Marco Briziarelli, Dana L. Cloud, Bryan J. McCann, and Mary E. Triece. Special thanks to those who spoke to viii

Acknowledgments

me about my work, critically, at the UDC meetings in Tallahassee, San Francisco, and Detroit, particularly, Steve Macek, Lee Artz, and Deepa Kumar. All have made incisive remarks about my work at crucial moments, which has helped me clarify arguments and positions. Finally, Dana Cloud has made substantially important comments to me at the meeting in San Francisco. Special thanks also go to Michelle Rodino-Colocino and T. C. Corrigan, who made me feel especially welcomed at the UDC meetings and suggested and (in T. C.'s case) nominated me for the organization's steering committee. I admire all of these folks for their scholarship, activism, comradeship, and community. I also have to thank others who have found the time to discuss and support my work at these meetings: John Anderson, Stevie Berberick, Dan Berger, Brian Creech, Stuart Davis, Brian Dolber, Aaron Heresco, Jeffery Masko, Anthony Nadler, Russell Newman, Allessendra Renzi, Rianne Subijanto, John Sullivan, Rich Templin, Doug Tewksbury, and Mary Triece. Finally, I wish to thank Robin Andersen, Matthew Crain, Aimee-Marie Dorsten, Dorothy Kidd, Cristina Mislán, Molly Niesen, Andy Opel, Christine Quail, and Chris Robe. I was pleased to meet and present with Zack Furness, whom I knew from his book *Punkademics* and also from CSA meetings. I'm lucky to have him as a friend, too. In so many ways, this book is a product of my sustained relationship with the UDC and with all of you.

Since the 2013 Cultural Studies Association meetings in Chicago at Columbia College and also at the Rethinking Marxism and American Association of Geographers meetings I've received attention, support, and insight into my work from Marxist scholars and Gramsciani whose work I've read and admired prior to meeting them. I have to begin by thanking Joseph A. Buttigieg, Marcus E. Green, and Joel Wainwright, all of whom have facilitated the presentation of work that has gone into this book, in some form, and who have been kind, generous, and supportive beyond the mere organization and facilitation of panels. In particular, Joseph Buttigieg has made it possible for so many of us to have access to Gramsci in the English language. He's simply a wonderful person and welcoming to so many early career scholars focused on Gramsci. Marcus Green is an extraordinarily sharp and focused scholar of Gramsci. He's already contributed so much to the current wave of Gramsci scholarship. I owe him an enormous debt of gratitude. Other Gramsciani who have been helpful, kind, and supportive are Alessandro Carlucci, Giovanni Pizza, Peter Ives, and Nicola Short. Alessandro, Giovanni, and Peter's work has helped me craft this book. I've received support and am grateful for the work and friendship of Joseph Zompetti. At CSA meetings, I had the good fortune to talk with Julian Ammirante (especially), Antonio Callari, Daniela Mussi, and also S. Charusheela, Peter Hudis, and Azfar Hussain—the latter two I've been acquainted with prior to these meetings. Finally, Bob Jessop was the respondent on the panel at the Geography meeting. His enormous stature as a scholar is met by his enormous capacity for gentleness and generosity in critique. Kate Crehan, who also presented at the Geography meeting, was a joy to meet and speak with, however briefly. I am grateful for her work and am enjoying her latest book.

The following thanks go to my new CSA friends, as well as old friends and colleagues in cultural studies with whom I've had the longest association. I want to begin by thanking Christopher M. Sutch, Sean Johnson Andrews, and Pablo Andrés Castagno with whom I formed close relationships and remain in thrall of their intellectual contributions. I would also like to thank Jaafar Aksikas, Wendy Burns-Ardolino, Katy Razzano, Paul Smith, Eero Laine, Chris Alen Sula, Stefanie A. Jones, Andrew Culp, Ricky Crano, Eric Morales-Franceschini, Christian Quaresma, Don Hedrick, Gilbert B. Rodman, Helen Kapstein, Jodi Davis-Pacheco, Lia Uy-Tioco, Charles Thorpe, and Michelle Fehsenfeld.

I would also like to thank members of the International Social Theory Consortium whom I met at a panel at the joint meeting of the Midwest Sociological Society and the North Central Sociological Association in Chicago in 2016: Lauren Langman, Michael J. Thompson, and Harry F. Dahms. All three are generous and inviting colleagues with whom I have had important conversations in the context of critical theory that have helped to shape how I am thinking about some of the contributions that this book may make. I would also like to kindly thank Devin Lefebvre, Dan Krier, Fred Schiff, James Block, Arnold Farr, and Stefan Gandler.

At Texas A&M University I want to thank the following people from the Department of International Studies for their help and support: Bob Shandley, Stefanie Harris, Nathan Bracher, Maddalena Cerrato, Fabiana Cecchini, Bilge Firat O'Hearn, Ashley Passmore, Dinah Hannaford, and, especially, Jun Lei, and from the Departments of Visualization and Architecture Susanneh Bieber. Finally, I'd like to thank John Eason and Hazal Hürman from the Department of Sociology and Kate Siegfried from the Department of Communication.

I owe a special debt of gratitude to Hilario Molina II, who is one of my dearest friends, a supporter of my work, a collaborator, a great and dedicated scholar, and one of the best humans I have known.

Similarly, John O. Gibbs, another of my dearest friends, has put up with endless hours of me talking to him about this book over coffee and games. He is a sharp mind and a dear friend.

The work in this book began, in earnest, with the writing of my dissertation, although the former bears little resemblance to the latter. Joseph O. Jewell, who chaired my dissertation committee and who saw the value in the project, deserves my deepest thanks. Joseph, in particular, wanted to see much of this work make it into print and he helped me begin to envision this particular book project. He was an invaluable guide, is an excellent scholar, and will never know just how much his intellect and kindness mean to me.

I want to extend this gratitude to the other members of my dissertation committee: Robert Mackin, Sarah N. Gatson, and John J. McDermott. McDermott, too, was insistent about my dissertation turning into a book project. He has provided unconditional moral support and friendship to me.

I also wish to thank Anitra Grisales and the two anonymous reviewers. All provided excellent and concrete suggestions as to how to improve this work.

A special thank-you to Roger N. Lancaster, whom I am lucky to have as a friend, guide, and teacher. Roger has produced some of the best academic writing that I have read and I strive to be at least half as talented as he is. I owe him a debt for his help in crafting my proposal for this book.

Finally, I want to thank my daughters Ayira and Angela Amina for their love, their Magna-tile sessions, and for keeping everything very real. My partner Shona N. Jackson, who is a model of high erudition and exquisite scholarship and my greatest love, deserves all my thanks. I apologize to anyone that I've neglected to thank here.

Publishers Taylor and Francis and John Wiley and Sons granted permission to reprint portions and use content from the following articles in this book: "Ideological Contention: Antonio Gramsci and the Connection Between Race and Social Movement Mobilization in Early Twentieth-Century Italy," *Sociological Focus* 49 (2016): 1, 28–43, DOI: 10.1080/00380237.2015.1065700, reprinted by permission of the North Central Sociological Association, www.ncsanet.org; "Agile Materialisms: Antonio Gramsci, Stuart Hall, Racialization, and Modernity," *Journal of Historical Sociology* 26, no. 4 (December 2013): DOI: 10.1111/johs.12023.

Tactics and Practice

Culture and Tactics focuses on the racial determinants and racialization processes through which Antonio Gramsci was able to mobilize an ethnically, culturally, and linguistically diverse group of workers. It theorizes the role of tactics as a substantive and articulatory form of practice and, in doing so, positions Gramsci as a theorist of race. *Culture and Tactics* links an original organizational and ideological theory of tactical practices to contemporary analyses of race and power in cultural studies and critical race theory. The mediations that produce connections between race, and the tactical practices that are involved in mobilization efforts, give rise to new concepts through which to analyze the intersections of race and power.

The book begins by demonstrating how tactics can be understood more broadly as interventions into social forces. It intercedes into the predominant view of tactical effectiveness in contemporary social science research. In this book, I argue that tactics should and must be considered as more than the means through which specific goals are achieved. In a more expansive and concrete framework, tactics must be viewed as a form of practice. Tactics are what set social movement participants on a path of collective action; they also represent an active declaration of grievances and demands. The tactical, public demonstration of grievances point out injustices to others and, in turn, make just demands. *Tactics are transformative practices*, they convert ideas into actions and, sometimes, actions into broad mobilizations, *and yet, tactics have not been analyzed as a transformative practice. Culture and Tactics* is a work of social, cultural, and political theory that aims to demonstrate how tactics effect movement organizational structures, strategic programs, and political ideologies; it also shows how tactics in turn are affected by them. It demonstrates that regardless of whether a specific goal or set of goals are achieved or whether movements rise or fall, tactical successes are broadly and collectively resonant beyond the movement and its specific purposes. In specific, *Culture and Tactics* interprets, across several historical and contemporary contexts, Gramsci's use of an innovative repertoire of tactics to bridge perceptions of racial differences between factory workers and subaltern groups, the latter denigrated into a position of subhumanity by a complex Italian national racial economy. It discusses the organizational and developmental context in which Gramsci was embedded in order to both understand and develop a tactical framework through which he was able to intervene in and affect the trajectory of society and history during the time that he lived through broad-based mobilizations of racialized groups in a context of class struggle.

In the work that follows, I show that Gramsci consciously mobilized against both class exploitation and racial domination. However, with regard to the latter, Gramsci's legacy as a theorist of race has not been fully taken into account. Through an examination of his efforts to mobilize veterans, peasants, and industrial workers, I demonstrate that Gramsci both understood the racial, national, and pseudoscientific context in which he was engaged in mobilization efforts, and through an analysis of those mobilization efforts, *traces of a racial-theoretical perspective emerge and beg both interpretation and connection to contemporary theoretical frameworks on race, culture, and politics. Culture and Tactics* offers both a substantive set of theoretical perspectives on tactics as a practice (in the framework of political subjectivity, organizational structures, ideology, and collective memory) and an interpretation of Gramsci as a theorist of race, articulating connections between Gramsci's perspectives and contemporary theoretical approaches to race through new concepts. The focal point for this book requires situating tactical practices that articulate twin responses to class exploitation and racial domination in historical, social, cultural, and conceptual contexts. To establish this framework and the methodology it depends upon, it is necessary to briefly review the positioning of the concept of practice as it relates to the concept of culture in the humanities and the social sciences.

Culture and Method

Culture is the mediations between the ideational and concrete; it is a potentially transformative medium and, in turn, a medium that is transformed by its political articulations and societal concretizations. In each of the subsequent chapters, I specify, through analysis, the political direction, intensity, and the role of tactics in both reproducing and transforming cultural forms and social relations. I contextualize specific mediations and derive theoretical and conceptual insights from each of them. These insights pertain, specifically, to social determinations that concretize race and class and, also, the political interventions and mobilizations that upset these determinations to produce social interventions that concretize class struggle and struggles against racial oppression and domination. In order to derive theoretical insights from inquiry into historical events that illustrate the dynamism of these struggles, I rely on two approaches. The first is sociological and the second is a cultural studies approach. I will explain them and how they connect to one another.

However, first, it is important to explain that what is predominant in both approaches is the centrality of theory in cultural studies. It is quite literally textbook to claim, as Barker and Jane (2016) do, that "a significant work in cultural studies is not empirical but theoretical" (42). However, it is important to add that cultural studies approaches are neither crudely empiricist nor purely theoreticist but, rather, recognize that theoretical categories are always already implied in empirical research and that such a recognition needs to be a part of the framework through which a study is approached. A cultural studies approach, then, relies on reflexivity to frame and consider the ways that theories derived from careful scholarship and analysis are, in fact, narratives "with implications for action and judgement about consequences" (Barker and Jane 2016: 42).

It is also, at this juncture, necessary to add that the way in which a significant work in cultural studies is theoretical is not only a product of its reflexivity (which is an ethical injunction that indicates a sensitivity to the positionality of the researcher and to their intervention into the phenomenological webs that constitute our understanding of culture, which might also be shared by cultural anthropologists and sociologists) but, rather, is a product of cultural studies' approach to analysis. A significant work in cultural studies is theoretical to the extent that the analysis of empirical examples, which may be texts, results in a broader transformation of theoretical perspectives, the genesis of theories and concepts that are both appropriate to what is being analyzed and, at the same time, indicate and demonstrate a reorganization of the transdisciplinary theories and concepts that have contributed to what has become over the course of analysis a changed theoretical perspective. Analysis should transform theory; a transformed theory, dependent on analysis, transdisciplinary interpretations, and mediations between these disciplines is precisely what is theoretically significant in a work of cultural studies. Stuart Hall is clear about what these implications, for both ethics and epistemology, mean and how they work. For him, the uses of theory in cultural studies are central to the project in the way that they relate to empirical examples. Responsibility for concepts, quoted as follows, indicates both reflexivity and the process of producing knowledge. Hall states:

> [O]ne can only begin to theorize phenomena by breaking into this apparently seamless phenomenological web . . . with concepts which are clearly formulated and which belong to a theoretical paradigm. One has to take responsibility for the concepts one is generating in relation to that empirical material. Only in that way can one break down the material into forms amenable to proper conceptualization and theorization. (Hall 2016: 112–113)

Reflexivity in cultural studies then requires not only that one cleave to the way that a specific theoretical paradigm is essential to the production of knowledge about phenomena, but also that one take responsibility for how one's study is positioned within the broader theoretical and discursive frameworks that are constitutive of one's meanings. The ethics of a cultural studies approach depend upon recognizing the politics of knowledge and one's participation within it. It also requires generating concepts and theories, the reinterpretation of knowledge and its positioning, and this, in short, is the process that marks a contribution to cultural studies. So, the proper organization of empirical examples, conceptualization, and theorization depends, in this book, on selecting a sociological approach, to demonstrate a transdisciplinary relationship. It must be an approach that is designed in such a way that it incorporates secondary sources—that are both analytical and historiographical—and, also, theoretical frameworks alongside of empirical examples into the theoretical insights that drive the originality and the ethics of developing cultural theories that are—in the case of *Culture and Tactics*—antiracist and anticapitalist.

The sociological method that I rely on in this book is a "limited-depth case study" approach because it simultaneously establishes the centrality of theory to the study and produces the potential for the empirical material that comprises the case study to be generalizable beyond the boundaries of the study (Mills, Durepos, and Wiebe 2010). It is a sociological method that is the best fit with a cultural studies approach. The advantage of this approach is based in its intended design, which is predicated upon the illustration of a new theory by focusing on the relations, processes, and dynamics that are the most important for the determination of analyses and theoretical inquiry. Reinharz explains that limited-depth case studies are designed "to illustrate an idea, to explain the process of development over time . . . to explore uncharted issues . . . and to pose provocative questions" (1992: 167). Broadly situated within other research, by relying on materials "like documentation of events, quotes, samples and artifacts" (Wilson 1979: 448), the limited-depth case study approach provides a means to organize a depth of context in such a way that it is *self-consciously* directed toward what is most significant for analysis and most important to theorization and conceptualization. Mills, Durepos, and Wiebe (2010) describe limited-depth cases as "draw[ing] upon existing analytical accounts of key social processes to illuminate key features of the case." They continue by explaining the sociological impact and contribution that comes from using this method: "On these bases it is possible to envisage that limited-depth but theoretically directed case studies could sometimes meet the criteria for effective case study research" (2010: 531–532). In this way, *Culture and Tactics* is intended as a contribution to the study of society, specifically, to social theory, social movement studies, and critical race theory.

The cultural studies approach that I use in this book is developed from Stuart Hall's discussions of the concept of articulation.[1] I claim that Gramsci's tactics are predicated on the articulation of race to class across various contexts or moments that occur between 1916 and 1925. Positioning race in historical and social contexts and Gramsci's organizational, strategic, and tactical responses to them are the bases for my entire theoretical and conceptual framework in *Culture and Tactics*. The discussion of tactical practices in this book fall within traditions of Marxist theory. Cultural studies' or Hall's interpretation of Marxist theory is, in part, consonant with my approach in *Culture and Tactics* and also a part of the Marxist tradition. In a series of foundational lectures delivered in 1983 at the University of Illinois at Urbana–Champaign entitled "Marxism and the Interpretation of Culture: Limits, Frontiers, Boundaries" and collected in the recently published book *Cultural Studies 1983: A Theoretical History* (2016), Hall states in his concluding lecture, "Lecture 8," that in order for cultural studies to effectively theorize multiple societal contradictions, especially, those pertaining to race, capital, and class struggle:

> The only alternative is a Marxist politics which recognizes the necessary differentiation of different struggles and the importance of those struggles on different fronts, that is to say, a Marxist politics which understands the nature of a hegemonic politics, in which different struggles take the leading position on a range of different fronts. Such an understanding does not suppress the autonomy and specificity of particular political struggles, and it rejects reductionism in favor of an understanding of complexity in unity or unity through complexity. The reality of this complexity is not merely a local problem of organizing but the theoretical problem of the noncorrespondence of the mode of production and the necessary relative autonomy of different political and ideological formations. . . . This is, after all, the site of the emergence of cultural studies . . . (Hall 2016: 185)

The theoretical problematic that cultural studies addresses is precisely related to articulation: determining in an analytically derived and specified conjuncture the strategic connection between the contradictions manifest within the structural organization of capitalist social relations and the autonomy and plurality of struggles that emerge in the space of that contradiction. It is only then that, through identifying articulatory dynamics, a hegemonic project for class struggle and within the framework of resistance to racial domination and oppression might be identified as the democratic impulse for any future politics.

Peter Thomas's groundbreaking philological investigations into the concept of hegemony beginning in *The Gramscian Moment* (2009) and his explicit focus on subaltern groups serve, in this context, to specify the role of subaltern groups as the broader base of progressive elements involved in political struggle. They echo aspects of my positioning of articulation in *Culture and Tactics*. Thomas states:

> Gramsci posed the question of how a hegemonic project could be constructed out of the immense richness of all the different interest

groups—sometimes even conflicting interest groups—that constitute what he came to call the 'subaltern social groups', or popular classes in the broadest sense; that is, all the groups or classes that are oppressed and exploited by the current organization of society. . . . Political actors aiming to build a hegemonic project must continually make propositions, test them in practice, correct and revise them and test their modified theses once again in concrete political struggles. This process results in an ongoing dialectical exchange and interchange between the existing political conjuncture and attempts to transform it, and even more crucially, between leaders of a political movement and those who participate in them. A political project of hegemonic politics thus comes to represent a type of 'pedagogical laboratory' for the development of new forms of democratic and emancipatory political practice. (Thomas 2013: 27)

Gramsci's organizational and mobilization efforts were designed to stretch the boundaries that constituted party cadres and affiliated trade unions by listening to and working directly with subaltern groups that had been excluded or instrumentalized by other political organizations. These organizations had accepted the racial construction of various subaltern groups in the framework of Italian nationalism and politics. *Culture and Tactics* demonstrates the dynamics of racialization, subaltern political participation, and the indefatigable strategic, organizational, and ideological efforts made on the part of Gramsci and others to build political-organizational structures that challenged both racial domination and labor exploitation by focusing on, supporting, and developing the tactical activity and political participation of the subaltern classes. In short, if the central theoretical problematic that cultural studies addresses is precisely related to articulation, *Culture and Tactics* places itself squarely within this problematic; it is a work of cultural studies as much as it is a work of social and cultural theory. To specify, articulation and elaboration are forms of mediation. But, how this functions in the framework of political organization requires taking the following perspectives: First are theorizations that take account of the social determinates that political and social organizations introduce. These determinants include a reconstructed conception of ideology (that is built from Gramsci's conception of ideologies as historically organic and, furthermore, W. F. Haug's concept of societalization—a historically robust interrogation of the concept of "ideological powers" that originates in Engels's work) as well as a structural analysis of the various ways that social movement organizations are composed. Second, the concept of articulation must be reconceived, at the political level, through a tactics of articulation based on Gramsci's project and concept of hegemony in relation to subaltern classes.

In summary, if culture is the mediation between the ideational and the concrete, articulation is a concept that specifies how mediation works, how it may be understood as developmental and transformative.[2] Articulation, the elaborate relational connection between a possibility and the means to act upon it, is an essential cultural dynamic in the context of this book. This dynamic is demonstrated in chapter 1, "The Epistemological Status of Tactics," through the development of a transdisciplinary theoretical framework of tactics that shows the ways that it functions as the concrete mediation between cultural traditions, values, and sentiments and their transformation. Gramsci's organizational efforts demonstrate that in the politicized crucible of national class struggles that depended on mobilizing peasants, veterans, and tertiary workers from the southern regions of Italy along with an industrial proletariat affiliated with various trade unions, factory councils, and political parties, tactics can work to articulate a durable connection between these struggles. The role of tactics is explored, further, in theoretical and conceptual detail in chapter 2, "Ideological Contention," which specifies the role of tactical practices into a theoretical-articulatory framework that includes organizational structure, strategic plans, and the unique conception of ideology as a generative and concrete force that catalyzes disparate groups into waves of struggle and contention. In chapter 3, "Expanding Ideological Contention Theory," I explore the conceptual frameworks that contribute to rethinking the role of ideology in the framework of social and political organizations that are organic to the contexts within which capitalist social relations produce a myriad of contradictions, contradictions that cannot be resolved through normative political means. Here, "ideological contention" provides the basis through which social and political organizations generate and regenerate structural durability, organizational and coalition-based continuities, and communicative frameworks. Across all of these chapters, culture is provisional to both the means for political mobilization and the act of articulation. The concept of articulation is explored both within theoretical discourse and as a part of the political process within society and history in chapter 4, "Agile Materialisms." Here, articulation is the act of rendering the material necessity of a set of political strategies so that a strategic plan is more than merely intelligible or resonant but, rather, affirms, as the end of the second chapter shows, the substantive, material, and historical struggles of groups that already comprise the necessary front in a broader political project. At the same time the persistent strategic deployment of articulations in specific strategic contexts advances various fronts in a struggle collectively. Chapter 4 looks, specifically, at Gramsci's perspective on peasant struggles in 1925 and the problems that peasant organization encountered in the context of the Catholic modernization movement; it also includes a discussion of the role of the Popular Party in the South of Italy. It demonstrates, in Gramsci's work, how his specific concerns about how to develop connections between the Communist Party framework and peasant struggles in the South of Italy are based on fomenting concrete connections by articulating the cultural foundations of peasant struggles along with the goals of the Italian Communist Party. Chapter 5, "Conceptualizing *Aporetic Governmentality*," the concluding chapter of the book, uses critical race theory centered on the concept of colorblind racism to expose some of the limits of the concept of institutional racism, specifically, how race and power work at the level of the state and governance. It rethinks the conceptual positioning of practices when the potential for producing political subjectivity for race resides in a societal lacuna or aporia—an irresolvable contradiction internal to theories of subjectivity and self-governance—that reappears through the reproduction of racialization as modalities of exclusion in the framework of the US state. Critiquing and working with Foucault's conceptions of power and subjectivity, I rely on various theoretical perspectives on race and Marxist perspectives on class to argue that there is a productive asymmetry to the theorization of class exploitation and racial oppression and domination that exposes the way that exploitation and domination get reproduced, as limits to collective subjectivity, through ideology in order to lay bare what is at stake in the development of black subjectivity in a context where the most antihuman forms of racist practice emerge within a context of colorblind postracialism.

Articulation becomes an indispensable part of the process and the development and structuration of a political project.[3] In relationship to politics, the function of culture, the function of *articulating* an effective political strategy precisely presumes modes of exchange must be *inclusive of diverse and, in some cases, divergent groups* within the framework of a broader political project.[4] At the same time, the meditative cultural processes require the cultural foundations of these groups to remain intact to allow for the development of their understandings and justifications—upon which mass solidarities are built—for action, intelligibility, expressive qualities, or a "voice." Then strategy, built through the twin rubrics of culture and politics, opens the gateway, broadly, to transformative mass mobilizations.[5] Reciprocally, tactics bridge the politically manifest cultural desires with the attempts toward a societal concretization of that desire. The concrete realization and implantation of that desire into society necessarily transforms the structure of power (that organizes certain aspects of culture outside of itself into marginal, liminal, or invisible spaces) such that what was, at one point in time, marginalized, liminal, or invisible culture has seized social space through political means.

In *Culture and Tactics*, both the political articulations and societal concretizations that lead culture into a range of transformative configurations culminate in tactical practices. In chapter 1, "The Epistemological Status of Tactics," I excavate the roots of the theoretical framework that comprises the meditative dynamics of ideational and material culture through a critical analysis of various disciplinary approaches—culminating in Gramsci's singular approach—to the relationship between culture and tactics. Across the analyses and theoretical framings in each of the subsequent chapters, culture involves the *communicative* development of experiential, phenomenal, linguistic, and sentimental aspects of perspectives, shared collectively, into a broader critical, social, and materialist perspective that is active, systemic, and that can form the expressive basis for politics; the prolegomenon for any collective constitution of a new society. Gramsci clearly draws each of the threads mentioned in the previous sentence into a developmental definition of culture where the production of culture, or the reorganization of these threads, is necessary to the metaphysics, or theory, of positioning the subaltern classes within politics—within hegemonic struggle. The transformation of these metaphysics into a philosophical fact—a thing that can be realized by tactical means or through vital action—is the impetus toward class struggle; the democratic ideals that were once the provenance of a small group of intellectuals and ultimately reflect a limited scope are rearticulated and necessarily expanded through the sundering of the class structure. According to Gramsci:

> Creating a new culture does not only mean one's own individual "original" discoveries. It also, and most particularly, means the diffusion in a critical form of truths already discovered, their "socialization" as it were, and even making them the basis of vital action. . . . For a mass of people to be led to think coherently and in the same coherent fashion about the real present world, is a "philosophical" event far more important and "original" than the discovery by some philosophical "genius" of a truth which remains the property of small groups of intellectuals. (Notebook 11, §12; Gramsci 1971: 325)

Tactical practices concretize the transformations that are expressed culturally, hence, it is important to describe the positioning of practice within the cultural theoretical perspective that informs this book.

Practice

Practice is a concept that does not travel easily across disciplinary boundaries. Positioning a practice as an object of inquiry within a specific field of knowledge introduces constraints on how it is conceptualized. These constraints vary from field to field. They are a product of the epistemological configurations that have been introduced through the disciplinary scope and framework within which the concept of practice is embedded. The disciplinary combinations and classifications include the social sciences (specifically, the study of politics, culture and society in political science, sociology, anthropology, and in some cases, communications and geography); humanistic fields of inquiry (which also include areas of cultural anthropology, cultural sociology, and sociological theory along with literary studies, continental philosophy, and, also, media studies, communications, and critical and cultural geography); the study of aesthetics (which includes performance studies, literary studies, art history—any field that focuses on cultural objects, texts, and performances).

Although there are obvious overlaps from one disciplinary framework to the next and, also, strong similarities between concepts of practice—for instance, cultural and social forms of practice and aesthetic and cultural forms of practice—there remain distinctions between social practices, cultural practices, and aesthetic practices that can be located in the field within which the practice is theorized and analyzed, in some cases, the object to which the practice is oriented, and differences among the enactments of practices. In the introduction to *The Practice Turn in Contemporary Theory* (2001), Theodore R. Schatzki explains that despite overlaps in the approach to practice distinctions remain; in this case, "it is not surprising that there is no unified practice approach" (11). In "Two Concepts of Practice" (2001), Joseph Rouse notes that with regard to the politicization of knowledge around the concept of practice, disciplinary boundaries work to justify and specify the concept of practice. He states: "There will always be conflicting interpretations of ascendant scientific disciplines, as well as marginal and alternative ways of knowing, which have at least the potential to support critical perspectives upon dominant practices ..." (207). Despite similarities in the concept of practice across areas and disciplines of study, there remains a lack of reflection on the concept's multidisciplinary presence and an equal lack of an articulatory framework to produce an interdisciplinary and reflective perspective on the concept itself. Although this book is not an abstract treatise about the concept of practice, it does seek to demonstrate how an interdisciplinary perspective on practice might enliven how we approach tactics. To articulate the concept of practice across disciplinary limits, the constraints expressed in the various theories of practice must be placed in relation to one another. These concepts and theories must be pointed at a particular practice. It is from out of the arrangement of productive conceptual and theoretical relationships between different disciplines—by placing the concept of tactics as a practice into specific points of contact with one another—that interdisciplinary theories and concepts emerge.

In its broadest conceptual formation, a practice is something that someone does. In each of the fields of study mentioned earlier, a practice implies *a community of influence* that may be relatively strong or weak, structured or unstructured, formal or informal, direct or indirect, present or absent. Practices may be enacted or performed individually but they are not individual acts (i.e., not spontaneous). Although, a practice may be creative both within and also beyond the community that influences it (e.g., Raymond Williams's [1977] practices may be emergent from out of and not a reaction to a dominant cultural framework). Finally, practices may be designed (conceived of by someone) as destructive, as an intervention within a field of practice. They may be intended to be disruptive or negative (i.e., negation).

Tactics, as a form of practice, are destructive, creative, and performative. Destruction, negation, and conflict is a precondition of the performative and generative quality of tactical practices but these forces, when expressed, are compounded—they combine and overlap—within the enactment or demonstration of a specific tactical practice. Effective tactical practices are a part of an analytical and deliberative process that entails the establishment of a strategic program and specific articulations of strategies in contexts where a range or "repertoire" of tactical practices would be most appropriate. The analytical and strategic determination of tactical practices and the establishment and maintenance of an effective strategic program requires an organizational form, a community of influence. The communal organizational body is composed of individuals engaged in deliberation and debate. The stakes entail agreeing on a program that contains pointed strategies that will take the form of tactical practices every member is expected to perform. At a minimum, each person has a direct stake in the community of influence that results in what they will do: their commitment to act through a range of tactical practices. Tactics, in turn, *impact upon the community of influence*, whatever organizational form that this may take; they also impact upon the political or ideological expression that represents the communities' social-organizational position.

These claims are explored throughout *Culture and Tactics* but, for now, can be illustrated by three examples: the Black Bloc formation in the contemporary alter-globalization movement and current antifascist mobilizations; the "Love-in," popular in the protests against the Vietnam War in the mid-to-late 1960s and into the 1970s; and the "Sit-in" especially popular during the civil rights movement. I follow these examples with a brief overview of the book describing the intervention that it makes in the study of social movements, its focus on the unique contribution that Gramsci offers to our understanding of tactics, and, specifically, the relationship between race and mobilization that can be derived from an analysis of Gramsci's writing and political activity.

Demonstrating Tactical Practices

The Black Bloc Tactic

Participants in and commentators on the Black Bloc formation have linked its origins to the Europe-wide (especially German) expression of Marxist and anarchist-based autonomy movements (e.g., Autonomia in Italy and Autonomen in Germany) in the 1980s (Douglas-Bowers 2014; Dupuis-Déri 2013). Since then, the Black Bloc formation has appeared in Brazil, Canada, the United Kingdom, Italy, France, across the United States, Egypt (against the Muslim Brotherhood), and, again in Germany. Black Bloc formations often appear in anticapitalist, antitotalitarian, and antifascist contexts protesting against the G8 and G20 Summits, the World Trade Organization meetings, the Universal Exposition in Milan, the London anti-cuts protest, and, more recently, appearing alongside students and in antifascist protests (Andersen 1999; Bacchi, Iaccino, and Mezzofiore 2015; Byrne 2010; Fernandez 2008; Kettley 2017; Mackey et al. 2013; Mason 2012; Moynihan 2013; Waldram 2013). Print news media like the *Washington Post* and *USA Today* have described the Black Bloc as a tactic echoing participants' accounts.

The Black Bloc tactic illustrates the conception of tactics as a form of practice. It is undeniably expressive: participants in Black Bloc tactical actions dress in black from head-to-toe. The phenomenal appearance expresses solidarity in the unity of a tactical force. In the framework of a protest action that contains a range of groups—social movement organizations, political party members, and groups and individuals expressing an alliance with these groups or an affinity toward the issues driving mobilization efforts—the Black Bloc stands apart. The notoriety that the Black Bloc has established as tactically aggressive, within a demonstration that exhibits a range of tactics that are often not physically confrontational, is exhibited both sartorially and through demonstrating in a formation. It allows demonstrators to put physical distance between themselves and the Black Bloc formation where the latter is easily identifiable. A further implication of the sartorial presentation and physical grouping together of Black Bloc participants is that the Black Bloc also identifies itself in advance to the police; it draws policing efforts toward itself within a broad demonstration, taking responsibility for confrontational tactics in a mobilization framework that is variegated in how it expresses grievances and demands. The Black Bloc formation, then, gives allies and others who are a part of the demonstration and the social forces monitoring and policing the demonstration a means by which they may identify Black Bloc participants. The sartorial representation of the Black Bloc tactic contains an ethic of responsibility in the framework of a broader movement engaged in a differentiated set of tactical practices.

The tactical practice itself, though, contains an explicit relationship to a complex strategy, strategic program, and ideological framework. The strategic framework for the Black Bloc tactic necessitates an agreement among participants. Often in a meeting prior to a protest action, participants agree, in advance, to a select group of targets and actions appropriate to those targets. By strategically limiting the scope of the tactical practices and coordinating actions, the Black Bloc tactic effectively maximizes individual actions as long as those actions conform to the strategy agreed upon in advance (Van Deusen and Massot 2010). Regarding the broader strategic program of Black Bloc tactics, participants can come from any organization as long as they agree to the guidelines established, in conversation, in advance of a protest action. A strategic program that is open to alliances across organizations (on the left, in this case) represents a United Front strategy catalyzed in the collective protest actions around a tactical practice. This builds capacity for a coalition of social movement organizations—or for a larger organizational framework—that may be heterogeneous in their ideological perspectives but that can accommodate a specific strategic program, plan, and tactical practice. As I have argued elsewhere, the demonstration of the Black Bloc tactic also builds momentum, or extends a cycle of contention, through the adaptation, escalation, and transformation of its tactical practices in new contexts (Carley 2019b). Finally, the Black Bloc formation demonstrates, visually and sartorially, solidarity as well as a coordination of efforts, however the agreement with regard to select actions maximizes the individual autonomy of participants during a demonstration. Black Bloc tactical actions maximize the mobility and autonomy of individual participants while framing their creative responses to contextual conditions within a broader strategic plan and program; arguably an embodiment of an anarchic ideology (Carley 2019b).

By way of a transition to my next example, A. K. Thompson (2017) links Black Bloc tactical practices, like property destruction, to Herbert Marcuse's discussion of "one-dimensionality." He states:

> [I]t is necessary to first highlight and then foster those pedagogical moments when protest turns violent and when violence tears at the representational screen that envelopes us all. Through these tears, it is sometimes possible to glimpse another politics and, in turn, another world. (Thompson 2017: 166)

Later, specifically regarding Black Bloc tactics, he states: "Nevertheless, by its [the Black Bloc's] ability to point out *the possibility* of an outside to this 'comfortable, smooth, reasonable, democratic unfreedom,' it has already proven felicitous" (167). As Peter Marcuse (2016) notes, Herbert Marcuse had a complex relationship to violent protest tactics. However, he did not rule them out, explaining that they were a part of the right to resistance in certain circumstances despite what he thought were almost inevitably problematic repercussions (due to the distribution and imbalance of legitimate violent force in society). Marcuse also thought that violence ought to comprise a part of the left's political tolerance of tactics (Marcuse 1965, 1970). However, Thompson's previous larger point specifies that, as a transformative practice, tactics are often violent and certainly confrontational. Tactics transformative qualities draw upon violent reprisals from opponents; they indicate the limitations to the political expression of specific social issues as a part of the broader dynamic of an emancipatory politics.

The Hippie Love-In and the Greensboro Four

In "The Problem of Violence and the Radical Opposition" (1970), Herbert Marcuse discusses hippies participating in an antiwar protest in Berkeley, California, where students—who were permitted by the police to demonstrate—went off course to a military railroad station. The antiwar protest targeted the station for obvious reasons—the deployment of munitions and wartime tools, technologies, and so forth. However, the moment they entered state (military) property they became legitimately subject to state violence, in this case, "10 rows of heavily armed policemen outfitted in black uniforms and steel helmets" (1970: 92). Marcuse then describes a creative tactic: student marchers approach the rows of police in riot gear; they form their own echelon that cordons off the protesters willing to engage with police. After tensions heighten, protesters sit in the street, occupy the space, and perform a "love-in."

What was important about this tactical shift is that it took on the tactical quality of a *feint*; it began as the implication of aggressive confrontation and turned into a deliberately nonviolent protest tactic. This specific love-in creatively combined direct confrontation with a relatively new form of social protest expressing two nonallied tactical approaches simultaneously. It was also creative in its apparent spontaneity; it represented an adaptation of tactical approaches to a contentious and potentially violent context. Finally, and most significantly, faced with state violence, protesters chose to literally demonstrate the society as they wished it as opposed to the society they were confronting, exhibiting two very different spirits of "democracy." The love-in presented the polar opposite of the violence suggested, given the contemporaneous context as well as the location. In short, protesters performed an immanent critique in the streets dramatizing the extraordinary contradiction, or gulf, between the abstract de jure democratic society that needs to be viciously protected, that is, held in place and extended militarily, and the de facto democratic society that the wave of protest actions (this, a part of that wave) seeks to bring into being.

As a tactical practice, the love-in represents a demonstration that is both unique to the hippie subculture (its community of influence) and the context of protests against militarization, specifically the Vietnam War. In short, the love-in is a unique tactical practice; it represents a direct expression of a subcultural group and it is the extension of a cultural practice into a political and tactical context. Though a unique and emergent practice, as a tactic, it signifies more broadly with the "sit-in" tactic. There are however significant differences between practicing, or demonstrating, a love-in and a sit-in. These differences are organizational, strategic, and contextual. They demonstrate the necessary and sufficient conditions for variance in tactical practices. For example, the Greensboro lunch counter sit-in at Woolworth's in North Carolina in 1960 was designed to disrupt an unjust social practice—racial segregation—still prevalent in parts of the Southern United States. Formally, these sit-in protest tactics were a social practice; they can be understood as what sociologists refer to as a "breaching experiment." However, not an experiment, the strategic plan of the Greensboro Four involved a direct personal risk of violence not only in the form of state (police) reprisal but, rather, a broader violent public response by Southern whites. The tactic was designed to demonstrate that racial segregation and racial violence was a broadly accepted social practice. It was the demonstration of an injustice and a demand for justice: leveraging pressure on Woolworth's to desegregate its lunch counter and inspiring others to engage in similar tactical practices to do the same in segregated spaces. It was successful. Since this was the first sit-in of this kind that led to a "sit-in movement," it was not expressive of a cultural practice but, rather, was designed as a specific social response to unjust laws. Also, it was not the organizational response of a political movement or party but, rather, was linked more loosely to the civil rights movement; it had been inspired by Dr. Martin Luther King's practice of nonviolence protest tactics. The sit-in, in this case, was experimental and strategic.

A cursory discussion of tactical practices based on the previous examples demonstrate some analytical distinctions as well as an overlap among cultural, social, and political practices. Black Bloc tactical interventions have an expressed political intention and design. Yet, the phenomenology of the Black Bloc tactic relies on classical cultural practices like sartorial and ideological expressions of tactical purpose. The example of the "love-in" from Marcuse's (1970) observations appear to be the translation of a specific and unique cultural practice into a political context where the demonstration of a love-in as an expression of a desired society deeply troubles the context where the supposed defense of democracy is a defense of the expression of militarism and imperialism in the framework of national self-interest. The contradictions of American democracy are laid bare at home, where the democratically constituted "people" are prevented from expressing opposition to the institutional and proprietary presence of state frameworks that their tax monies engender and that they wish to take back. It also expresses the contradiction that for American democracy to flourish, at home, the national right to self-determination of other nations must be prevented with grave costs to human life, the environment, and democratic free expression. The physical and emotional expression of love through a tactical practice, or in the context of political expression, takes on a range of different character-istics and meanings external to the framework of hippie subculture. Finally, the Greensboro Four insert their bodies into a social space that is regulated through both laws and customs. They design a tactic that, as a social practice, draws out a history of racist social practices from behind the law, a law that conceals the persistent historical legitimation of racial violence in the United States behind what is a barely democratic "separate but equal" facade. The Greensboro Four produce a context that belies the US conception of "sep-arate but equal" as the democratic justification for racial segregation (and the abeyance of seething racial hatred) in the South.

Overview of the Book

Each aforementioned example also alludes to both communities and means of influence upon tactical practices that differ in their constitution, imple-mentation, and effects. These examples illustrate tactical practices, but they fail to fully capture the relationship between organizational and ideological frameworks, and tactical practices, as well as the resonant qualities of tac-tical successes and failures. The goal of *Culture and Tactics* is to capture and explain this specific dynamic, which frames the conception of what a tactical practice is. In the literature on social movements, tactics have been placed in relationship to the tangible goals or the results of social movement activity. Tactics have been analyzed, primarily, for their relative strengths and weak-nesses in achieving outcomes. Tactics have been viewed as effective or inef-fective, radical or pragmatic, sustainable or untenable, and incendiary or reconciliatory as they relate, more broadly, to the polity. However, *tactics have not been analyzed* as an event out of which a social movement orga-nizations' ideology is shaped, reshaped, and changed. *Tactics have not been understood* as impacting the organizational structure of social movements. *Tactics have not been viewed* as a variant of transformative social, cultural, or political practice. But as I will show, tactics are an expressive practice. Tactics are what social movements do; they are a collective form of public expression. They draw in bystanders based on how a social movement frames and demonstrates injustices and makes demands for justice through the tac-tical repertoires that they develop and use.

Culture and Tactics offers an analysis of the importance of tactics going beyond the sociological study of tactical effectiveness or the ability of tactics to produce tangible goals. Specifically, it identifies, interprets, and analyzes the tactically mediated relationship between race and mobilization in Gramsci's work to establish the conceptual basis of tactics as a practice across a range of disciplines in the social sciences and humanities. *Culture and Tactics* investigates Gramsci's innovative use of specific tactics and, through these investigations, produces new concepts and theories that explain race, class, and mobilization through organizational, ideological, and strategic frameworks. By articulating the relationship between racial domination and class exploitation to peasants and veterans from Southern Italy, in the context of a wave of protest actions against manufacturing firms in Northern Italy and the postwar Italian state, this book provides an interpretation of how Gramsci successfully mobilized subaltern groups alongside of trade unionists, socialists, and various fractions of the Italian left and builds upon these interpretations through new concepts and theories. It is the broader theoretical goal of this book to connect Gramsci's insights about the political mobilizations of racialized subaltern groups to contemporary critical race theory and cultural studies of racialization and racism through an interpretation of how Gramsci's work influenced Stuart Hall's concept of culture, hegemony, and race and, also, a by introducing an original conception of the role that ideologies play in the reproduction of racism in the framework of critical race theory.

In short, *Culture and Tactics* breaks new ground by envisioning Gramsci as an early and salient theorist of race in a broader context of social struggle. The following chapters demonstrate Gramsci's attention to race in at least two ways. First, in 1919, Gramsci uses language, as a tactic, to articulate and broadly mobilize common demands between Sardinian veterans from World War I, industrial workers of Southern peasant origin and Northern industrial workers in the Piedmont region. Gramsci skillfully code-switches between a subaltern peasant imaginary and the ideological expressions of the Italian Socialists, for whom he was engaging in organizational activity, linking racialized expressions of peasant injustice to contemporary socialist political strategies for fighting labor exploitation. Second, Gramsci creates an organizational framework, "ward councils," to connect workers from the Southern, racialized, regions of Italy to trade unionists and Italian Socialist Party members, giving subaltern groups an organizational basis through which to participate in strike actions and, more broadly, in politics.

In a broad interdisciplinary conversation with contemporary social theory, social movement studies, and theories of race in sociology and cultural studies, *Culture and Tactics* offers a range of original concepts to assist in the interpretation and analysis of the tactical practices associated with protest activity where race is a central factor in both mobilization and state violence. In this book, I begin by examining Gramsci's approach to creating innovative tactical practices and organizational structures to link industrial workers and racialized subaltern groups together in common struggle. Based on the examination of Gramsci's development of tactical approaches, innovative organizational frameworks, and the articulation of common struggles, I develop a broader theoretical framework to explain the relationship between organizational structures, strategic programs, political ideologies, and the collective memory of participants and allies involved in social movements. I demonstrate how tactical practices impact the organizational structure of social movements and, also, shape, reshape, and shift the ideological framework that informs social movement politics. I end the book by placing specific interpretations that emerge from new insights into Gramsci's work in conversation with contemporary theoretical inquiries into the racialization process and racism in the fields of cultural studies and critical race theory.

In the field of cultural studies, Stuart Hall is responsible for a significant essay on Gramsci's relevance for the contemporary study of race and ethnicity. Hall's essay represents an intervention into the theoretical grounding of contemporary cultural studies. In it, Hall describes Gramsci's epistemological position as both Marxist and nonreductionist. During the time that Hall wrote this piece, he, along with other notable scholars connected to cultural studies, was attempting to establish a plurality of theoretical and methodological perspectives that would set cultural studies apart from contemporary interpretive disciplines and, also, the social sciences. Hall, also, was writing about the different ways that race had been studied and the problems that arose from nonaligned methodological and theoretical approaches to race. Gramsci, for Hall, not only offered a way to analyze race, racialization, and racism in contemporary society, he also provided a way to bridge nonaligned approaches to the study of race. Hall demonstrates *how* Gramsci is relevant to the contemporary analysis of race and ethnicity. I demonstrate *why* Gramsci is relevant. By analyzing Gramsci's perspectives on the social forces that were attempting to constitute typologies of racial characteristics, I show that Gramsci not only attacked the reductionist—in this case, Catholic humanist and sociobiological—classifications and schemas of human typologies, but, more importantly, Gramsci understood both the interrelation of authoritative and "expert" knowledge and political forces that would use these new schemas to justify inequalities, political nonparticipation, and persistent forms of domination and exploitation in the framework of a modern democratic nation-state. Through his mobilization efforts, Gramsci links together the structural and cultural expressions of racialization. In short, for Gramsci, the mobilization of workers and peasants required a focused articulation based on excavating and developing different conceptions of oppression, exploitation, and domination into a united front against a state that supported not only the industrial development of capitalist social relations but also regional distinctions within Italy that, through a racialized discourse, fractured the potential for political and social mobilizations.

Critical race theory shares a common affinity with Gramsci's concept of hegemony since both perspectives are interested in the forces that maintain power structures. Several scholars, including Hall, who analyze racism have used Gramsci's concept of hegemony to explain rhetorical, discursive, and cultural changes that point toward what seem like progressive social impulses but that, overall, maintain both structural racism and racist practices. Taking cues from critical race theory, the last chapter locates, within both the hegemonic racial and broader societal disciplinary frameworks, an aporia for racialized subjectivities. The term aporia, here, refers to an irresolute social and historical contradiction that persistently blocks the collective and self-directed subjective formation of blackness in contemporary society. One recent example that I discuss in the last chapter is the murder of Walter Scott during a traffic stop in South Carolina in 2015. Scott was shot multiple times in the back by a police officer while fleeing and was only hailed by the officer after the shooting began. This event demonstrates that Scott was not offered by the state the marginal privilege of an interpolated subjecthood. For him, and for many other recent black victims of disproportionate state violence, the repressive experience of being hailed and interpolated (which, in this case, is negative) is at least an acknowledgment and affirmation of subjectivity. But for Scott and so many others it is absent. The exclusion from productive schemas of power that offer subjecthood, discipline, and self-governance represents a broader phenomenon that points to an aporia. By focusing on contemporary racial violence directed, especially, against black bodies and black collective expressions of self-determination, I argue that productive social schemas of subjective development reproduce exclusions in the case of race. Racialized groups are met with domination, destruction, and erasure. I link these racial exclusions to class exploitation through the ideological mechanisms that, in the case of Marxist state theory, reproduce the class structure and, at the same time, conceal class relations. Gramsci demonstrates how in Italy the consolidation of political expression and activity defined appropriate behaviors, forms of conduct, and cultural discourse. Behavior, conduct, and culture, Gramsci shows, were grounded powerfully in social institutions constituting both the modern "public" and, also, the practices that shape and direct reality itself and that circumscribe some within the boundaries of social reality and exclude others. I demonstrate that although there is an affinity between the ideological concealment of class relations and race, in the case of racial exclusion the historical and social forces that reproduce it work within fundamentally nonproductive and destructive schemas. These schemas, I argue, reconstruct an aporetic space, a lacuna or hole, for the collective determinations of racial subjectivity. Out of this aporetic space, the most vicious racist practices continue to erupt into the present alongside declarations of "colorblindness" and "postracialism" and produce severe limitations for the subjective realization of race and class power both politically and socially. The last two chapters of *Culture and Tactics* demonstrate Gramsci's perspective on race, racialization, and racism and connect it to contemporary analyses of race, class, mobilization, and power.

It is the goal of *Culture and Tactics* to offer an analysis of the importance of race in Gramsci's work and to elaborate Gramsci's unique insights about race and mobilization across a range of disciplines that are interested in understanding the various forms that antiracist struggle can take. It is the purpose of *Culture and Tactics* to strengthen our understanding of the tactical use of framing in the social movement literature, to expand our understanding of the concept of practice in sociology and cultural studies, and to offer new theoretical insights pertaining to racialization processes and antiracist forms of struggle. As the examples in this introduction lay bare, tactical practices are interventions into social reality. They serve as a starting point through which social movement participants can begin to understand and craft a collective agency that mobilizes their ideas, demands, desires, and selves into a world that is opposed to who they are, what they represent, and what they do. Tactics serve as a way to test and to know both how to navigate within a framework of opposition, what that framework is, and what is successful in challenging it. Chapter 1 will explore, broadly, the relationship between tactics and knowledge across several disciplines and interpret and develop Gramsci's unique contributions to how we can conceive of tactics especially in the context of race and mobilization. The discussion in chapters 2 and 3 will be expand upon the first chapter by interrogating the positioning of tactics in strategic, organizational, and ideological frameworks; these chapters theorize the broader effects of race and mobilization on social movement organizations. The last two chapters of the book, chapters 4 and 5 will focus on how we might understand Gramsci's legacy for contemporary theories of race in the context of contemporary cultural studies and critical race theory.

The Epistemological Status of Tactics

What is the status of tactics for knowledge, in thought or in theories? In the case of Marxist materialist thought, tactics are the *pivot-point* upon which theories are tested and from which new theories emerge. I demonstrate this claim in two ways: First, as it concerns Gramsci's thought, I refer principally and extensively to Notebooks 13 and 15 as well as to some sections in Notebook 6. In these notes, Gramsci addresses several themes, most importantly: ideology, strategy, and strategic political analysis; economic, political, and societal forces; conceptions of reality and the effect of forces on reality; democracy and political organization; and agitation and propaganda. Second, as it concerns Gramsci's experiences organizing workers in Turin between 1916 and 1919, I focus on his mobilization strategies with Sardinian workers.

In this chapter, I demonstrate the centrality of tactics across three sections, where tactics are an object of theoretical inquiry or analysis in humanistic and social-scientific disciplines. The approach to the analysis of tactics in this chapter is to, first, analyze it as a concept through a series of limited-depth cases in humanistic and social scientific fields to establish a broad scope for the concept of tactics. I provide a greater depth of analysis by anchoring the study of the concept of tactics in Gramsci's insights about mobilization, organization, and political subjectivity. I follow the analysis of the concept of tactics with a limited-depth historical case study of Gramsci's development of durable organizational frameworks and strategic plans and deployment of tactical practices that specify, through language, articulatory frameworks to connect the mobilization of various subaltern groups to class struggle within a strategic conjuncture. The goal of this chapter is to demonstrate how the relationship of a multidisciplinary conceptual rendering of tactics and practice, and how the theoretical insights that emerge from the relations among these concepts, is materialized through the co-organization and culturally specific articulations of antiracist and anticapitalist mobilization.

In the first section, I explain how contemporary and integral Marxist materialist approaches to texts, genres, and other forms of categorization—including theories of culture, literature, and aesthetics—advance inquiries and analyses that rely upon tactical frameworks to demonstrate the necessary and absent forces determined and catalyzed in class struggles. The forces that shape the world, as we find it, understand it, and interpret it, are not only a product of our collective social and cultural relationship to the natural world; but, more significantly, the social and ideological justifications that symbolize the world and render it intelligible as culture conceal its collective making. Specifically, they conceal the struggles against oppression and exploitation that disrupt its seamless cultural symbolization. Relying on critical Marxist analyses of the politics of cultural interpretation, these analyses demonstrate that canonical forms of cultural expression and the traditions of cultural interpretation both exclude class dynamics and limit or frame class representations. In response to the deracination of cultural and aesthetic criticisms and representations, Critical Marxist analyses of culture also incorporate concepts and interpretive frameworks that were expressed in "liberation," socialistic, and communistic political and organizational contexts connecting radical political critics and theorists to normative aspects of interpretive traditions. The conceptual mechanics of tactics as a pivot-point between "theories" and "practices" (between knowledge-acting-knowing-new knowledge) come from a note of Gramsci's about how and why to analyze the relations of force at a particular moment in time.

The second section of this chapter critically reviews the discussion of tactics in contemporary social science research, specifically as it pertains to the study of social movements. The subfield of social movement research that looks at tactical choices, changes, and relationships represents the singular and contemporary study of tactics in historical, societal, and political contexts. Although this literature is not directly concerned with the interrelation of epistemology and tactics, I locate it there by interpreting the questions posed in this research as well as some of its implications for building up and breaking apart political communities. What this literature demonstrates is the substantive role that tactics play in relationship to mobilization efforts, movement organizational structure, leadership roles, the acquisition and distribution of crucial resources, the constitution of political discourses, and the polity in general. Rather than imagined as a "pivot-point," tactical forms of expression and decision making in the social movement literature become a centripetal force around which many other variables orbit. Tactics are not only considered a primary and necessary condition of social movement organizations and mobilizations but, more specifically, have a powerful effect on movement communities. I develop the specific effects that tactics have on social movement communities through a discussion of the ontological and subjective effects of tactical actions. These effects are intimated in the literature but not developed. Specifically, I demonstrate how certain subjective orientations toward organizational complexity are both the product of sustained tactical interventions against structured forms of authority, and, at the same time, these sustained tactical intercessions give rise to a collective and participatory framework. These organizational frameworks, I argue, mediate both movement ideology and tactical practices and offer movement participants a hand in shaping their political subjectivity.

After reviewing and building upon the positioning of tactics in the field of social movement studies (which also gets addressed and developed more fully in the next two chapters), the third section of this chapter demonstrates the core of its main claim through an analysis of tactics from different sections in Notebooks 13, 15, and 6. Here, Gramsci discusses tactics in the service of organizational questions and debates, political science, political analysis, and the role that social, political, and economic forces play—at various levels—and, finally, the significance of internal forms of political organization and, also, "prediction" in determining tactical action.

Finally, the link between thought, tactics, and race is made through the following example: In 1919, Gramsci uses language, tactically, to articulate and broadly mobilize common demands between Sardinian veterans from World War I, industrial workers of Southern peasant origin, and Northern industrial workers in the Piedmont region (this is taken up and expanded across the next three chapters). Gramsci makes reference to the lessons of this mobilization in his final pre-prison writing, "Some Aspects of the Southern Question" ([1926] 1995b), which is analyzed and discussed in greater detail in the next chapter.

In this chapter, I set the tone for the remainder of the book by positioning tactics into a broader epistemological field, interrogating the relationships that tactics both require and engender. I demonstrate how tactics develop through relations that often strain the political communities that work to come to agreements about their form of practice. I show the organizational work through which effective tactical practices develop. Finally, I demonstrate the scope and degree of analysis required (both within the organizations that are building their capacities and, also, of the broader social and political forces contained within it) to develop tactical repertoires. Most importantly, I illustrate how tactics are a form of practice. Tactics are acts that, when effective, articulate relations for the political communities contained within a movement. They also articulate the movements' broader relations with external political forces and social forces. Finally, tactics demonstrate concrete instances of how political communities can intervene in, bend, and shape the world around them, transforming it, at least, for a time. Tactics, then, engender practices by articulating connections and demonstrating the viability of those relations in the context of a broader political, social, and cultural framework. Participating in practices that are transformative and that become the instruments that are the warp and woof of a political community's experiences and expectations alter the political subjectivities of movement participants who engage in these practices. As long as the political community contained within a broader organization remains an integral part of the strategic planning and tactical realization of strategy, the organizational framework is changed as are the ideas that give an organization (not merely an identity but) life—that allow it to survive and thrive. The organizational context, which becomes the collective locus of struggle, takes on a specific dynamic that I explain across the next two chapters through my original conception of ideological contention. Though tactical practices are central to the dynamism of an organization and the ideas that give it shape, the effect of tactical practices on the organizational structure of movement groups and the way that ideas in the movement change need to be explained as a relationship. I argue that tactics affect the ideological framework and organizational structure of a movement, and they also shape the collective history of political and social struggle through collective memory. My argument about tactical practices articulating connections that affect political organizations and ideas takes its shape by considering how race is positioned as a necessary concern in mobilization efforts. The historical and social context through which Gramsci mobilized workers, peasants, veterans, and others was a context in which racial domination played, at least, as substantial a role as did labor exploitation. In the remainder of the book, I show that for Gramsci the tactical innovation in the framework of his mobilization efforts raise questions, for him, about the framework through which Southern Italian peasants were racialized—questions that he addresses in ways that resonate with and can inform contemporary cultural studies and critical race theory. I theorize the connections between Gramsci's efforts to organize and mobilize peasants in the context of a racialized, or racist, national environment and contemporary frameworks that theorize the contemporary role of racialization processes, institutional racism, and racist practices.

Unearthing Class

Metaphors of turgidity, stolidity, and density are often used to mark the traditions of literature and criticism as "sediment": the earth compressed and striated or stratified (Jameson 1981). This trope frames the aesthetic values that form a canon and (to borrow a turn of phrase from Karl Mannheim's *Ideology and Utopia* [(1926) 1997]) a partial expression of culture as total. Class, then, sits forgotten (not visible to us, not a part of our consciousness) beneath these layers, the rock formation that holds everything in place and, yet, only it has the capacity to shift everything.

Locating the class relations beneath high forms of cultural expression requires an approach and a methodology that is distinct; many forms of interpretation and analysis add to, complicate, and reify implicit cultural values expressed textually as well as critically. In *The Political Unconscious: Narrative as a Socially Symbolic Act* (1981), Fredric Jameson introduces a sufficiently complex methodological approach to texts embedded in society through traditions of interpretation *and reading practices.* "Metacommentary" (Jameson 1971, 1981) is an interpretive operation linked, explicitly, to a Marxist analysis of meanings as well as the practice of reading—"the absolute horizon of all reading and all interpretation" (Jameson 1981: 17). Metacommentary locates analyses of texts beyond the page, extending the horizon of interpretation beyond texts and their critics to ideology and the class contradiction that forms of cultural expression and critical reflection contain and conceal. As such, meaning and interpretation are called into question by the *structuring determinants* of the text: the political terrain that engenders and limits concrete possibilities, the ensemble of social and quasi-private institutions in which those possibilities are rooted and from which they may be eliminated, and the relations and practices that are enabled and constrained through power and its numerous presences. Metacommentary links meanings to the formal aspects of the text, especially including its cultural and intellectual production, and more significantly, places the onus for interpretation and analysis upon the political and social forces that determine, in the main, the conjuncture in and through which the text is extended. The political and social forces themselves, and not their expression, become the target of analysis through which a text is produced, authoritatively interpreted, and, finally, reproduced.

The Political Unconscious (1981) is touted, by many, as Jameson's most important book (LaCapra 1982; Poster 1981; Punter 2001); it provides a methodological approach for Marxist cultural and literary criticism beyond what Jameson offers in *Marxism and Form* (1974) and *The Prison-House of Language* (1972). His approach requires critics to engage texts through the *cultural instance* of their *historical production* (besides also evoking Marx and Engels's [(1845) 1960] "First Premises of Materialist Method" as well as Marx's 1846 "Letter to Annenkov" and his 1859 "Preface to a Contribution to the Critique of Political Economy"). Jameson develops a dialectical approach to locating the analyses of texts historically. According to Jameson:

> The historicizing operation can follow two distinct paths, which only ultimately meet in the same place: the path of the object and the path of the subject, the historical origins of the things themselves and that more intangible historicity of the concepts and categories by which we attempt to understand those things. . . . [W]e are thus confronted with a choice between study of the nature of the "objective" structures of a given cultural text (the historicity of its forms and of its content, the historical moment of emergence of its linguistic possibilities, the situation-specific function of its aesthetic) and something rather different which would instead foreground the interpretive categories or codes through which we read and receive the text in question. . . . Texts come before us as the always-already-read; we apprehend them through sedimented layers of previous interpretations, or—if the text is brand-new—through the sedimented reading habits and categories developed by those inherited interpretive traditions. (Jameson 1981: 9)

Put simply, the form as well as the ideologies of literary and cultural interpretation and the conjuncture in which they are shaped become the analytical target of "metacommentary." As such, the act of analysis and interpretation situates both the text and the various "readings" or methods of approach historically—neither uncovering truth nor establishing an authoritative interpretation but rather calling both into question (and placing both into the pathway of analysis) as acts of politics and power (within the necessary encumbrance of historical development). Hence, what is latent to the general reader—as well as the close literary reader and disciplined literary scholar—is exposed: political content or—concerning the dual pathways of subject and object—the substantively political as an aesthetic form.

This delineation marks a crucial moment in Jameson's analysis. As I noted, the political and social forces appear substantively within the conjuncture. Jameson's analysis depends upon delineating specific horizons or frameworks that both locate and move analysis through strategies of interpretation based on the limitations inherent within specific fields of meaning. The limitations represent political, social, and economic forces that, determined and combined (overdetermined), constitute varying degrees and intensities of class struggle that are expressed culturally across horizons, from texts to genres. Specifically, the decomposition of political, societal, and historical and economic unities framed within texts and groups of texts is the act of analysis that allows for criticism. Criticism reorders the "unconscious" political forces in the ideological field (or third horizon) into a representative form so that it may be analyzed and criticized. These forces, "all together project . . . a formal conjuncture through which the 'conjuncture' of coexisting modes of production at a given historical moment can be detected and allegorically articulated" (Jameson 1981: 99).[1] After determining the broadest historical representation of forces constitutive of the cultural fields that produce a range of discursive possibilities and limitations, a conjuncture is identified and *the act of concrete analysis (articulation) becomes possible.*[2]

More than two decades following *The Political Unconscious*, Timothy Brennan's *Wars of Position: The Cultural Politics of Left and Right* (2006) describes how the class-rooted presumptions of cultural and literary theorists lead to a rewriting of the prehistory of contemporary theory associating Mikhail Bakhtin with the Russian Formalists, Raymond Williams with popular cultural studies, and Henri Lefebvre with poststructuralist thinkers—not with political activity and contexts. Brennan points to a more vigorous and, in some cases, more intentional (than Jameson) act of producing interpretations of the literary and cultural interpretive tradition from dominant ideological positions. Aesthetic form is unified, constituting a substantively politicized field precisely by willfully vacating critics' political histories. By erasing these theorists' associations with political organizations and by delinking their critique from the political conversations in which it was embedded (e.g., Lefebvre and Althusser with French Liberation and the French Communist Party) and, also, the intellectual and ideological frameworks where class struggle finds new energies and challenges, contemporary theorists come to these theories as reified. Theories that have a basis in Marxism but, more importantly, are focused on the strategic, tactical, and political positioning of classes engaged in class warfare in democratic capitalist society, become objective and expressive forms of bourgeois society often articulated through political categories that are pluralist in their logical ends. These theories are decoupled from their foundational critique and standpoint epistemology. Also, more radical critiques are constrained by normative frameworks within democratic theories (e.g., politics of recognition, identity politics, radical and critical paradigms linked to radically performative political practices, etc.).[3] Where Jameson exposes the political contents embedded in critics' writing about texts, Brennan exposes the political contents embedded in critics writing about other critics. Brennan forces the field of cultural criticism to confront its politics in the form of disciplinary and arbitrary boundaries, creative revisions to omissions, misprisions, and the like.

Importantly, Brennan makes a *specific* point that becomes central to the approach I take in *Culture and Tactics*. As he discusses the rewriting of the historiography of certain theories (e.g., postcolonial theory, cosmopolitanism, Hardt and Negri's *Empire* and *Multitude*, and the lack of state and organizational analyses across the academic left), he notes that in the specific case of revisionist history as it pertained to Henri Lefebvre, his "intellectual resources came not from Ferdinand de Saussure or Claude Lévi-Strauss but from the French Liberation, and were tempered *in debates over tactics and strategies within the French Communist Party*" (Brennan 2006: 2, my emphasis). To be clear: Lefebvre's *singularity within the theoretical field* of French and continental theory comes neither from his reinterpretation of the metaphysical tradition or an alliance with the materialist departure point of Marx; nor is it connected to any fundamental disagreement about the meta-organizational patterns of thought—being space or time—that constitute the categorical shifts in intellectual historiographies and give names to theories and theoretical fields. His singularity neither emerges from an abstract synthesis of Marxism with urbanism or geography nor from competitiveness within French cultural theory around the issue of categorical or cultural intelligibility of contemporary urban daily life (e.g., de Certeau). Although, certainly, Lefebvre's singularity as a theorist is *informed* by his intellectual biography, it is developed by the positions that he takes, in each instance, on concepts, theorists, and traditions to develop a political perspective, principally, through Marxist thought. However, *singularity* marks the constitutive elements of theoretical knowledge (according to both Jameson and Brennan) that work to differentiate theoretical approaches and give rise to *decisions* that resulted in specified positions or standpoints. These theoretical standpoints emerge from *the question of tactics* (in the organizational contexts of class struggle).[4] The primary concrete mediation is debate. Higher order mediations include political organization and the (empirical) positioning of that organization in the context of social forces as well as the political field (polity).[5]

Jameson locates in both the formal and substantive aspects of culture a broad yet differentiated class struggle as its concrete content; the political unconscious that determines the descriptive fields of sentiment, what might be referred to as the production of literary structures of feeling. In so many expressions of culture and across so many texts and images, the substantive descriptions and representations, the techniques that have wrought these cultural objects, and the *similarities* in representation and technique that constitute categories and genres—in short, the taxonomy of aesthetic thought and production—conceal *the deep political structure of that reality. The deep political structure of reality is the class struggles within the broad and diversified organizational forms that alienate and exploit human labor power, on the one hand, while offering narrow and hobbled societal and economic subjectivities on the other*. At the same time, these struggles must be understood as the dead labor that, for generations, was animate (in this context) in the following way: It worked the countryside, constituting the object for the pastoral, the picturesque, and the sublime: a protean literary and aesthetic fetishism—a kind of primitive accumulation of literary cultural capital.

As previously mentioned, Brennan describes how the singularity of theoretical production—the intellectual resources constitutive of the kernel of a theory—is matured, honed, and sharpened in the context of political organizational forms, through debates pertaining to how, when, and in what way to act. In this instance, a theory is produced through dialogic forms that are mediated through internal, organizational, and external societal constraints with the scope of the dialogue focused on producing an effective range of tactical practices. Jameson and Brennan point their analyses toward the layers, encumbrances, and sedimentation inherent in elevating culture to its mass and high forms. Both offer a concrete analysis of the forces that hold culture in the thrall of an authoritative interpretation. That analysis is the basis for understanding—for politics, but most significantly for tactics. Gramsci recognizes this, too, but reorders it so that tactics mark the continuance of thought and analysis:

> The most important observation to be made about any concrete analysis of the relations of force is the following: That such analyses cannot and must not be ends in themselves (*unless the intention is merely to write a chapter of past history*), but acquire significance *only if they serve to justify a particular practical activity*, or initiative of will. They reveal the points of least resistance, at which the force of will can be most fruitfully applied; they suggest *immediate tactical operations*; they indicate how a campaign of political agitation may best be launched, what language will best be understood by the masses, etc. (Notebook 13, §17; Gramsci 1971: 185, my emphasis)

The Centrality of Tactics

In my view, tactics are *the crucial and singular implementation of strategies*. Strategies are *hypothetical forms of actions*. A tactically guided action is organizationally and contextually driven. Neither strategies nor tactics can be decoupled from history, culture, or the ideational or ideological framework or frameworks through which a political organization understands, explains, and justifies its actions to its members and to others. To be clear, in the framework of the Marxist tradition and, also, in Gramsci's thought, tactics are politically dependent for their efficacy in no small way on the strategic orientation of any social movement or political project.

The discussion of tactics in the framework of Gramsci's thought and, also, more broadly, within the Marxist tradition demonstrates this claim while, at the same time, prioritizing the necessity of analyzing tactics. In "Revolutionary Adventurism," an article written for *Iskra* in 1902 and reprinted in volume 6 of *Lenin Collected Works* (1964), Vladimir I. Lenin writes that "any popular movement assumes an infinite variety of forms, is constantly developing new forms and discarding the old, and effecting modifications or new combinations of old and new forms. It is our duty to participate actively in this process of working out means and methods of struggle" (Lenin 1964: 192–193). According to Daniel Egan (2018) the text of "Revolutionary Adventurism" is situated in an early revolutionary context of state insurrection (as opposed to the latter context of Soviet power and international strategy) and, more broadly, in a tradition of theorizing the relationship between strategy and tactics in the work of Engels,

Trotsky, Lenin, and, later, Mikhail Tukhachevsky and Ho Chi Minh. Egan notes in the context of state insurrection and within the framework of the Marxist tradition that explicitly theorizes strategy and tactics that "tactics, however, unconnected to any kind of centralized political leadership and ungrounded in a revolutionary mass movement were a form of 'revolutionary adventurism' " (Egan 2018: 54). Briefly, the analysis of the organization of political and social movement structures is a central feature of the theory and analysis in subsequent sections in this chapter and, also, the next two chapters. However, Egan's larger point is twofold: First, the popular distinction between Lenin and Gramsci—where the former, Lenin, is viewed as positing a strategy of workers' insurrection that is centralized and militarized and the latter, Gramsci, is viewed as positing a broad democratic participatory counterhegemonic strategy with cultural and developmental foundations—is false. Both, according to Egan, understood that modifications to movement organization required a persistent reorientation of strategy, a constant working-out of the means and methods of struggle so that tactics, to be effective, could be organized into and a product of the strategic orientation of a political organization. This point is addressed, directly, in the third and fourth chapters. To continue, according to Egan, Lenin and Gramsci have more in common with regard to the tactical positioning of political organizations within the broader framework of civil society.

But, second, and more importantly, the strategic conjuncture within which anyone might imagine a strict distinction between strategy and tactics (based on Clausewitz's perspective in the early nineteenth century) where "[t]he importance of the individual battle as the building block of strategy" was changing in the context of the twentieth century, it "had given way to that of a sustained series of operations" (Egan 2018: 87). The interpretation of Gramsci's military metaphor—where positioning political organizations institutionally, in alliances with other organizations, in frameworks of solidarity or mutual aid with social and cultural groups represented a broad *strategy* that culminated in maneuvering a political organization, a party, into a position to seize state power through *tactics*—was, according to Egan no longer sustainable as the twentieth century experienced an increasingly more complex and persistent context for class struggle. Egan explains that the concept of operations suggests a higher level of political struggle where the binary, strategy: planning based on the implementation of a successful repertoire of tactics/tactics: the implementation of strategy grounded in tactical success and experience is less useful. For Egan, as the framework for political struggle becomes more challenging, "maneuver no longer was limited to a specific event but had to be sustained in a more consistent manner. . . . Maneuver and position were increasingly integrated within the operation. . . . the basis on which Gramsci's military metaphor could distinguish the war of maneuver as tactical and the war of position as strategic was becoming increasingly problematic" (Egan 2018: 87). Although Egan relies on the concept of the operation as a more fluid and more advanced framework within which the binary between strategy and tactics is collapsed, the nature of political organization itself is changed to a more horizontal framework where this new fluid dynamic can be viewed as "a strategy of counter-hegemonic revolution as the integration of a number of operations across time and space" (2018: 87). In this context, Egan argues that "the action of such organizations can best be seen as tactical" (2018: 87).[6]

The tactical practices, especially those of subaltern groups engaged in contemporaneous and differentiated sites of political struggle, outpaces what Lenin describes as the "process of working out means and methods of struggle" and, as Gramsci calls it, a "centralism" in movement—that is, a continual adaptation of the organization to the real movement" (Notebook 13, §36; Gramsci 1971: 188). In this book, then, the focus on tactics at the organizational level signals an attempt to come to grips with its effects across a context of persistent contention. This and the following two chapters explore how the result of tactical actions impacts the organizational structure, ideological framework, and future tactical engagements of political coalitions that comprise social movement organizations. Tactical failures and successes, both, ripple through the fabric of a political organization, placing strategic planning as well as the ideological framework of the organization in question. Tactics are an intervention into bounded knowledge. They shake, shift, or pulverize the ground upon which theories are built. Their destruction is creative: as tactics open up possibilities not yet extant within current theoretical horizons, new explanations, new theories, become necessary. Finally, the process of agreeing on a tactical way forward is (in this context) fundamentally nondeterministic; it is deliberative and conflict based (as I will discuss further in chapters 2 and 3), since both the democratic core of the organization and the organization itself are at stake in the process of agreeing upon strategies and implementing—participating in—tactics in protest actions. This also introduces at least two additional variables into political analysis: 1) the form of the deliberative process within the political organization; 2) the effective determination and judgment or measurement of contextual elements—both internal and external to the movement—that would direct strategy and effect forms of tactical implementation, suggesting flexibility within organizational and ideological parameters.

The response to indeterminacy in the Marxist tradition is collective action. Of course, collective action implies organizational forms, planning, strategy, and the implementation of tactics. Further, it requires Marxist thought to develop guidelines by which to analyze and determine a contextual understanding of when and how to act. Knowing how to establish the concreteness of a context—what comprise the organizationally and politically durable yet societally (and also politically) vulnerable elements of a context upon which to act—is a particular kind of knowledge: analysis. *Understanding the range of options* through which to insert action into a context relies upon yet another kind of knowledge: strategy. Finally, all of the implications and approaches come down to the application of tactics within a broad range of strategic possibilities based upon an effective appraisal of the situation that a specific organization is confronted with at a given moment in time. The moment from which any theory or idea may be advanced is through and after tactics—it is from these moments that the intellectual resources of Marxism are birthed.

There is, however, no explicit field of study focused on the place of tactics in the development of the intellectual resources of theoreticians or philosophers. The two closest existing categories of thought linked to collective political action as tactics are 1) the philosophy of praxis, which is not, in fact, about tactics but, rather, represents the expressed combination of materialist method with the substantive, phenomenological, or sociological aspects of class (group) consciousness and *is both a precondition for and a condition of tactical action* in the Marxist tradition, and 2) the contemporary analysis of strategy and tactics—often framed alongside other variables and theories—in social movement studies.

The Epistemological Status of Tactics in Social Movement Studies and Political Subjectivity

"What is to be done? This question of tactical choice is a persistent one for social movements. Tactics are the essence of collective action" (Ennis 1987: 520). Borrowing from Lenin, James G. Ennis (1987) introduces his case study of collective tactical choices and societal and strategic contexts (dubbed "tactical repertoires") by raising and settling a fundamental epistemological question. Although his three lead sentences are meant to illustrate, generally, the centrality of tactics to all collective action (a guiding presumption of the social movement studies literature), his utterly normative claim (however, framed through a question posed by Lenin) *that tactics are the essence of collective action* within the field of social movement studies allows for a bridge between the question posed in this chapter, about the epistemological status of tactics in Marxist thought, and the body of research that analyzes contemporary movements.

Tactical repertoires—the range of tactics that have been used in social movements—represent the culmination of several significant studies that demonstrate different facets of how tactics are used by developing categorizations from historical accounts of several similar cases (e.g., Evans 1995), comparative historical cases (e.g., Chibber 2006; Skocpol 1979), and smaller but significant cases (e.g., Ennis 1987; McAdam 1982, 1983; Morris 1981). McAdam's groundbreaking study of "black insurgency" in the United States between 1930 and 1970 (McAdam 1982) and his demonstration of "tactical innovation" through the same data (McAdam 1983) position tactics as the preeminent solution to the problem of powerlessness and institutional political impotence (1983: 735).[7] McAdam discusses the "level of indigenous organization" in a movement containing multiple organizations and their "organizational readiness." Together these structural factors comprise the necessary conditions for tactical innovation; organizational readiness allows an organization to "furnish the context in which tactical innovations are devised and subsequently carried out" (McAdam 1983: 736).

Aldon Morris's (1981) research into black insurgency (which provides support for McAdam's necessary structural factors) describes the role of long-term and immediate rational planning in tactical innovation, including left-militant elements within the National Association for the Advancement of Colored People (NAACP), who, due to the democratic organizational structure of the NAACP, drove discussions of confrontational tactical forms contributing directly to tactical innovation. Significantly, a heterarchy of activist experience between formal leadership and activist militancy (in the context of a formal hierarchy) determined the responses to tactical questions while threatening the parameters of the political community. The democratic and organizational framework of the NAACP allowed militants to remain in the organization as a key element of the organization's community, whereby the community's needs, as well as its deliberative and democratic framework, stretch the bounds of legitimacy between the poles of formal and conservative leadership and militant actions. Morris "fleshes out" the bones of McAdam's concept of tactical innovation. More to the point, Morris's research *substantively* demonstrates how a collective and intersubjective deliberative democratic organizational context operates. Morris's work "furnish[es] the context in which tactical innovations are *devised and subsequently carried out*" (McAdam 1983: 736, *my emphasis*).

This sharpens a key point with regard to tactics and epistemology: Ennis, quoting Lenin from 1902, implies that any response to his question is *substantive*—both analytically and then tactically. Therefore, it concerns the context where tactics are devised (where, in part, external forces are analyzed) and where tactics are implemented (subsequently carried out). The question is posed contextually; that is the only way it can be posed. And, of course, Ennis demonstrates an answer to a more specified version of this question; as we would expect, he responds sociologically (but neither historically nor philosophically) by demonstrating how collective tactical choice is constrained and facilitated by movement ideology, parameters of political community, the capacity and ability to mobilize resources, organizational structure, and a group's position within a broad political field. The construction of a field allows Ennis to determine *tactical repertoires* that operate through criteria of effectiveness and legitimacy for the group deploying them, in his case, in the singular context of a specific social-movement organization prohibiting the research and development of nuclear weapons.

Like Gamson (1975) before him and Staggenborg (1989) after, Ennis also effectively demonstrates through his research what is *not* to be done. Ennis uses the category of "legitimate political community" to demonstrate that the relationship between certain types of tactical action and the ideology and organizational structure of a social or political organization is connected. The term "legitimate political community," de facto, encompasses ideological standpoints as well as the organizational structure of social movements without focusing, directly, on these variables. Despite this, his analysis gives priority to the implementation of certain kinds of tactics that, when implemented, have the ability to either stretch or break what members share as the core of their political legitimacy. So, the deliberative approach (demonstrated most effectively in Morris's example) to tactical action has both an epistemological dimension as well as a "political-ontological" dimension.

This raises a question with regard to political subjectivity.[8] If tactics are the essence of collective action and if the integrity of the social movement—its organizational structure, legitimacy, and community—depends (both necessarily and sufficiently) upon how it responds, repeatedly, to the question of "what is to be done," then who responds, how, and under what conditions not only comprise the phenomenal, substantive, and effective responses to social problems and political conflict in the form of tactical practices. More significantly, a social movement's tactical practices that comprise the responses to social problems on behalf of the groups affected by them represent the political expressions of racial, ethnic, and religious groups as well as citizens and workers. They activate these categories in political frameworks and give them a historical life both laying the groundwork for ethnic, racial, and class-based political subjectivities and, at the same time, rescuing them from the easy and enormous condensation of posterity. What, then, might we ask is a laborer? Someone who converts resources into socially useful things. One answer is as good as another. Only under certain conditions does a laborer become a contractor, a small-business owner, a technician, an industrial programmer/operator, a member of an occupational interest group, a trade unionist, a militant trade unionist, a member of a political party, a community organizer, a union organizer, an operative in an AstroTurf organization, a token, a politician, a subversive, a political prisoner, a proletarian, a revolutionary. What are the conditions? In the most general and categorically all-encompassing sense, there must be a robust democratic state where rights are maximized in the political and civil sphere.

Lenin sets these conditions in his argument with both Karl Kautsky in "Nationality and Internationality" ([1907] 2009) and Rosa Luxemburg in *The National Question and Autonomy* (1909) regarding the self-determination of nations. In *The Right of Nations to Self-Determination* ([1914] 1970), in the first chapter, "What Is Meant by the Self-Determination of Nations?," Lenin explains that

> [t]he bourgeois nationalism of every oppressed nation has a general democratic content which is directed *against* oppression, and it is this content that we support *unconditionally* while strictly distinguishing it from the tendency toward national exceptionalism, while fighting against the tendency of the Polish bourgeoisie to oppress the Jews, etc., etc. . . . . It is only policy in the national question that is practical, that is based on principles and that really furthers democracy, liberty, and proletarian unity. (Lenin [1914] 1970: 211)

In short, the conditions that provide the right to free association and political assembly allow the establishment of trade unions and, more importantly, political parties—the most complete assertion of political capacity and power that would enable a transition to socialism. In both a complementary and converse sense, the increasing complexity of civil society—the division of labor, new enterprises, the role of independent research in private use, and

intellectual property rights, for example—increases the legal reach and specificity of the democratic nation-state.[9]

What, then, is a *political subject*? It is someone (experientially) *subject
to* the presence of all of these conditions in their institutional, legal, bureaucratic, and organizational forms; the degree of their presence as either a historical and durable societal and political force; and the development of a
legislature that guarantees a range of inalienable rights whereby minimum
rights entail the freedom of collective political expression. Within these limitations, a political subject can determine or become the subject of / subject
to these organizational forms and to a range of choices.[10] The political subject
exercises the ability *to choose from, or, more importantly, create the terms of his
or her own subjecthood* by developing organically (i.e., from the grass roots),
a range of representative political, religious, societal, and cultural organizations in which a political subject has relatively broad opportunities for representation (or participating in the process of subjectivization) as well as
some degree of agency to direct (collectively and democratically) the ability
of the organization to represent their interests, which, though ideologically
diversified, are collective interests. In this case, constraints upon the subjective development of political consciousness are external and, at the same
time, a part of the internal development of the ideological and organizational process. Gramsci takes the dynamics that constitute political subjectivity beyond the bounds of these effective and real constraints, whereby
subjection and subjectivization are transformed, marking the emergence
of a historical and political subject. To do this, the organizational forms
that determine real and effective political subjectivities must change so
that political subjectivity can be expanded beyond the level of constraint
that marks the apotheosis of the modern democratic nation-state in the
framework of a capitalist economy. The organizational form may not simply
crown itself at the height of the extant social and political reality; rather, it
has to transcend this reality.

Constraint is a common thread connecting cultural and literary critics
to sociologists. Both subjectivity and meaning are determined by constraint.[11] The sociological analysis of structural factors that are both internal
to an organizational form and the external structure that contains political
forces and institutional frameworks represent constraints at the broadest
level. The institutional factors and political forces combine with meaning
and expressive cultural forms that contain action—what a subject can know
and do. Conversely, tactics open political institutional forms and the terrain
upon which they exercise power, as well as the organizational and ideological

frameworks that contain the desires of political subjects as a collectivity or a community—including the cultural traditions, meanings, and interpretations that contain, produce, and reproduce these traditions for new possibilities and realizations. This breathes new life into durable and meaningful ideational frameworks, suffusing language with shifts in consciousness indicative of the struggles that constitute organic political subjects and subjective forms.[12] The analysis that brings the political, societal, and cultural elements together with tactical action, and that demonstrates the shifting terrain of struggle, comes from Gramsci.

"Modern Prince," "New Science"

> For Gramsci theory does not simply reproduce practice; it systematizes it, rectifies it and formulates it at a conceptual level. And by the same token, practice itself raises new questions for theory. (Buci-Glucksmann 1980: 231)

> Because this philosophy has its starting point in praxis, in the class struggle, and not in philosophy, something has to be added to political science, i.e. a gnoseology of politics. . . . . Marxist philosophy . . . consists . . . in a change of terrain, the status of the dialectic having nothing to do with any abstract, formalistic or universalist (*a priori*) logic. This is a logic of the real object in the strong sense, requiring a different structure of knowledge. The gnoseological question that is specific to Marxism is by no means resolved simply in Engel's alternative of idealism or materialism, which is never more than a starting-point. The gnoseology finds its operative concept only when "the realization of a hegemonic apparatus is a philosophical fact." (Buci-Glucksmann 1980: 236)

> The whole thrust of Gramsci's work in prison is to unmask the complexity of the concrete situation which is the basis for the activity of the party and to delineate the terrain of political struggle. The ability of the party to relate to the concrete situation depends on its having accurate knowledge of the historical moment in which it is working. The very object of political science, according to Gramsci, consists in "The study of how 'situations' should be analyzed." (Sassoon 1987: 180)

In the introduction, I discussed how practices are embedded within communities; what differentiates practices from action is their collective nature. The community imbues upon the act a collective influence and depending on the nature of the practice it has the ability to impact upon the community. In a political framework, tactical practices are directed toward a range of social problems and are designed to challenge and disrupt specific political forces that legitimate and support the social forces that a movement organization has targeted. This chapter has demonstrated the essential relationship between knowledge and tactics. It has focused on, in detail, the intellectual, cultural, societal, and political contexts in which tactics represent transformative practices.

In the beginning of this chapter, I discuss how, in the absence of a Marxist methodology, all meaning—cultural texts, objects, and practices, especially cultural criticism—reproduces, willy-nilly, an architecture of aesthetic values that is organized in seamless continuity through canons of cultural representation and traditions of interpretation. These canons and traditions exclude the question of how meaning is produced and reproduced and, more significantly, they organize texts and critics into categories that are indicative of specific reading practices that, due to the force of authority, become general or universalized representations of aesthetic, cultural, and literary thought. More significantly, however, they aestheticize class relations into representations and objects that both contain and hide class struggles and they arrange the political and organizational frameworks through which Marxist critics directed their work (toward social and political problems that determined class positions) into interpretive schools. These interpretive schools represent a continuity of interpretive historiographies; a taxonomy of literary and interpretive concepts that masks the political work that gave rise to these theories (Brennan 2006; Jameson 1981). A Marxist or political tradition is pulled away as chaff from the wheat of interpretive and theoretical traditions that nourish the interpretation of texts and aesthetics. The emptying out of political-theoretical content within theoretical and interpretive traditions could be claimed about both Althusser and Lefebvre (as well as Gramsci) as I've noted and, most famously, about Edward Said's contributions to Palestinian liberation politics over and against his work in literary criticism and interpretation (Bové 2000; Said 1979).[13] In each of these cases, political and tactical thought is relegated to the margins of these authors' work or it is denigrated, hidden, excluded, or constitutes the basis for an apologia in the traditions of interpretation and criticism.

In social movement studies, tactics are an essential expression of collective action. Authors writing on tactics through the traditions that analyze collective action describe a relationship between tactics and political community where certain tactical practices threaten to undermine the political communities that engage in organized struggle. Both a sense of what comprises legitimate forms of tactical practice and the organizational structures through which tactical practices are exercised lock participants in place. The political community becomes a product of its social location in a broader framework of institutions, law, and politics. Transcending the social location through which organizations operate politically requires not simply a more radical theoretical posture toward society and a more aggressive repertoire of tactical practices but, as Buci-Glucksmann explains in the first two quotations, both a real and conceptual change of terrain that demonstrates to the individual subjectivities fomented in an oppositional political community the actual potential for a critical transformation of society through the ways in which they act upon it collectively. Theory systematizes practice if and only if practices intervene in reality in ways that begin to open up new possibilities that command new knowledge, new approaches, in short, a new framework or a change of terrain. This, as Sassoon states, is the basis of Gramsci's work in prison: to understand a shifting political terrain that is the product of the party's activity in political struggle; to understand how the subjective forces contained within the party begin to lay the groundwork for a new reality that reflects these forces; to insert the party into a position of command within the framework of a reality that is shifting and changing—opening up new situations through which the party can seize territory and further position itself tactically.

Buci-Glucksmann and Sassoon, as quoted, are discussing the conditions, in thought, that can be realized, that can be made real (i.e., a gnosis—a philosophical and political practice that both penetrates and reorganizes the political forces that lock the society into a totality through an operative knowledge and that confronts the essential productive forces that reproduce power relations). I will discuss and demonstrate three registers of reality that are, at the very least, analytically distinct from one another to establish the contextual levels in which tactical practices are situated. They are refractory reality, effective reality, and concrete reality. The latter, concrete reality, is a conceptualization of the objective conditions constitutive of reality, including a subjective (a predictive and perspectival) element—this is the intervention of the (collective) analyst and their movement organization as both an analytic and decisive event.

In the beginning of Notebook 13, §2, Gramsci introduces the determinants of analysis that constitute his Marxist political science, an analysis that finds its conclusions in strategic plans and tactical inquiries. He describes:

> The study of how 'situations' should be analyzed, in other words how to establish the various levels of the relations of force, offers an opportunity for an elementary exposition of the science and art of politics—understood as a body of practical rules for research and of detailed observations *useful for awakening an interest in effective reality and for stimulating more rigorous and more vigorous political insights*. This should be accompanied by the explanation of what is meant in politics by strategy and tactics, by strategic 'plan,' by propaganda and agitation, by command structure or science of political organization and administration. (Gramsci 1971: 175–176)

In order to understand "effective reality"—the combination of economic, social, and political forces that pose an immediate constraint to the present (conjuncture)—any political analysis must concern itself with questions pertaining to the contents of that reality. Political insights, denotatively, mark the passage from analysis to an operative political subjectivity directed toward achieving a societal transformation through the characteristics of political science: an organizational and administrative capacity that enables the development of a plan, strategies, and the collective will to implement the program tactically.

Later, in Notebook 13, §36, Gramsci discusses characteristics pertaining to organization and administration. Debates pertaining to the organizational form of the communist parties in general and the Italian Communist Party in specific (Stalin's "Third Period Policies" Lyons Theses [1926] [in Gramsci 1978: 340–375]),[14] frame, for Gramsci, how the penultimate political organizational form can most effectively render itself as a solid, inclusive, and agile political force in the context of effective reality or, put more specifically, in a context where the forces of political opposition maintain powerful allegiances, command resources, enjoy greater organizational capacity, and maintain a predominant ideological position. A political organization must continue to both struggle and grow its ranks in this context, all the while depending on the progressive elements within its ranks and providing support to them. A democratic structure must be adaptive to real, concrete struggles in such a way that party strategy understands and effectively strategizes the tactical thrusts of the rank-and-file members, understanding, meeting, and supporting their most crucial needs in the framework of a concrete political reality. Sassoon specifies this point as follows: "The fact that organizational questions must be resolved in terms of a concrete political reality is emphasized by Gramsci's discussion of democratic as opposed to what he calls bureaucratic or organic centralism" (1984: 162).

In these notes, Gramsci categorizes a range of bureaucratic and administrative forms. In Weberian fashion, Gramsci explores a logic of means noting that bureaucratic centralism finds its apotheosis in expressions of vulgar vanguardism and expressive charismatic-authoritative forms.[15] Complementary discussions of the party from *Note sul Machiavelli* (1949) describe the internal composition of social relations across the party form in general, whereby any organizational form runs the risk of participants seeing it apart from themselves. He describes the breaking of an organic link between the collective political community and the organization:

> If each of the individual members sees the collective organism as an entity external to himself, it is evident that this organism no longer in fact exists, it becomes a phantasm of the mind, a fetish. . . . What is astonishing, and typical, is that fetishism of this kind occurs too in 'voluntary' organisms, not of a 'public' or State character, like parties and trade unions. The tendency is to see the relationship between the individual and the organism as a dualism; it is towards an external, critical attitude of the individual towards the organism (if the attitude does not consist of an enthusiastic, acritical admiration). In any case a fetishistic relationship. The individual expects the organism to act, even if he does not do anything himself, and does not reflect that precisely because his attitude is very widespread, the organism is necessarily inoperative. Furthermore, it should be recognized that, since a deterministic and mechanical conception of history is very widespread (a common-sense conception which is related to the passivity of the great popular masses), each individual, seeing that despite his non-intervention something still does happen, tends to think that there indeed exists, over and above individuals, a phantasmagorical being, the abstraction of the collective organism, a kind of autonomous divinity, which does not think with any concrete brain but still thinks, which does not move with specific human legs but still moves, etc. (Gramsci 1949: 157–158, cited in Gramsci 1971: 187, note 83).

The problem with a party that forces its collective body into movement with strong command and political and cultural detachment from its members is that, over time, it disintegrates the democratic impulses that engender it. More significantly, however, is that the internal process of collective analysis, collectivized information, deliberation, and dissensus is replaced with an authoritative framework that cannot take account of the political and tactical details in the context of class struggle; there is no communication from "below," no participation in the framework of the party. The accumulation of the experiences produced through class struggle become separate from the party; it ceases to be organic, rather it becomes merely administrative. Taken together, all the elements internal to the political organization that denote political subjectivity and establish praxis at a specific level as a philosophy of becoming ever more conscious and active (as developing more rigorous and vigorous political insights) can either be nurtured or destroyed. In this case, it is destroyed and a party becomes independent from its "rank-and-file" members; it becomes authoritarian. It decides for the rank and file. Political issues and problems, then, become matters of morality, culture, and conduct that are imposed upon the rank and file within the framework of a political organization. They take the form of dictates from administrative strata. The party becomes an external force opposed to the consciousness of those it purportedly represents.[16]

Despite all the risks of developing party cadres that are interdependent in the internal and external constitutive framework of political processes and political power so that they can retain and foster independent and constituent critical subjectivities elements and maintain a progressive and inclusive line, Gramsci sees the internal constitution of a progressive political party structure as necessarily democratic and more than merely worth the risk. Sassoon states, in a footnote, that Gramsci's discussion of the political party (in Notebook 14, §34) demonstrates that, "for Gramsci, the type of internal organization of a party is an indication of its 'progressive' or 'regressive' nature" (1984: 239, note 4). I explore the theoretical and historical ramifications of this theme in greater detail in the second and third chapters. However, it is worth noting in brief here that a party where across the *organica*—or strata with positions and roles that contain authorities, jurisdictions over which authority is exercised, and rules of conduct, that include the flexibility and responsiveness of everyone involved—the development of political subjectivity (independent) becomes an expressive and intersubjective process (debate, dissensus, etc.).[17] Despite the risks of fractionalization and dissolution, every instance of collective political expression is also, at the same time, a litmus test, so to speak, of collective will (political intersubjectivity). Finally, a party that requires persistent contact between its rank-and-file members and its administrative structure is a party that has the capacity to reshape itself, to rebuild itself, to expand itself, to form coalitions, alliances, and so on. The persistent work of "articulating" the party builds the party; it requires the collective participation of all of its members. A party that is detached from its rank and file and maintains a strong line, opposing itself to building coalitions and making alliances, is a party that has limited its capacity to intervene politically in effective reality.

The political party must act upon political realities concretely. Indeed, this is the impetus for the logic of structure and argumentation in the third section, if not the entirety, of Sassoon's *Gramsci's Politics* (1987). The relationship between class struggle and thought mark the philosophical and historical investigations of Gramsci in Buci-Glucksmann's *Gramsci and the State* (1980), which give rise to her gnoseological conception of Gramsci's Marxism. Buci-Glucksmann's investigations allow Thomas in *The Gramscian Moment: Philosophy, Hegemony, and Marxism* (2009) to pinpoint the development of hegemony in a concrete historical fashion. Thomas fleshes out, further, the bones of Buci-Glucksmann's gnoseology, investigating and explaining the full philological thrust of Gramsci's thought in the crucial period "between 1931 and 1932, between the description of hegemony as a 'metaphysical event' and the discovery of a type of hegemony that would be a 'philosophical fact,' " sustaining a new wave of Gramsci scholarship (Thomas 2009: 39, 2013).

The category of concrete reality is, then, of the greatest importance in understanding the special and active role that analysis plays as indicative of a transformative system of thought. Tactics implemented upon extant political realities become the entry point into reality itself; marking an intervention into the social structures through a force of political power that develops originally and organically on the terrain of economic production from the agents of working and subaltern or popular classes. The accumulation and articulation of the experiences won through a repertoire of tactical practices inform the adaptive strategic plan of the party as a whole—making the experience of struggles within the party both live and concrete. As each of the preceding sections discuss, tactics, more than merely acts, play a central role in proving hypotheses; building knowledge, community, and subjectivities; and tactical practices give rise to the departures into knowing, otherwise shaking and shifting the epistemological traditions that have weighed on the social, cultural, and political consciousness of the majority of the population for so long.

Concrete reality must be understood through the complex of social, economic, and political forces that comprise reality at various distinctive levels. These forces move with various degrees of stolidity and responsiveness and in various ways. Concrete reality, then, is an empirical and analytically derived reality that—most importantly—is an expression of the "subjective elements" described earlier: political communities, political strategies, and an active presence within the social forces that shape history (e.g., party, program, and tactics). Reality, in this sense, is understood as an analytical and political potentiality that can only be realized collectively, subjectively, and in action (this is why the debate pertaining to the internal politics of the bureaucratic form of political organizations, expressly the political party, is of significance in the discussion of concrete reality). This is why, for Gramsci, maintaining and elaborating the democratic impulses in the organizational structure of the political party is a central concern. The empirical determinants of concreteness find their ontological rhythm in tactical responses to the external and internal political conditions and constraints through which the party members intervene, in struggle, in effective reality (in the *realpolitik*). As I describe further in the next chapter, the expression of a concrete reality is part of Gramsci's original theory of ideologies as "historically organic." Any transformations in political practices that see strategies implemented through programs that give rise to assemblies that intervene, for instance, upon the contemporary and original terrain of economic production change reality and, as a result, give rise to ideologies organic to this change (Texier 1979).

The realization and canalization of concrete political force in the form of practices and the party's institutional presences correspond to the analyses of the relations of forces; they mark effective and real fronts in the war of position.[18] In order to fully understand how an intervention into and a transformation of effective reality happens, a conception of concrete reality is necessary. Effective reality represents the social forces that are produced, shaped, directed, and reproduced through political forces—hegemony—supported by institutions, ideology, law, policies, customs, and traditions. The shift to a reality concrete to the political subjectivity and organizational form that seeks to wrest the power of the state through incremental and durable societal changes emerges from praxis constituted in class struggle. It is important to understand the aspects of Gramsci's thought that contribute to the relationship between political subjectivity, political organization, and effective and concrete reality.

The quotations that describe concrete reality are rooted in Gramsci's discussion of the party form as derived from his reading of Machiavelli's *The Prince*. Notably, Benedetto Fontana's authoritative analysis of Gramsci's relationship to Machiavelli's work in *Hegemony and Power: On the Relation between Gramsci and Machiavelli* (1993), provides a clear statement of the ontological basis for Gramsci's thought in the historical context through which political forces play a role in shaping the direction of history.[19] Fontana states:

> Interpreters of Gramsci have rightly noted that his political philosophy is fundamentally humanist—or rather, as he himself puts it, 'neo-humanist.' Human beings, for Gramsci, are not 'givens' whose nature is immutable and fixed: they are not 'essences' whose existence is already determined. They are a 'becoming,' ineradicably rooted in the historical process. Indeed, human beings are history, both as actors who through their practical activities make history, and as thinkers who contemplate themselves in history. (Fontana 1993: 1)

Fontana captures the constructivist nature and ontological thrust (Gramsci's neohumanism) of Gramsci's theory as it is realized historically. The philosophy of praxis advances elements of a reality that, though ineradicably an essential, organic, contribution to economic production,[20] is buried by the effective reality of social and political forces that obscure, alienate, and hide these relations of forces in plain sight through the structural and juridical form of the nation-state and, also, directly and politically at every turn whenever and wherever they become manifest. Gramsci's political theory, then, takes on the characteristics of what Buci-Glucksmann describes as a gnosis: establishing a special and active political knowledge and insight that is designed to penetrate the mystical, yet real, presences of power and unveil and confront them through an analysis of the essential productive forces that reproduce power relations economically, socially, and politically.

Levels of Reality

The relations of forces, at their most solid, durable, and highest (macro) level, are described by Gramsci as a "refractory reality" in Notebook 13, §17, under a long note that discusses the levels and moments of forces in combination and movement. Although it is not possible to "move" on the terrain of a "refractory reality," the analysis of this level of force is indispensable to understanding "hegemony as a philosophical fact"—whether "the problem of the relations between structure and superstructure" can begin to be "accurately posed and resolved" (Notebook 13, §17; Gramsci 1971: 177).[21] It is here that a sustained tactical campaign of agitation, propaganda, and mobilizations can be envisioned and, in the main, may become warranted. The identification of specific conjunctures where, from out of the polity, an effective reality expressed through political forces mounts a vigorous albeit limited defense of the existing societal structure (see, also, earlier in Notebook 13, §17; Gramsci 1971: 178). Gramsci describes this "refractory reality" as "a relation of social forces which is closely linked to the structure, objective, independent of human will, and which can be measured with the systems of the exact or physical sciences" (1971: 180). He goes on to explain:

> The level of development of the material forces of production provides a basis for the emergence of the various social classes, each one of which represents a function and has a specific position within production itself. This relation is what it is, a refractory reality: nobody can alter the number of firms or their employees, the number of cities or the given urban population, etc. By studying these fundamental data it is possible to discover whether in a particular society there exist the necessary and sufficient conditions for its transformation—in other words, to check the degree of realism and practicability of the various ideologies which have been born on its own terrain, on the terrain of the contradictions which it has engendered during the course of its development. (Notebook 13, §17; Gramsci 1971: 180–181).

The accurate analysis of economic forces, "refractory reality" is a necessary condition for the war of position. It provides information about the most effective strategic plans; it identifies weaknesses; it suggests effective tactical practices. Pointedly, Gramsci identifies the terrain upon which the political forces express aspects of refractory reality. These ideological or political expressions of economic suture and societal overdetermination (the amplification and transformation of existing ideological tenets) become the target, in a conjuncture, for propaganda and agitation.[22] Political ideologies move upon the terrain of effective reality. As several structural Marxists have written, based on Gramsci's construction of civil, social, and state alliances within the framework of hegemony, a relatively strong integral state may adjust aspects of refractory reality (through, for example, direct partnerships between private industry and the state or through policies that have an indirect but broad and general effect on several fractions of the capitalist class) to make ideological proclamations effective in society. Attempts to address structural problems that give rise to conjunctures mean, first, that hegemony moves both ideologically and politically on the terrain of effective reality for the purposes of avoiding a crisis of political authority. At the same time, the party as a guiding counterhegemonic force militates—through agitation and propaganda—against these tenuous policies and practices issuing out of positions of power. In each conjuncture, realizing the possibility to advance counterhegemonically, by making real concrete interventions into social problems and establishing alliances, building party capacity, providing aid, winning social and economic concessions, and so forth, demonstrates both how and indeed that struggles can be won. These successes link the political subjectivity of the political community within an organization to the strategic program and tactical practices that produced a real and palpable change. The ideological expression of these victories, however small, reflect real events that were the product of the coordinated tactical action of party members and allied groups and individuals who engaged in struggle to the benefit of both their immediate needs and, also, to the benefit of the broader class position. The ideology both reflects a historic event and is organically linked to the struggle itself (Notebook 13, §17; Notebook 7, §19; Gramsci 1971: 178, 376–377). As a result, an ideology organic to working and popular class fractions and to a party or coalition of left parties strengthens the political position of the left as a whole. The collective, subjective framework of the left becomes real, concrete, and durable as it advances further into the effective political reality—as it realizes its program through a range of tactical interventions.

Effective reality represents the society expressed through the polity, the real constraints of hegemony. It consists of the organizations and agents, the intellectuals, that are organic to it in both the state and civil society. Effective reality is the preeminent domain of entrepreneurs, investors, industrialists, their vast support staff, and the bureaucrats, jurists, and official and unofficial ideologues of the hegemonic state. Gramsci also discusses diplomats, politicians, and even political scientists operating within the national norms of their discipline. All have a stake in either maintaining or advancing the conditions of hegemony for the capitalist state. Each, however, is constrained by the institutional forms, procedures, and the refractory forms of reality that, disembedded from society, require a response that often results in the state acting either at the behest of class fractions that are strongly allied with the polity, class fractions that provide essential social services and goods (through market forces), or those that operate in the interests of stabilizing sectors of the society. Gramsci, in Notebook 13, §16, describes the relationship between the pragmatics of realpolitik and effective reality, arguing, "Too much (therefore superficial and mechanical) political realism often leads to the assertion that a statesman should only work within the limits of 'effective reality'; that he should not interest himself in what 'ought to be' but only in what 'is' " (Gramsci 1971: 171).

However, Gramsci also makes an important distinction between the active politician who wishes to transform societal conditions and politicians whose consciousness, analysis, and range of actions is limited by maintaining hegemony as it exists. Intellectuals who articulate amplified or even extremist versions of mainstream ideological currents might seek to upset the balance of political and social forces to favor a broad or specified set of policies for capital accumulation—in some instances fundamentally transforming the relationship the state has to private industry and finance (both fascism and the "neoliberal revolution" of the 1970s are cases in point), making a political program concrete. But these shifts in the balance of forces have two significant and problematic results. First, they often upset the societal status quo, potentially resulting in a longer-term instability with sets of unintended consequences (for example, the vast array of contemporary, post-2008, political responses on various scales to the "neoliberal revolution"). Second, the limitations to imagination and action must move upon the terrain of effective political reality culturally, rhetorically, ideologically, procedurally, legally, and so on, to transform the balance of political and societal forces. This requires significant time, massive resources, and mobilizations, as well as new cleavages within the polity—cleavages that may be detrimental to both the integration of civil society into the state and long- and short-term hegemony. Regardless, economic, political, and cultural elites' access to the state, even within the extreme ideological parameters of the existing polity, mark a continuity of and not a challenge to hegemony. Political transformations of this kind also require a relatively integral state in the short term (articulated and experienced under different political and economic conditions), the continuity of cultural and political traditions (building relationships with some elite, traditional intellectuals), and maintaining and improving capitalist society. The transformation of political forces maintains class society.

Concrete reality represents an intervention into the polity and the social forces that it shapes and supports through waves of tactical action maintained through a political organization or organizations that are broadly interrelated. Concrete reality renders the struggle against hegemony as concrete by establishing footholds in the war of position through organizational positioning, developing ever broader relationships, maintaining and further developing strategic posture, and pushing counterhegemonic struggle further into the effective or extant political reality through tactical action. The distinction between an "active politician" and a politician whose function it is to maintain hegemony introduces the categorical shift to "concrete reality." Gramsci uses Machiavelli as the model of an active politician; it allows him to introduce the category of "concrete reality." He states,

> A distinction must be made not only between "diplomat" and "politician," but also between political scientist and active politician. *The diplomat inevitably will move only within the bounds of effective reality, since his specific activity is not the creation of some new equilibrium, but the maintenance of an existing equilibrium within a certain juridical framework.* Similarly, the political scientist has to keep within the bounds of effective reality in so far as he is merely a scientist. But Machiavelli is not merely a scientist: he is a partisan, a man of powerful passions, an active politician, who wishes to create a new balance of forces and therefore cannot help concerning himself with what "ought to be" (not of course in a moralistic sense). Hence the question cannot be posed in these terms, it is more complex. It is one, that is to say, of *seeing whether what "ought to be" is arbitrary or necessary; whether it is concrete will on the one hand or idle fancy, yearning, daydream on the other.* The active politician is a creator, an initiator; but he neither creates from nothing nor does he move in the turbid void of his own desires and dreams. *He bases himself on effective reality*, but what is this effective reality? Is it something static and immobile, or is it not rather a relation of forces in continuous motion and shift of equilibrium? *If one applies one's will to the creation of a new equilibrium among the forces which really exist* and are operative—basing oneself on the particular force which one believes to be progressive and strengthening it to help it to victory— *one still moves on the terrain of effective reality, but does so in order to dominate and transcend it (or to contribute to this). What "ought to be" is therefore concrete.* (Gramsci 1971: 172, my emphasis)

The quotation represents (as can only be the case) a dynamic definition of "concrete reality." It contains the following elements: 1) Political subjectivity, organizational position, and role determine one's relationship to either concrete or effective reality or the continuum that moves one between these two realities. 2) Acting in such a way as to intervene within political and social forces requires a distinction between a political ideology and a program; the latter demonstrates the realization of a politically expressed desire for social transformation. It follows that "ought to" signifies only on the surface of ethics.[23] However, in this case, "ought to" signifies changing social constraints that the effective reality of existing politics struggles to leave in place for the dominated class, and the differential and varied or changing effects (over time) across working-class fractions. 3) The pure ideologism of what "ought to" be is challenged when that question is approached through "effective reality" or what is. 4) Collective organizational will (the subjective element) links the desires of the counterhegemonic political community (the organization) to the ideology, strategies, and tactics that produce and demonstrate "what ought to be" or the process of transcending effective reality. 5) Finally, concrete reality is predicated upon the subjective element; how one acts upon, and through, the balance of existing forces depends upon *one's goal* in relationship to hegemony. If the active politician uses political means to reorganize and rearrange or shore up the balance of forces in favor of a progressive social force or to *transcend* the current basis for social organization, they contribute to either transformation or revolution, respectively.

At the conclusion of this section, several insights about the analytical levels of reality must be brought into sharp relief. The first is that though a methodological distinction can cut reality into three levels, "they are aspects of a single phenomenon at a single moment in time" (Sassoon 1987: 184). The second insight has to do with the discussion of political consciousness and political subjectivity in relationship to tactics as the singular form of the imputation of a concrete reality that emerges, politically, through class struggle. Buci-Glucksmann's "gnoseology" and both Buci-Glucksmann and Thomas's discussion of hegemony as a philosophical fact mark a crucial distinction between effective and concrete reality. The realization of hegemony as a philosophical fact indicates that an organizational change both can be imagined and has occurred; the positioning of the organization within political forces has reached a position of significant political contention in the framework of society (or in effective reality).

This marks two important implications for political consciousness and political subjectivity. The consciousness of political power—the limitations and constraints within which a political organization and its members operate—implicitly establishes the range and modalities of political antagonism, such that one's consciousness of the object world of political forces as well as one's location and range of movement within that world—one's subjectivity—is expressed through the planning and tactical frameworks that make up struggle. The heavy triumvirate of levels of reality weighs upon consciousness and action. In this context, both political consciousness and subjectivity express revolution as both ideologism and desire while, at the same time, attempting to make revolution concrete within the boundaries established through political forces gaining footholds in civil society, which decreases the burdens and alleviates constraints that are immediate to both consciousness and subjectivity (e.g., higher wages, reduction in work time, increases in benefits). A "trade union mentality" finds its apotheosis in the realization of class corporate limits. The same may be said for "parliamentary" socialism and communism in relation to the state. A revolutionary political consciousness and subjectivity may engage in the tactical framework that supports a trade union mentality, but it cannot cease to be active and must move beyond class corporatism (to the extent that political consciousness contains and expresses, intellectually, revolutionary theory). Then, to move beyond the bounded aspects of political forces and vie for hegemony, it would follow that political consciousness and political subjectivity are no longer bound by its existence in refractory reality or by the limitations of social forces that seem to be or are detached from political forces. The realization of hegemony as a philosophical fact requires subjective factors to have access to the full societal and political terrain. As Sassoon states, "It is at this stage that the subjective forces can have full play for it is only now that the class goes beyond its structural existence and exists fully at the level of the superstructure. When this happens, the realm of necessity or constraint by material conditions recedes and the realm of freedom or of subjective force emerges" (1987: 186).

It is my contention, here, that the concrete path toward the realm of freedom happens through the incremental intensification of tactical practices. If the goal is to intervene in effective reality in such a way as to make concrete the communal political consciousness, political subjectivities, then, are actively developed and shaped through tactical action. Tactics are the collective yet directly experiential means of intervention. They are the subjective development, transformation, and realization of the subjective forces that have been expressed ideologically, realized tactically, and honed into programs that are the product of debates about strategic action. Finally, the full theoretical and expressive array of political consciousness and the ontic, epistemological, and experiential contents of political subjectivity become real and concrete. Political consciousness is developed and unified as the organization, its political community, and each member sees their planning take shape through the mobilization of their bodies on the plane of an oppositional political and societal reality that, up to this point, has produced only ill-fitting, uncomfortable, and torturous subject positions.

From Effective to Concrete Reality: Demonstrating Tactics

The conclusion of this chapter is designed to demonstrate the *tactical* intervention into *effective reality*: the conversion of a theory into a strategy and, finally, tactically, into a *concrete reality*. Further, the epistemological and ontological role of tactical action is evidenced through Gramsci's careful, deliberate, and precise linguistic design of "propaganda" and "agitation." The indispensability of tactics—tactics as both culturally and politically expressive—and, most significantly, the successive tactical interventions as productive of an inaugural political subjectivity not only draw together the preceding conceptual threads, they show how the concept of the conjuncture works (on the terrain of effective reality concretizing or making real the organizational, theoretical, and subjective elements of counterhegemony). The following example brings together Gramsci's analyses of forces with his concept of the conjuncture and concrete reality, demonstrating this chapter's core claim regarding the tactical pivot: the realization of praxis, intersubjective political consciousness and revolutionary will through action. Taken pari passu, we can demonstrate through passages from Notebook 13 key concepts contributing to the role of tactics. The first passage describes how tactics must be positioned in relationship to the relations of force at a given moment in time through *analysis*; the characteristics of that moment comprise the concept of the conjuncture; the sustained tactical intervention beginning within a conjuncture is paired with the various societal and political forces that mark the progressive development of political struggle in the context of hegemonic struggles with *effective reality*.

Analyses:

> acquire significance *only if they serve to justify a particular practical activity*, or initiative of will. They reveal the points of least resistance, at which the force of will can be most fruitfully applied; they suggest *immediate tactical operations*; they indicate how a campaign of political agitation may

best be launched, what language will best be understood by the masses. (Notebook 13, §17; Gramsci 1971: 185)

Conjuncture:

> [T]he conjuncture is the set of immediate and ephemeral characteristics of the economic situation.... Study of the conjuncture is thus more closely linked to immediate politics, to 'tactics' and agitation, while the 'situation' relates to 'strategy' and propaganda, etc. (*Passato e Presente*, 1951: 148–149)

> These incessant and persistent efforts (since no social formation will ever admit that it has been superseded) form the terrain of the 'conjunctural,' and it is upon this terrain that the forces of opposition organize. These forces seek to demonstrate that the necessary and sufficient conditions already exist to make possible, and hence imperative, the accomplishment of certain historical tasks. (Notebook 13, §17; Gramsci 1971: 178)

Effective and concrete reality:

> If one applies one's will to the creation of a new equilibrium among the forces which really exist and are operative—basing oneself on the particular force which one believes to be progressive and strengthening it to help it to victory—one still moves on the terrain of effective reality, but does so in order to dominate and transcend it (or to contribute to this). *What "ought to be" is therefore concrete.* (Notebook 13, §16; Gramsci 1971: 172, my emphasis)

These quotations both summarize and demonstrate the insights discussed at the end of the last section and Buci-Glucksmann's gnoseological conception of Gramsci's theory, whereby it "finds its operative concept only when 'the realization of a hegemonic apparatus is a philosophical fact' " (Buci-Glucksmann 1980: 236). This, also, is the substantive and philosophical aspect of what Peter Thomas identifies as the "Gramscian Moment"[24] (2009: 38–39).

I build upon an example drawn from Alessandro Carlucci's book *Gramsci and Languages: Unification, Diversity, Hegemony* (2015).[25] Carlucci discusses the efforts of the Turin Socialists (especially Gramsci and the *L'Ordine Nuovo* group) to demobilize the Sassari Brigade through a sustained campaign of agitation and propaganda organized and led by Gramsci between April and July of 1919. Carlucci's contribution uses archival research in the Central State Archives, Interior Ministry, Headquarters of Public Safety, Division of General and Confidential Affairs (ACS Ministero dell'Iterno, DgPS, Divisione Affari Generali e Riservati) as well as many Italian-language secondary sources and firsthand accounts.

Although Carlucci's book is most the complete English-language discussion of the events specific to the demobilization of the Sassari Brigade that occurred prior to the international general strike in solidarity with the Russian and Hungarian Soviet Republics (planned for July 20 or 21) it is important to briefly set the historical context in which this event took place.

In late March, the Sassari Brigade arrives in Turin months into the Biennio Rosso (Two Red Years) (Fiori 1971 120; Gramsci [1926] 1995b). According to Gwyn Williams and Alistair Davidson, since 1916 Gramsci had been immersed in the working-class movement in Turin (Davidson 1977: 114, 118; Williams 1975: 92; see also Galanaki 1986). Davidson recounts correspondence with Palmiro Togliatti and testimony from Giovanni Parodi—a radical and well-respected worker who was an ardent supporter of Gramsci from early on:

> In this ceaseless contact with the workers and in the mutual exchange of education, lay the secret of Gramsci's success. Years later he wrote to Togliatti that he had succeeded in linking his position with that of the workers by "never taking action without first sounding out the opinion of the worker in various ways . . . so that our actions always had an almost immediate and wide success and seemed like the interpretation of a diffuse deeply felt need, never as the cold application of an intellectual scheme." Sometimes he would speak three times in an afternoon, and his staunch followers from the Youth Federation emulated him. Parodi said simply that he had completely "proletarianized" himself. (Davidson 1977: 118)

Briefly, according to Walter L. Adamson (1983), and repeated in the testimony of an unnamed militant worker, Gramsci's relationship to the Turin working classes enabled him to introduce an original organizational structure—ward councils or clubs—that combined each craft within a factory and unorganized workers in other occupations (Adamson 1983: 52–53; Zuckert 2011). By the time Gramsci embarked upon his campaign to demobilize the Sassari Brigade and clear space for the subsequent wave of strikes, he had been in constant contact with Italian laborers in Turin for four years and had organizational experiences that were affirmative, significant, and resonated broadly among the working population.

As Giuseppe Fiori notes in his biography of Gramsci, the Sassari Brigade consisted "largely of Sardinian shepherds and peasants" (1970: 120; Carlucci 2015: 38, note 74). During this time, Gramsci's principal concern was with establishing and building *L'Ordine Nuovo* into the organ of the factory council movement, especially after the momentum from his "Workers' Democracy" article written with Palmiro Togliatti on June 21, 1919, about the factory "internal commissions." The internal commissions were the nascent form from which the factory council movement develops until it is subordinated to trade union control by Tasca at the conclusion of the general strike in late April 1920. Gramsci was also "exasperated" by the ignorance of the Italian Socialist Party (PSI) toward the peasants (Cammett 1967: 132). Gramsci wrote several articles in the late months of 1919 and the early months of 1920 in *L'Ordine Nuovo*: "Il Rivoluzionario e la Mosca Coccheria" (The revolutionary and the coachman flies), "Fuori del Dilemma" (The problem of force), and "Cos'è la Reazione?" (What is reaction?), attacking the liberal position that advocated an alliance between skilled labor and technicians in the North with capitalists at the expense of the Southern peasants. The liberals viewed the peasants as suspicious of, if not antagonistic to, socialism, believing that the PSI would take back gains made during the beginning of the Biennio Rosso. Seratti's leading position in the PSI met the broadly imagined and alleged antagonism that the Southern peasants held for socialism with, quoting Tasca, "suspicion and ill will" (in Cammett 1967: 132). As Gramsci will recount in his last piece of writing before his incarceration, "Some Aspects of the Southern Question," if the terrain of Italian politics, in particular, the "bourgeois parties" and the Socialist Party, shared anything in common, it was their belief that the Southern peasant was "the ball and chain that prevents a more rapid progress in the civil development of Italy; Southerners are biologically inferior beings, either semi-barbarians, or full out barbarians, by natural destiny" (Gramsci [1926] 1995b: 20).

Gramsci was exasperated because he knew, firsthand, that the accounts of the left and center-left were untrue. "Workers and Peasants," published in *L'Ordine Nuovo* on August 2, 1919, unpacks Fiori's description of the Sassari Brigade as Sardinian shepherds and peasants. Gramsci describes, in no uncertain terms, the historical peasant and shepherd shaped by modern forms of militarization and discipline. Whereby the Southern peasant, prior to the war,

> was reduced to a tiny sum of primordial feelings (real feelings remain hidden) caused by the social conditions created by the parliamentary-democratic

state: the peasant was left completely at the mercy of the landowners and of their sycophants and corrupt public officials, and the main worry in their lives was to defend themselves physically against unexpected natural disasters, against the abuses and barbaric cruelty of the landowners and public officials. The peasant has always lived outside the domain of the law, without a legal personality, without moral individuality: he has remained an anarchic element, the independent atom in a chaotic tumult, held back only by fear of the *carabiniere* and of the devil. (Gramsci 1977: 84)

After the war, for the Southern peasant,

> [i]ndividual egotistical instincts have become blurred, a common unitary spirit has been formed, feelings have been equalized, a habit of social discipline has been formed: the peasants have conceived the state in its complex greatness, in its unmeasured power, in its complicated construction. They have conceived the world, no longer as an indefinitely large thing like the universe and tightly confined like the village church tower, but in its concreteness of states and peoples, of social strengths and weaknesses, of armies and machines, of wealths and poverties. Links of solidarity have been formed which otherwise only decades and decades of historical experience and intermittent struggles would have caused; in four years, in the mud and the blood of the trenches, a spiritual world emerged eager to affirm itself in permanent and dynamic social forms and institutions. (Gramsci 1977: 84–85)

In short, the peasant now possessed the prerequisites for political mobilization. Having been organized and disciplined (militarily) but, also, controlled, deployed, and used, the mysteries of power and how it is exercised that, according to Gramsci, the peasant had made a career of evading, now became a social fact or an effective reality, one that could now be confronted politically and organizationally. However, the composite Southerner-now-Northern-industrial-worker and Southerner-now-veteran provided, for Gramsci, the basis to demonstrate that "unearthing" the "hidden feelings" that were the shared basis for a peasant imaginary (the dynamics of oppression and exploitation as a national-cultural experience) could be achieved, tactically, with the historical advantage of many Southerners having an expanded world-view—a product of the effective social and political reality of a postwar and postindustrial Italy.

The goal of the Turin Socialists and the group associated with *L'Ordine Nuovo* was not merely to prevent the Sassari Brigade from mobilizing against the striking workers in July of 1919. It was, rather, to construct connections between the Turin workers and the soldiers; to communicate the solidarity of social class in the face of a contrarian elite rhetoric of both regional differences and the privileged status of industrial workers through direct communication, leaflets, and articles. The key to the entire campaign was Gramsci's strategic use of Sardinian to address the context in which the Sassari Brigade had been immersed but, more importantly, to get the Sassari Brigade to recognize that it played a broader role, both socially and politically, within the framework of this strategic conjuncture. Through archival documents, Alessandro Carlucci demonstrates the complexity of the situation that Gramsci had to navigate. He states:

> These documents confirm that the sense of belonging to the same region was also an element used to promote solidarity between the soldiers and the Socialist militants who came from Sardinia but lived in Turin. This use of regional identity was instrumental to the following ends: encouraging as many soldiers as possible to share the revolutionary enthusiasm of the working classes; and propagating modern political views based on the belief that social progress would be the result of class conflict. Regional identity was not presented as a form of identity to be admired or preserved. We shall see that many of those who collaborated with Gramsci later recalled that the Sardinian language was used during this campaign. Yet this use of Sardinian was also functional in the attempt to bring the soldiers onto the side of the popular masses, while it did not entail praise of linguistic otherness as a value in itself. (Carlucci 2015: 44)

Carlucci recounts through workers' testimonies and archival research that Gramsci's use of language had to demonstrate or represent, broadly, workers' respect for Sardinian people. Although, in specific, a sense of respect had to be conferred upon the Sardinian soldiers, Gramsci used language to bridge the workers and the Sardinian soldiers, not to affirm the specialness of Sardinian identity, which could have played easily into the contrary rhetoric that separated soldiers and workers. Carlucci puts it as follows:

> Gramsci knew what the linguistic repertoire of the Sardinian soldiers was, despite the internal variation associated with the different local origins of the soldiers. In most situations, Sardinian was likely to be perceived as the

language of solidarity, as well as the language that symbolically evoked the common destiny of all of those who could understand it and use it. . . . Gramsci did not indulge in an idealization of Sardinian cultural and linguistic identity. Nor did he snobbishly condemn Sardinian as a language (or a group of language varieties) which an intellectual committed to the cause of social and political revolution should not use. As we have seen, he offered some brief accounts of the life and history of the subaltern classes in a geographically marginal region, as Sardinia was at the time. At the same time, this attention to the past and present culture of the Sardinian poor was accompanied by recognition of the vitality of their language, which Gramsci did not refrain from using. Yet he did not turn to the regional language as a symbol of identity with which boundaries might be erected, leading to the exclusion of those who do not share that particular identity. On the contrary, he emphasized the common demands of peasants in southern Italy and the working-class population of the North; and he used Sardinian words in a manner that was functional to the achievement of this inclusive goal. (Carlucci 2015: 47)

Carlucci demonstrates *how* Gramsci was able to link the demands of the workers and the Sassari Brigade to translate or make intelligible to members of the Sassari Brigade not simply an ideology or, more crudely, an action. Rather, by switching cultural codes and paying attention to regional differentiation (linguistic markers) within dialect, Gramsci bridged a Sardinian imaginary that was embedded socially and culturally through tradition with the concrete terrain he had been working to establish and advance with socialists, and others, and for the workers in Turin. Gramsci needed to make the desires of the Sassari Brigade consonant with the demands of the workers (while at the same time driving a wedge between the Sassari Brigade and the military and industrial elites in Turin) but, more importantly, he needed to demonstrate that these desires (and their bearers) had a place in reality—a reality not at all dissimilar to the workers' demands, which the Sassari Brigade had been sent to quash. He did this with a carefully chosen, single, word.

Gramsci uses the word "commune," a word with broad and multifaceted ethnoreligious, traditional-experiential, and modern revolutionary significance. Commune was a word that would signify differently for different classes but, more importantly, it was a Sardinian word that contained a deep spiritual resonance (that was not chiliastic) and, at the same time, indicated autonomous forms of regional governance and functional forms of communalism. According to Carlucci, Gramsci pens two articles upon the arrival of the Sassari Brigade in April, one using "commune," the other discussing the patronizing way that the soldiers had been received and the nature of General Carlo Sanna's (well regarded by Sardinian soldiers) remarks, which, delivered in Sardinian, were designed to drive a wedge between the Turin workers and soldiers. By July, the word "commune" is developed into a slogan linking workers to Sardinians in a broad and contemporary rendering of a political community.

In no uncertain terms, Gramsci is able to intervene in a contentious environment—one that would, likely, have resulted in mass violence and transform the effective political reality into a concrete political rendering of societal forces that represent, most closely, the class places of the participants involved in the episode. Gramsci spends four years developing relationships to the workers in Turin, giving speeches on an intensive and intensifying schedule, writing articles, editing a new paper, organizing workers, and transforming the organizational basis of political class composition to expand the political community of workers so that he can move, effectively, within the bounds of social reality.

The central point, however, is that Gramsci uses language and culture to unearth expressions of class forces that have been absent from the national discourse, from the language and strategies of political parties, and canalizes and advances these forces through the careful tactical use of language, through relationships, and through simple and appropriate terms that resonate, powerfully and broadly, for and against classes in society.

Carlucci discusses the work of Camilla Bettoni, a cultural linguist. He states, "As explained by a leading expert, Camilla Bettoni, loyalty and affiliation to a certain cultural-linguistic background can be conveyed by using even just a few words" (2015: 49). This is echoed in the social movement literature by Meyer N. Zald, who, precisely, explains how an "ideological catchphrase" resonates. He states:

> Ideological concerns may be manifested in elaborate, relatively coherent, and integrated systems of beliefs that have long histories and are widespread in a civilization, or they may be manifested in catch-phrases and metaphors that have mainly local resonance. Cadres and leaders of social movements are likely to have more developed and coherent systems of beliefs than casual adherents, sympathizers, and by-stander publics. (Zald 2000a: 4)

Gramsci, it seems, has achieved both criteria, simultaneously, as Zald describes. He is able to embed systems of beliefs into an ideological catch-phrase with deep transformative effects. As Zald notes, Gramsci, par excellence, had a more developed and coherent system of beliefs but, strikingly, he was able to articulate it, tactically, to effectively demobilize the Sassari Brigade. Gramsci's ability to produce a body of deeply effective verbal and written propaganda by recomposing and making intelligible class struggle also had the effect of increasing or unifying oppositional societal fractions or groups, expanding the boundaries of political community and affecting the political subjectivity of at least a group of soldiers. To demonstrate, in "Some Aspects of the Southern Question," referred to hereafter as "The Southern Question" ([1926] 1995b) Gramsci notes the following:

> These events . . . have had results which still subsist to this day and continue to work in the depths of the popular masses. They illuminated, for an instant, brains which had never thought in that way, and which remained marked by them, radically modified. . . . We can recall dozens and indeed hundreds of letters sent from Sardinia to the *Avanti!* editorial offices in Turin; letters which were frequently collective, signed by all the Sassari Brigade veterans in a particular village. By uncontrolled and uncontrollable paths, the political attitude which we supported was disseminated. (Gramsci [1926] 1995b: 26–27).

This particular event, which developed through sustained tactical intervention, is remembered as the basis for new political community and had a fundamental role in the development of the Sardinian Action Party, which was, at its inception, a socialist party. This event also, as Gramsci notes, transformed the way in which the Sassari veterans, returning from World War I, thought about society, politics, and their potential to act.

Conclusion

An effective and transformative action, agreed upon and applied collectively, is not merely transformative; it exposes novel ways of knowing that may not be present on the terrain of an "effective reality" but become "concrete," materializing class-based political subjectivities fighting to position and expand their political community. In this chapter, the heuristic that I am using to explain, first, the epistemological positioning of tactics in Gramsci's thought and, by extension, Marxism, and second, the role that tactics play across different analytical and interpretive approaches, is based on my interpretation of Gramsci's thought and the discovery (by Alessandro Carlucci) and discussion of significant events leading into the Biennio Rosso.

Gramsci *implements* several *strategies—hypotheses* he developed through interaction with the Turin workers (as Davidson [1977] notes). The circumstances, in 1919, demonstrate how tactically guided action is driven by both contexts and organizational forms and capacities. Most importantly, the success of the campaign to demobilize the Sassari Brigade shows how strategies and tactics are coupled to history, culture, and the ideological frameworks through which, at the time, Gramsci, working under the aegis of the PSI, understands, explains, and justifies its program, broadly. In this case, the success of Gramsci's tactical use of language resonated through the workers' movement. Gramsci's use of tactics, here, marked a significant intervention into bounded knowledge about the mobilization of Southern peasants; setting up a long-term strategy for the Italian Communist Party's theorizations with regard to peasant mobilizations. Last, the deliberative process within the political organization and the constant feedback from workers and sustained engagement with the Sassari Brigade developed and directed strategy and tactical implementation. The ward councils and factory councils represent original and innovative organizational forms through which a broader political composition of classes was possible. In specific, these groups demonstrated flexibility within organizational and ideological parameters. This is true of the ward councils, in particular, but as Davidson claims, the secret of Gramsci's success, in general, depended upon the deliberative and democratic form through which Gramsci could understand the conscious development of the subjective elements that allowed him to intervene in "effective reality."

The use of language with tactical precision, excavating and breathing life, politics, and community into an expressive culture, is how Gramsci makes his intervention. Gramsci's revitalization, rearticulation, and transformation of the traditions, through language, that informs the imaginary of the Sassari Brigade connects the examples from the social movement literature to the literary critical analysis at the beginning of the chapter. Gramsci "unearths" perspectives buried deeply within the tradition and culture of a peasant imaginary and mobilizes them, in an articulatory combination, with the industrial fraction of the Italian working classes in the North of Italy through innovative tactical and organizational means. The substantive aspects of Gramsci's experience in Turin set against his insight made, much later, in the 1930s, bear repeating. Furthermore, as the following quotation illustrates, Gramsci connects cultural, traditional, and linguistic expressions to the tactical act and the act to the forces that constitute the open-endedness of the real events that constitute a conjuncture. This is illustrated fully when Gramsci states:

> The most important observation to be made about any concrete analysis of the relations of force is the following: That such analyses cannot and must not be ends in themselves (*unless the intention is merely to write a chapter of past history*), but acquire significance *only if they serve to justify a particular practical activity*, or initiative of will. They reveal the points of least resistance, at which the force of will can be most fruitfully applied; they suggest *immediate tactical operations; they indicate how a campaign of political agitation may best be launched, what language will best be understood by the masses*, etc. (Notebook 13, §17; Gramsci 1971: 185, passages in italics and bold, my emphasis)

The campaign that Gramsci launches begins in 1916. It used language to articulate cultural positions and political futures between peasants and workers leading into a broad and, during its time, successful mobilization. However, over the course of those four years, Gramsci had to build capacity and structure a mobilization. Articulation implies the work of connecting separate parts. The next chapter focuses on the contention and correspondences between different parts of what may or what does comprise a broad-based movement. Gramsci had to use language to signify a series of cultural, traditional, and political contents in such a way that it was broadly resonant. As such, he produced an inclusive political-ideological framework and, alongside it, an organizational structure that was ready to both accommodate and demonstrate the ideas that were resonant for so many and poised them to act in common. In what follows, I theorize these relationships through the concept of ideological contention.

CHAPTER TWO

Ideological Contention

Rethinking Race and Mobilization during the Biennio Rosso

This chapter has two goals: to introduce the concept "ideological contention" into the study of social movements, and to demonstrate the concept through an analysis of the relationship between race and mobilization in modern national contexts. In this chapter, I expand my analysis of Gramsci's tactical and organizational work with a focus on the tactical and organizational efforts of Sardinian Southern Italian veterans and communists that also occur in 1919 and into the Biennio Rosso. A part of this expanded context establishes the contentious racialized political environment in which Southern Italian veterans and communists mobilized alongside industrial workers in Turin, building upon the context, case study framework, and analysis set up at the end of the last chapter.[1] Specifically, the analysis links the emergence of scientific racism to the period of large nation-state consolidation and the development of liberal political ideologies across Western nations. By broadening the scope of my analysis through a focus on racial and class struggles at the national level, I am able to articulate tactical practices in a broader theoretical framework.

The main claim that this chapter demonstrates is that movement struggles within the context of a national ideological framework impact movement ideology, such that the ideology of a movement effects their *organizational structure, the process of ideological elaboration, strategic choices,* and *tactical practices.* Specifically, I will argue that the internal struggles over the framework and interpretation of tactical practices, strategic programs, and the outcomes associated with protest actions including the development of successive waves of protest action depend upon understanding ideology as a contentious process within and against a movement that shapes it. This chapter explores how ideology organizes, coordinates, and mobilizes movement members in political processes through a study of the Sardinian worker and peasant and communist struggles in the context of a modernized and industrialized Italy (1917–1920). I expand upon the discussion of Gramsci's mobilization of racialized groups in Italy by demonstrating that, first, there was a strong pseudoscientific and political context that, collectively, generated a "racialized" common sense rather than an explicit coding of racism at the highest institutional levels of state governance. I argue that reevaluating the theoretical and empirical relationship between ideology and the frame perspective could strengthen analyses of social movement struggles. Specifically, I demonstrate that the concept of ideological contention and the conceptions of the tactical implementation of frames as "frame alignment" can be understood in a complementary manner. The modification of frames implies a process of articulation that is entirely like Gramsci's efforts to link the beliefs and sentiments of different groups (how they understand and express their domination and exploitation) in the interest of mobilizing them, in common, through a broader ideological framework of class struggle. Gramsci's articulation becomes inclusive of multiple perspectives and this is reflected in the debates about the organizational composition of the Communist Party (between 1921 and 1925), in "Some Aspects of the Southern Question" written in 1926, and, finally, in his conception of the bureaucratic organization of political parties (written between 1932 and 1934 in Notebook 13, §36). In short, these writings demonstrate my concept that there is a relationship between the ideological framework, organizational structure, strategies, and tactical practices that are both mutually constitutive and transformative.

This chapter analyzes the connection between race and mobilization in the context of early twentieth-century nationalism. Across Europe, just before, during, and immediately following the consolidation of large European nation-states in the late nineteenth century, theories of racial "degeneration" and evolutionary arrest were being issued by evolutionary scientists, medical psychiatrists and, in Italy, the newly "discovered" field of criminal anthropology (Gibson 1998; Pick 1989). In Italy, anthropologists and psychologists studied the Southern population with a particular investment in the hypotheses that degenerate physical and mental traits were stable and unchangeable (with some focused on the cultural and social effects upon heredity) and, also, that race ordered human variety in a hierarchy where Northern European characteristics resided at the top of the hierarchy and Southern Italians were near the bottom. Southerners were perceived as a social problem, and the Italian Society of Anthropology and Ethnology was founded on a research program based in these hypotheses in the interest of unifying modern Italy (Cimino and Foschi 2014). In the United States, Samuel George Morton's method of craniometry gave empirical grist to the mill of national discourses of racism—especially in the latter half of the nineteenth century (Gould 1993). A racialized scientific lens enabled national ideologies, following the period of consolidation, to "admit" racialized populations into various state structural frameworks, even in the context of liberal ideologies, within "limited terms." These "limited terms" were linked to the perceived inferiority of ethnic and racial populations. After the period of consolidation, it became legitimate through liberal and national lenses to see these populations as liminal in terms of full citizenship (both formal and informal); according to this logic, black, brown, and red peoples only had a partial capacity with which to participate in the economic, civil, and social life of modern democratic nation-states. Racism, then, was legitimated through (pseudo)scientific study and experimentation. These studies were incorporated into national ideologies as the legitimate basis for institutional legal racism and racist attitudes.

In *Making Race and Nation* (1998), Anthony Marx conducts a comparative study of nation-state racial formations going back at least as far as the period of nation-state consolidation in the late nineteenth century. He uncovers an important power dynamic, with regard to race, at the national level:

> Where and when states enacted formal rules of domination according to racial distinctions, racism was reinforced. . . . [C]hallenges from those subordinated eventually emerged, and major racial conflict ensued. *Where racial domination was not encoded by the state, issues and conflicts over race were diluted.* (Marx 1998: 267, emphasis mine)

Even in instances where ideologies did not directly encode racial domination into certain state forms, issues and conflicts with regard to race were present but masked. I explore this claim more thoroughly in the last chapter of this book in the context of the United States. The racialized context in which national consolidation occurs would suggest that racism is imputed into the process of consolidation through ideological forms whether these forms were explicit or not. These conflicts were increasingly complex, interacting with other social forces and given over to other forms of expression. Though no doubt present, they require a more intensive investigation and explanation of the determinants through which racial categories of social struggle and protest action occurred and were expressed.

Ideology is the predominant means through which nation-states can diffuse racial struggles and promote racist policies, and it is also the political terrain upon which contests with regard to race are staged. Ideology is the expression of the national consolidation of power, whether one takes Karl Mannheim's ([1926] 1997) view of ideology, that a *weltanschauung* or worldview that is evinced through institutions and practices is "total" in scope; or Marx and Engels's ([1845] 1960) view that ideology expresses the views of a dominant class as preeminent; or Althusser's (1971) view (a further theoretical development of Marx and Engels's position) that ideology implants itself within all institutions to produce a "soft" and "hard" system to ensure its dominion. However, Althusser describes how the reproduction of the conditions of capitalism across the varied stratifications present in society requires an ideational framework predicated on an illusory, yet active and structurally supported, personal sense of independence. Put succinctly, my point is that race-based struggles within ideological contexts have parameters bound by specific nation-state formations. However, the scientific justifications for racism and the effect of racialization upon populations within national boundaries take root in a discourse that is seated at the basis of all national ideologies, a national discourse that shares common features with regard to the links between pseudoscience, politics, and popular conceptions of national identity. The link between scientific discourses of race and national political ideologies, in the context of social movement struggles, needs to be explained and analyzed.

The scientific justifications for racism and the effect of racialization upon populations take root within a national political discourse that is articulated in ideological justifications. These justifications present themselves in a dense field of pseudoscience and associated authoritative historical, social scientific, and literary discourses of, or pertaining, to race between 1850 and the late 1890s: *in Italy*, Lombroso's "criminal science" focused on "forensic atavisms," which directly influenced Niceforo and Orano's "zones of criminality"; *in France*, Morel's "degeneration" or reverse evolution (the Italian and French examples based in the study of "cretinism"), which directly influenced Buchez's psychology and Taine, Le Bon, Sorel, and Zola's focus on "crowd regression"; *in Vienna*, Krafft-Ebing, an admirer of Morel, uses "degeneration" in his *Psychopathia Sexualis*. A similar pattern develops in Britain, the United States, Germany, and later Brazil (Gould 1993; Haas 2008; Heatherington 2010; Pick 1989; Portelli 2003; Reiter and Mitchell 2010; Stauder 1993). Despite differences in both geographical location and social concern, all pseudoscientific justifications for structural forms of racism occur at around the same time and in the same way: science turns its lens toward social and political issues after the formal ending of slavery in the United States, as colonialism begins its decline, and as peasant populations become increasingly incorporated into modern national and industrializing contexts. To the extent that national ideology during this time was expressing societal concerns based in but not expressed directly through racial pseudoscience, it is also possible to locate a coordinated response to the national and political expression of racism, a response that was also expressed ideologically and politically. Such a response presumes some level of organization and activity on the part of a social movement.

The analysis in this chapter demonstrates that the literature on social movement framing contains limitations in the way that it assesses the role of ideology, especially as it pertains to political organization, movement strategy, and protest tactics. Although there have been significant insights into how ideology guides behavior (Zald 2000a), how it affects organizational structure and collective action (Miller 1999; Westby 2002), and the dynamic forms of constituting resonant ideological frameworks (Raboy 1984), there is no independent perspective on social movement ideology. Gramsci's unique and underdiscussed conception of ideologies as historically organic to social groups embedded in various social strata assist in identifying a constitutive process that captures the relationship between social movement organizations, ideology formation, and mobilizations. The key descriptors of historically organic ideology are that they are *necessary* to a structure, they constitute a space for political subjectivity, communicate strategic presences or stances, and shape struggle. In the previous chapter, I demonstrated that organizational innovations and tactical practices introduced through the efforts of Gramsci and others were based on Gramsci articulating connections between industrial workers, veterans, and peasants and, also, providing organizational frameworks that made the potential for political action concrete. This chapter demonstrates how these organizational innovations and organic expressions of ideological contention create the conditions for Sardinian peasants to mobilize against Sardinian and other national elites in a racist national context. I lay out a framework within which the dynamics of ideological contention operate. Ideological contention explicates aspects of Gramsci's conception of historically organic ideology through the identification and demonstration of these dynamics. Political organization, movement strategy, protest tactics, and collective memory are active and expressive determinants of historically organic ideology, and they also comprise the substantive elements of a theory of ideological contention.

This chapter builds on the discussion of the Biennio Rosso from the last chapter. It analyzes the historical case of a social movement that is comprised of Sardinian (Southern) peasants: a population racialized, in general, as biologically inferior and, specifically, as a group of mixed Italian and African (also Arabic) ancestry—(this is related, historically, to the North African conquest of the early Roman empire by Hannibal). Although the struggle analyzed in this chapter was not explicitly racial, I demonstrate the means by which it was a racial struggle. Part of this relates to how racist scientific discourses contributed to the project of forming a modern Italian nation-state, national identity, and ideology. In Italy, Cesare Lombroso was the chief proponent of this racial discourse. His studies of the peasant population of Italy occurred just before and during the consolidation of the Italian nation-state into its contemporary form. Furthermore, as Silvana Patriarca notes, the introduction of official statistics just before the unification of the Italian nation-state amplifies the research of the Criminological School in Italy as an authoritative expression of social problems at the level of the national population (Patriarca 1996, 1998). Lombroso establishes a discourse, strengthened by emerging statistical research, into the national population, within which Sardinian peasants, workers, and veterans struggle against regional Sardinian elites and larger national political discourses of inferiority.

I focus on a case that describes the Sardinian struggle against a predominant racial ideology and the struggle within their own movements to determine an effective political and ideological platform upon which to mount present and future struggles. This happened through ideological contention, a concept that captures how ideology works as a dynamic within political struggles. Ideological contention describes specific social movement dynamics; it affects social movement organizations (SMOs) and strategy, and it reorients the relationship between the concept of ideology and framing in the social movement literature.

The chapter begins with a review of the concept of ideology within the study of social movements. The review identifies and interprets specific ideological dynamics within social movement organizations. Specifically, how ideology actively identifies and organizes political consciousness, how it can be distinguished, analytically, as both internal (to a SMO) and external to it, how the tension between inside and outside shape political action, how ideological distinctions directly and indirectly shape an organization's purpose and intent, and how external ideological forces shape tactical responses. These disparate fragments that describe the impact and role of ideology in the framework of SMOs establish the need for a broader theoretical framework to explain the effect of ideology on SMOs: ideological contention. Next, I set the stage for the concept of ideological contention and the basis for its utility in analyzing the intersection of race and mobilization through a historical investigation of widespread racialization in Italy in the late nineteenth and early twentieth century. I demonstrate how the scientific and political justifications for racism were central to the ideological terrain of national politics following the period of national consolidation of large European nation-states between the 1860s and the early twentieth century. I explain the relationship between early demographic analyses of Italian regions, the racialized pseudoscience of the criminal anthropologists, and the routinization of these studies into politics and the national imaginary. In a context of structural racism supported by a racist "common sense," I demonstrate how racialized subaltern groups defy all racist typologies through organized mobilization efforts in a racial-political context where, in specific, regional elites attempt to demobilize subaltern groups through appeals to a common ethnoregional identity. Although there is widespread ideological heterogeneity among Southerners, the concept of ideological contention describes the discussion, debate, and dissensus internal to a movement.[2] These exchanges that fall between what Miller describes as "adaptive responses to external political forces" and the tactical practices that represent the political footprint of a social movement in a broader social framework develop through the internal relations within a social movement. They are, as Gramsci states, "rich in content and significance," precisely because they substantively shape the political subjectivity of social movement participants who have a direct stake in the organization. The internal struggles over the meaning of movement struggles, the strategies that develop from these struggles, the tactical practices that embed the collective substantive sorting out of meanings, political positions, and political possibilities as well as the ways in which protest actions lead to waves of protest all depend upon viewing ideology as a contentious process both within and against a movement that shapes both the movement itself and its goals. The contention in and around ideology, then, has a theoretical, scientific, and pedagogic function. The collective contribution of social movement participants coordinates the ideological standpoint from which political action can be understood and implemented through the tactical practices that constitute a mobilization in action.

Framing and Ideology in Social Movement Studies

In social movement studies, proponents of frame theory hold the view that frame processes, or, the means through which social groups and societies organize, perceive, and communicate about reality, are dynamic, and ideology is best conceived of as a repository of cultural resources (in the form of symbols, narratives, ideas, etc.) from which frames derive meaning.[3] As the inquiry into the relationship between framing and ideology developed across the literature,[4] proponents of the frame perspective have claimed that ideology cannot form a strong empirical relationship to data because it does not explain how ideas are mobilized politically as well as the framing perspective does.[5] Specifically, theorists are faced with the issue of maintaining methodological precision and finding a strong relationship to "macro" explanations or perspectives.[6]

In the literature on framing, the concept of ideology is derived from cultural values and is largely static in relation to its political expression, which occurs through framing that is considered dynamic. This presumption about ideology and framing drives analytic intent. This perspective seems to be exclusive to the framing literature in social movement studies and, as a result, may lead to some circularity regarding concept and analysis. Regardless, for advocates of the frame perspective, framing provides the strongest mediation between theory and data, stronger than other similar concepts, like ideology (Oliver and Johnston 2000a, 2000b; Snow and Benford 2000).

Even though the concept of ideology has not been expanded beyond its cultural definition in the context of social movement studies, with some notable exceptions,[7] research has demonstrated instances where specific conceptions of ideology explain certain empirical effects better than the frame perspective, specifically, regarding the relationship between culture and political organization;[8] the interrelation of ideas, beliefs, and values (Oliver and Johnston 2000a, 2000b); and the elaboration of movement strategies (Westby 2002). David L. Westby cites studies that demonstrate how ideology, within a single movement, provides standpoints that have different

empirical effects on movement messages, strategies, and organization.[9]
The scope of ideology, in this literature, encompasses a social movement
or a single SMO. Studies demonstrate that ideology, especially ideological
diversity within an organization or an entire movement, has the capacity to
both unify and fractionalize movements and organizations and, as a result,
can strengthen our understanding of not only how and why SMOs frame
grievances and events in particular ways but also the ideological dynamics
that lead to the development of strategic frames and the tactical deployment
of frames in certain circumstances. The following section is a critical review
of four distinct theoretical perspectives that describe the effects of ideology
on movement cohesion and the relationship between movement organizational structure and ideology. As such, these perspectives contribute specific
conceptual support to a more holistic conception of a theoretical perspective
that focuses on ideological dynamics within a SMO.

Social Movement Theories of Ideology

Ideologically Structured Behavior

Mayer N. Zald's theory of "ideological structured behavior" is defined as
behavior "guided and shaped by ideological concerns" (2000a: 3). It is an
attempt to introduce ideology analysis into the social movement literature.
Contested by resource mobilization theorists (Diani 2000; Klandermans
2000) who claim that resources should be privileged in the analysis of
movement behavior, Zald claims that ideology demonstrates connections
between movement participants' behavior, political socialization and mobilization, and cultural contexts. Zald defines ideology politically and culturally and seeks to enhance its status as a political concept in the social
movement literature.

Zald's theory of ideologically structured behavior expands the scope
and sharpens the analytical intent of framing to include a description or
typology of movement politics; it clarifies other social movement concepts
and theories (e.g., resource mobilization and collective action), and it provides a framework to explain mobilization across different political and cultural contexts. Specifically:

1. *Ideology is an issue of theoretical scope and analytical intent*: "If your goal
   is to describe and analyze specific movements or families of movements,

then it is highly likely that you must take into account the ideological diagnoses and prognoses that shape movement adherents' world view and programs of action" (Zald 2000a: 5). Also, "a SMO's ability to perceive and take advantage of political opportunity and its ability to acquire resources are profoundly conditioned by the world view of SMO leaders" (2000a: 6). Zald's concept of ideology contains two levels. The first is abstract and corresponds to the *weltanschauung* (Gramsci 1971; Mannheim [1926] 1997) of movement leaders. The second describes how ideas inform "behavior," that is, the implementation of strategies and the legitimation of tactics (e.g., nonviolent tactics only, property damage, armed insurrection).[10]

2. *Ideology is an issue of conceptual and theoretical clarification in social movement scholarship*: "Researchers interested in core issues of the resource mobilization/collective action or the political process program end up introducing ideologically related issues through the back door when they "code" or analyze specific issues, conflicts, and movements" (Zald 2000a: 5). This suggests that ideology represents an underconceptualized variable in social movement analysis. Ideology may be represented as an independent variable structuring the use of resources, describing the internal structure of a movement, or delineating the strategies and tactics in contexts of collective action. It can also, in this same vein, represent a dependent variable depending on the analytic intent of particular studies.

3. Ideologically structured behavior, when put at the center of mobilization concerns, makes it easier to understand mobilization efforts since ideologies conform to member's beliefs, even prior to an individual's participation in protest actions. Political ideology resides both inside and outside of movements, actively structuring or passively categorizing political standpoints. Ideology has the potential to broaden the scope of political analysis with regard to mobilizing allies (e.g., through the application of frame alignment processes), engaging with external political forces, or configuring the relationship between cultural values and forms of political and ideological expression, specifically contexts.

Zald offers the possibility of approaching social movement organizations' mobilizations through an ideological lens that takes into view the relationship between ideology and collective behavior. The comprehensibility of mobilization efforts, when approached through ideology, can mitigate between external political and social forces that are rendered intelligible through ideology and the ideological positions within a social movement organization. However, as Zald notes, the relationship between ideology and behavior conditions the means by which resources are acquired, distributed, and used. This is often overlooked in the literature that takes a neutral organizational posture to the mobilization of resources reflecting a normative perspective, despite the fact the political action drives the mobilization of necessary resources and the interpretation of what constitutes an opportunity is conditioned fundamentally by the ideological lens of movement members (Kendall 2006). Ideological contention captures the dynamics that constitute the political views of social movement participants. Where Zald links ideological perspectives to behaviors, ideological contention links participation, especially in the form of tactical practices, to the factors that shape strategic planning and organizational structure with a range of potential outcomes for the broader social movement.

Ideological Salience

Westby uses the term "ideological salience" to demarcate instances where ideology is an operative factor in frame processes, distinguishing it from the social movement literature's more static conception of ideology. However, Westby also argues that there are instances where ideology is not salient in establishing certain frame processes at certain moments. His examples include the justifications for mobilization around the Three Mile Island nuclear energy plant disaster, revisionist socialism in Europe, and the civil rights movement in the United States. Each case offers different examples where, Westby argues, political ideologies were either rejected, jettisoned for practical and political purposes, or oppositional ideologies were appropriated, respectively. Despite the absence of an ideology, Westby claims that movements were able to engage in successful framing activities nonetheless. One could also make the opposite point: In order for these movements to establish a political standpoint and engage in framing activity, they had to, in some way, define themselves apart, alongside, or within an ideology. Determining the political actions that an organization will commit to not only implies an ideology (an expressive and meaningful framework derived from a political response), it also implies that a range of perspectives will be brought to bear upon the mission of an organization, the types of strategies that will determine how the mission of an organization is carried out, and the willingness of participants to engage in specific forms of tactical practice. The issue—as

Westby puts it—is a theoretical one. However, it is also an empirical issue (Hallgrímsdóttir 2003).

Frederick D. Miller and Marc Raboy

There are studies and examples centered on the preceding ideological dynamics that Westby describes. These studies demonstrate that external societal and political forces impact the organizational framework of a social movement specifically because as participants in a movement commit themselves to a strategic program, they affect the organizational framework of the movement by shaping and reshaping the movement's agenda and, as a result, their political perspective (interpretation of events, opportunities, and effective forms of tactical practice) changes. Frederick D. Miller's studies of the relationship between SMOs' structure and ideology describe a dialectical process driven by participants' "adaptive responses" to external political forces (Miller 1999; see also Freeman 1972). As Miller (1999) states, "Both movement ideology and structure, which shape each other, are created by the members' adaptive responses to external forces. Once created, neither ideology nor structure is static; both influence strategic choices that organizations make" (304). Miller's concept of ideology breaks the frame: social movements identify and interpret problems, propose solutions, and mobilize participants (i.e., they organize and strategize) through ideology. As movement ideology is crafted and changed in response to external forces—to the extent that the movement survives and participates in politics, in whatever way—a social movement demonstrates the salience of its worldview. The movement's perspective survives in that it has an empirical foothold—it may achieve its goals—and members adhere to the ideology (as members, allies, and fellow travelers) believing not only in the ideology but the potential success of the sociopolitical program espoused through the ideology. Miller's theoretical framework captures dynamics that are described by the concept of ideological contention, but it leaves out the substantive and rich quality of ideological and political engagement.

Where Miller focuses his studies on the relationship between organizational structure and ideology, Raboy (1984) and Gramsci (1971, 1995) both discuss instances where the ideological struggles internal to a movement organization have specified and important effects on how a collective both remains unified and, also, fractures into new expressions of movement ideology resulting in new political groupings. The substantive and internal content of social movements is a product of tactical practices that mark interventions into social and political forces. These engagements generate discursive frameworks that become the stuff of ideology.

By way of two examples, in a study of Maoist and Leninist-based social movements in Canada, Raboy (1984) gives us some insight into the highly contentious ideological work that largely goes unnoticed by observers who summarize these movements' ideological standpoints with Marxist terminology. Raboy studies the highly contentious ideological work that occurred in Quebec among radical workers' "anti-reformist" movements (Marxist-Leninist and Maoist) during the 1970s and the early 1980s. Raboy points out that, empirically, ideology can be and, in his study, is demonstrated through persistent arguments around issues of political analysis. Citing Legaré (1980), Raboy describes "how important and relevant a *group* of articles on class analysis can be to a collectivity's political memory" (Raboy 1984: 147). One need not look any further than Gramsci's biography for an example. In Gramsci's own time the split that he and Amadeo Bordiga led, away from the Italian Socialist Party (to form the Italian Communist Party, in 1921) and the subsequent split, in 1926, between Bordiga (or the left-wing "Bordigist Tendency") and Gramsci—who assumes the position of secretary upon the split—is fraught with contention. Shortly after the split Gramsci authors (with Palmiero Togliatti) the "Lyons Theses" ([1926] in [Gramsci 1978: 340–375]); a work of ideological realignment and analysis.

Raboy's example of the centrality of arguments over analysis signals an entry point to understand the substantive aspects that manifest ideological contention. In Gramsci's specific case, ideological struggles with Amadeo Bordiga often took the form of public debates, published articles, motions brought before the party and subjected to voting procedures, and political positioning on committees. Contentious issues included debates about national and international united front tactics among left parties (especially the relationship between the communist and socialist parties), participation in electoral and popular political frameworks at the national level, and taking a national position on Italy's involvement in the war. Issues internal to the Italian Communist Party included the agrarian question, the trade unions, and political tactics, especially involving the guiding principles of the newly constituted party and its appropriate tactical course, and, ultimately, the issue of leadership. These debates went directly toward the reorganization and restructuring of the Communist Party, the publication of a new paper, the genesis of a new statement on party strategy, and the consideration of effective tactical frameworks in the face of fascist challenges. Raboy, similarly, indicates—as it pertains to the distribution of ideological principles and political analysis, that publications which demonstrated analysis reflected new forms of organizational composition and "greatly contributed to the creation of a radical intellectual understanding of . . . context" (Raboy 1984: 48). A new paper, through analysis and theoretical reflection, could introduce "a distinct style that . . . nourish[ed] . . . social movements . . ." (48). Most fundamentally, the relationships inside of a social movement that shape responses to political environments are born out of an ideological contention around the analysis of that environment and establishing, collectively, the appropriate tactical practices to which movement participants can agree to commit.

Ideological Contention and Gramsci's Contribution to Race and Social Movement Mobilization

Building off of Miller's (1999) claim that social movement structure and ideology shape each other, and Raboy's (1984) insight that a movement's ideological content is a binding aspect of any political collective, *ideological contention* is a concept that *focuses on ideological struggles within* a social movement or SMO. These struggles necessarily unfold within a larger framework of external political forces that are also elaborated ideologically and that influence *movement organization, the process of ideological elaboration*, and *strategic choices*.[11] Strategic choices that emerge from struggle become a point of contention that actively and persistently inform a collective" ideology or political memory in the form of planning, writing, debate, and so on. Zald (2000a, 2000b) demonstrates how ideology has a structured effect on movement members' behaviors; this is not a unidirectional or instrumental effect but, rather, provides a set of guidelines for strategies. Westby (2002) demonstrates how ideologies are heterogeneous and contend for a predominant position within a movement or SMO. In this vein, Westby (2002) also notes that the process of establishing an ideological perspective is multiperspectival and often contentious (i.e., not stable). I propose that *ideological contention* represents a "process definition" that considers a specific set of empirical factors; regardless of intent, *ideological contention* can often lead to movement fractionalization and, potentially, to movement dissolution.

Gramsci provides the most salient concept of the essential relationship between ideologies and organizations (of all kinds). Gramsci's experience organizing and building a party framework recounted earlier is captured in his unique conception of ideology. Gramsci distinguishes between the concept of ideology as a set of ideas and what he describes as "historically organic ideologies." He defines historically organic ideologies as "necessary to a . . . structure." He argues, "Ideologies are historically necessary . . . they 'organize' human masses, and create the terrain on which men move, acquire consciousness of their position, struggle, etc." (Notebook 7, §19, §21; Gramsci 1971, 376–377). Accordingly, organizations require both description and legitimation. Any organization creates, with itself, roles and a sense of purpose. Though analytically distinct, ideology and structure (including roles) are essential parts of any organization. Participants are specialized; they are responsible to their role in an organization and have a broad relational understanding of that role. Gramsci notes that, over time, members work to legitimate the social and political position of an organization. They become intellectuals. All intellectuals have or have had at one time a specific function and a social role in an organization. They operate beyond their specialized role and must do so to explain their own and their organizations' role. These social and political explanations are ideology.

As will be discussed in chapter 4, "Agile Materialisms," Gramsci's contribution to the study of race has often led to the adoption of his framework for hegemony to either the cultural or structural aspects of the study of racialization or racism (Hall 1986a; Omi and Winant 1994). Although these adaptations of hegemony as a concept that describes the persistence of racism are useful, the question of Gramsci's direct contribution to the analysis of racial determinants in the context of politics has only been intimated (Verdicchio 1995). The demonstration of Gramsci's contribution is a persistent theme in this book. It is worth noting that, recently, it is only through philological and empirical research on Gramsci's category of "subaltern" that the linkage between race and political power has been explored more fully,[12] even at the level of language, political organization, and the cultural and political-organizational engagement with "common sense" (Green and Ives 2009). Contemporary research contributing to analyses in this book, specifically Brennan's (2001), Green's (2011, 2013), and Crehan's (2016), shows that Gramsci's contribution to the analysis of racialization, political power, and social movements is demonstrated in his writing on "Southerners" and "subalterns." For example, Green states:

> The concerns of race, class, and religion all appear in *Notebook 25*— the "special notebook" Gramsci devoted exclusively to the topic of subaltern. . . . The major notes . . . include discussions of class divisions

and class politics, but Gramsci does not reduce subalternity to class. . . . Gramsci makes the point that the Risorgimento constituted a non-national popular movement that excluded the active participation of the masses and institutionalized the North's authority over the South. A stratum of Italian intellectuals . . . who were associated with absurd pseudoscientific notions—reinforced the undemocratic and semi-colonial nature of the Italian state with racist theories of Southern inferiority. . . . The interconnection of these separate lines of inquiry demonstrates how subalternity is intertwined with national and colonial processes, as well as with the power of intellectuals in shaping culture and political discourse. (2013: 117)

Put simply, as the categories of "subaltern" and "southern" have come under closer investigation, questions emerge about the historical and empirical basis for the broader racialization process that as I have previously described take root within modern national frameworks. Racial characteristics that are determined and defined societally, nationally, and otherwise are a fundamental part of those categories. Gramsci's response to the "Southern question" represents a challenge to the authoritative discursive nexus of race, science, and nationalism. His discussion of Sardinian political movements exemplifies his intervention into the widespread ideology of race in Italy. In order to add to the literature that investigates the categories of "Southerner" and "subaltern" in Gramsci's work, I specify the process of Italian nation-state consolidation in late-nineteenth-century and early twentieth-century Italy to develop a robust racial context and, also, to illuminate specific aspects of what Anthony Marx means when he discusses the encoding of racial domination through state mechanisms.

Italian Nation-State Consolidation and Early Twentieth-Century Italy

Specifying the Dominant Racial Ideology through Lombroso, Demography, and Criminal Anthropology

It is in this context that the contention over Italian political ideology demonstrates aspects of contemporary racial struggles on the terrain of politics and social movements. To begin, Cesare Lombroso plays a key figurative role in the rise and dissemination of scientific racism. Pick (1989: 118–120) and Moe (2002) have both noted that Lombroso's concern with the origins of the modern Italian nation-state and Italian unification drove his investigations into the racial composition of Italy. In the late nineteenth century, Italy's "Southern question" had established a strong foothold in Italian political discourse. It had become the predominant political perspective on race in Italy and had—at this point—strongly insinuated itself into Italian common sense at the national level.

Silvana Patriarca's (1996, 1998) work helps establish the means by which Italy's "Southern question" became rooted, deeply and unquestioningly, in the national imaginary. Patriarca's study of the role of official statistics as an attempt to come to terms with the ramifications of facets of modernity (governance, industrialization, urbanization, etc.) for the emergence of the Italian nation is, simultaneously, a study of how official statistics actually constituted the nation itself. Patriarca explains at the conclusion of her study how precisely this works and—for the purposes of the example here—how these studies contributed to the commonsense representation of the Italian nation. She describes:

Questionable new "sciences" such as criminal anthropology and the biological and racial readings of Italy and its people that these sciences proposed received unwitting support from the steady accumulation of statistical data on the physical characteristics of the population which was generated by state statisticians. In the mid-1860s . . . Maestri and his collaborators, in an attempt to provide a detailed picture of the national population, added the anthropometric data collected by army doctors to the yearly publication of data on nationality, mortality, and marriages. Colorful tables showing the differential distribution of the height of conscripts on the national territory began to be published by the Direzione di Statistica in the late 1870s and 1880s. These collections were important sources of data for those private researchers such as Niceforo and the other Lombrosians who were looking for signs of essential difference on the surface of bodies. . . . Statistics translated complex differences between the conditions of social life in various parts of the country into "facts," and established what the facts to be considered should be: by definition only those phenomena that could be translated into figures and actually only those that the state was willing and able to measure. Official statistics did something else too: by constantly presenting comparisons between the various Italian regions, and aggregates of regions, they reinforced the primacy of the regional grid in the reading and imagining of the country. . . . It was and it continues to be easy to forget that what we see is the result of aggregative procedures; that the figures are averages, means of means, summary measures which hide a great diversity of individual cases. (1996: 238–239)

Patriarca adds to the perspective regarding the twin processes of racialization and nation-state consolidation. Specifically, she demonstrates how the coincidence of including anthropometric data facilitated and, ultimately, widely disseminated the work of the Italian criminologists. Furthermore, the actual diversity of regions within the nation was masked by the practice of producing aggregates, which gave the nation and its regions "characters" that were complemented by "pictures" of individual differences. For her, the "Southern question" emerges from "scientific" investigation of the national population, the work of the criminological school, and the representation of this data as factual—an ever-present racialized character present within the national fabric that was unearthed through new modes of scientific investigation.

In the middle-latter half of the nineteenth century, Lombroso had begun to construct the theoretical and "scientific" basis for "criminal anthropology" based in "French and Italian positivism, German materialism, and English evolutionism" (Pick 1989: 111–112). Early in his career Lombroso was interested in cretinism in Italy—which, at the time, was considered a sign of mental and moral "degeneration" and that presented as bodily and facial deformities. During his early studies, as an army doctor (quite possibly contributing to the data that, as Patriarca notes, accompanied the official statistics) based in Calabria, Sicily, in the 1860s he began to refine "phrenological" techniques (the visual and pseudoscientific study of cranial features, based in primatology and forensic anthropology) into theoretical craniometry (a pseudoscientific hypothesis based on assumptions about the correlation between crania size and intelligence and applied through the modern measurement of crania) to study Sicilian peasants and "brigands." Lombroso paired craniometry to an evolutionary theory of race that would later form the basis of his criminal anthropology (Pick 1989).

The culmination of Lombroso's work led to a core perspective of the Italian school of criminal anthropology: that criminals could be identified visually through "atavisms" or pronounced physical differences from Northern Europeans. Not unlike primatologists and forensic anthropologists, Lombroso relied on visual markers to identify and classify differences (his research, in 1860 in Calabria, Sicily, is focused on developing a method for taxonomy). However, these visual differences were markers of "racial" and "moral" differences; they produced a racist optic under the guise of "scientific observation" and they provided the basis for racist "scientific" theories. In short, Lombroso believed that certain physical features belied a "criminal nature"; for him, height, skin color, and facial features told the story of a criminal and savage nature.

Lombroso's theories (no doubt bolstered by the coincident and emergent popularity of the school through the annual publications of the Direzione di Statistica—as Patriarca noted) had become popular across Europe. Shortly after the publication of his central work in 1876, *Criminal Man*, racist social-scientific theories began to make their way into Italian politics and remained rooted there in the beginning of (and arguably throughout) the twentieth century.[13] Also, it is significant that Lombroso's studies (in part their methodology) are adopted by younger members of his group. Alfredo Niceforo and Paolo Orano turn their criminological lens on Sardinia; Niceforo designates it as the "criminal nodal point of a criminal zone" or the source of contemporary criminality in Italy (1897: 41). Note how Green frames the interrelation between Italian criminology, ideology, and political forces:

> The logic of the Lombroso school precludes a critical or political interpretation of the South, since race is considered the determining factor of the "Southern problem." In effect, the Lombroso school depoliticizes Southern revolt by replacing politics with racial and biological determinism, in the sense that the construction of social life and the cause of social antagonisms are determined by biological, racial, and physical characteristics, not political forces. (2013: 121)

It is in the early twentieth century that Sardinians become an object of political concern, just as the "South" and its peasant denizens were an object of scientific concern for Lombroso in the latter part of the nineteenth century.

Expanding Ideology, Challenging Racism: The Southern Question, the Brigata Sassari (1917–1920), and the Sardinian Communists (1919)

Gramsci's 1926 essay "Some Aspects of the Southern Question" signals a break with the Italian political discourse on race. Gramsci notes that all ideological perspectives on race shared a common thread. He states that the South is and has been perceived as "the ball and chain that prevents a more rapid progress in the civil development of Italy; Southerners are biologically inferior beings, either semi-barbarians, or full out barbarians, by natural destiny. . . . The Socialist Party was in great part the vehicle of this bourgeois ideology" (Gramsci [1926] 1995b: 20). This demonstrates that the perspective on race in Italy, and Southern *people* in particular, is directly informed by Lombroso's work. More generally, peasants were perceived as an impediment to the growing industrial successes in Italy. According to all primary political factions, Southerners could not be organized for the purposes of occupation and, more importantly, into politics. However, during this time, Gramsci documents the role of Southerners, specifically Sardinians, in challenging this predominant racial ideology by organizing movements and establishing political collectives (as discussed in chapter 1) and parties over and against the received wisdom that Southerners could only participate in the national collective if dominated and controlled through a centralized administration (Gramsci [1926] 1995b; Rosengarten 2009). This is a false presumption, as the following case shows, but more pointedly, the racial presumptions about Southerners frame the elite attitudes toward Sardinians among both their elite representatives and the Italian state as a whole.

In Turin in 1919, a constituent assembly was held to inaugurate the formation of a regional political bloc under the auspices of the Giovane Sardegna (Young Sardinia) group. Not yet a political party (the Giovane Sardegna is the basis for what would, in 1921, become the Partito Sardo d'Azione or the Sardinian Action Party), the Giovane Sardegna held a meeting in Turin to demonstrate its platform to Sardinians living on the mainland through a series of speeches given by notable Sardinians. The goal was to create the conditions for a constitution and a representative Sardinian party. The meeting was well attended; it represented a broad class base but the majority of the attendees were poor Sardinians working on the mainland. Members of the Brigata Sassari, who had participated in Italian military actions with the Northern Armed Forces prior to and in World War I, were also in attendance. Significantly, part of the platform of the Giovane Sardegna was to pressure the government to keep promises (regarding remuneration) made to these soldiers during World War I. The idea of a Sardinian homeland that was more prosperous and somewhat autonomous was attractive to all Sardinians, especially those who could not make a living on the island.

According to Gramsci, "The Sardinian Communists, who numbered exactly eight, went to the meeting and presented their motion . . . to make a counter-presentation" (Gramsci [1926] 1995b: 24). The majority of speeches made prior to the communists' presentation "filled" those present "with enthusiasm to the point of delirium with the idea of a united bloc of all the generous sons of Sardegna" (24). In a hostile climate, the counterpresentation was a success. The eight communists present argued that a united Sardinian bloc would not improve conditions in Sardinia. They argued that only by uniting with workers of the mainland who were seeking to emancipate the poor workers and peasants did the majority of those present stand a chance of increasing their own quality of life. Most importantly, the communists drove home the point that the political allies of the Sardinian worker and peasant were other workers and peasants, not the economic and political elites of Sardinia.

This presentation was well received by the peasants and workers at the constituent assembly. Gramsci notes:

> The vote, by division of the assembly, was a tremendous success: on one side, there was a handful of smartly dressed gentry, top-hatted officials, professional people, livid with rage and fear, with a circle of forty-odd policemen to garnish the consensus; on the other side, there was the whole mass of poor folk, with the women dressed up in their party best, clustered around the tiny communist cell. An hour later, at the Chamber of Labor, the Sardinian Socialist Education Circle was set up, with 256 members. The founding of Giovane Sardegna was put off *sine die*, and never in fact took place. ([1926] 1995b: 25)

One year later, during the occupation of the Turin factories in 1920, the Brigata Sassari were sent to break up the factory occupation. Members of the Italian state and the military had believed that the Brigata Sassari—who three years earlier, in 1917, had quelled the worker's protests centered on demands for bread and withdrawal from World War I—would never consort with the workers occupying the factories. However, news of the Sardinian communists' intervention in the constituent assembly had reached many Sardinians. Political journalism, especially on the part of the communists, as well as direct communication among Sardinians, had played a central role. In this context, the attitude of the Brigata Sassari toward industrial workers had changed; thanks to the position that the Sardinian communists took at the constituent assembly in 1919, these protest actions were seen as having a broader base, one that included veterans. State actors at administrative levels had determined that the Brigata Sassari would be unwilling to fire on the workers occupying factories around Turin; they were sent away on the eve of a general, citywide, strike in July.

Ideology, Collective Memory, and Strategic Choices

The predominant political ideology regarded Southerners as biologically (racially) inferior, and capable only through subordination to others in positions of public and private administration. In this context, the Sardinian example demonstrates that various ideologies of racial, ethnic, and class determination intervened in this ideology, much to the surprise of Northern political elites. Despite widespread ideological heterogeneity among Southerners, a racial politics grounded in peasant-based movements was ascendant within Southern groups in Turin and elsewhere (Foot 1997). More significantly, Gramsci's "The Southern Question" is the only document that demonstrates a break with the predominant racial ideology (Ghosh 2001; Green 2013; Urbinati 1998a). His historiography of North-South relations in Italy demonstrates a record of political activism not thought possible by elites whose position was dependent upon Lombroso's and others' studies.

Regarding aspects of *ideological contention* that pertain to social movement ideologies, Gramsci's gives us a glimpse into how ideology becomes the standpoint of various political groups. These positions and protest actions disrupt the predominant racial ideology. The speeches, journalism, mobilizations, and demobilizations (in the case of the Brigata Sassari) comprise waves of protest and contentious politics throughout Italy. Toward the end of "The Southern Question" Gramsci—similarly to Raboy (1984) when exclaiming about the record of political analysis serving to unify political collectives' memories of struggle—makes the following statement:

> These events . . . have had results which still subsist to this day and continue to work in the depths of the popular masses. They illuminated, for an instant, brains which had never thought in that way, and which remained marked by them, radically modified. . . . We can recall dozens and indeed hundreds of letters sent from Sardinia to the *Avanti!* editorial offices in Turin; letters which were frequently collective, signed by all the Sassari Brigade veterans in a particular village. By uncontrolled and uncontrollable paths, the political attitude which we supported was disseminated. The formation of the Sardinian Action Party was strongly influenced by it

at the base, and it would be possible to recall in this respect episodes that are rich in content and significance. ([1926] 1995b: 26–27)

Italian racial ideology provided the framework and justification for the oppression of Southern workers and peasants. The wave of protest actions represents *ideological contention*. Its preconditions and results depend upon the presence of political collectivities, which demonstrate their own ideologies through struggle. Southerners become agents of their political destiny. They contribute to the intellectual basis of autonomous (Foot 1997), semi-autonomous, and party-affiliated protest actions as intellectuals of their own condition.

Ideology, then, is never static. If one were to perceive ideology as an abstract set of principles inessential to the struggle of social movements, it can only ever be understood as a hobbled category. This case demonstrates that ideology is eclectic within the parameters of a movement organization (Westby 2002). The internal politics among movement participants is the "engine" within social movement interventions into larger, oppositional political discourses. The struggles over garnering coherency within a social movement, the unfolding contention, *is* ideology. It is rendered, in my argument, concretely and as essential to both a movement organization and the broader political process. Gramsci's "historically organic ideology" is a conceptualization of ideology that is necessary to an organization's structure, to those participating in that structure, and to those outside of the organization. It is a category in constant movement, in contention both externally and internally.

So far, this chapter has focused on the relationship of national racial discourses to social movements that have an ethnic and racial character in either the composition of their membership or as a part of their political platform. My claim is that the internal struggles over the meaning of movement struggles, strategies, and goals, as well as the ways in which protest actions lead to waves of protest, depend upon viewing ideology as a contentious process both within and against a movement that shapes both the movement itself and its goals. The claim in Raboy about the memory of a movement's discussion of a crucial issue or moment in its history, and Gramsci's claim about the effects of the Sardinian worker and peasant mobilizations beyond the protest tactics discussed earlier could not be sustained if ideology were a static category. My goal, then, is to strengthen the relationship between ideology and framing by demonstrating and specifying the role of ideology (in the aforementioned case) and by suggesting that framing can be viewed in consort with *ideological contention*. One way to strengthen the relationship between framing and ideology is to suggest that specific categories of framing can be viewed as tactical responses to extending a movement's ideology. Cast back into the inventory of concepts that inform the study of social movements, *ideological contention* provides methodological and analytical guidelines that can contribute to concepts developed across the sociological studies of social movements: specifically, diagnostic, prognostic, and motivational aspects of framing as well as frame alignment.

Gramsci and Diagnostic, Prognostic, and Motivational Frames

Frame alignment provides an intersection between Gramsci's insights into the relationship between ideology and political tactics and the social movement studies discussion of frame process. The claim—repeated throughout the framing literature—that frames "assign meaning to and interpret relevant events and conditions in ways that are intended to mobilize potential adherents and constituents, to garner bystander support, and to demobilize antagonists" (Snow and Benford 1988: 198) is linked to the conceptual categories within the frame perspective. These categories are: 1) *diagnostic*, the identification of a social problem; 2) *prognostic*, proposing a strategy; 3) *motivational*, mobilizing movement members as well as others who may be affected by the problem (Snow and Benford 1988, 2000). But, stating that a frame—which describes the forms of cognitive, cultural, and symbolic connections between a movement, its members, and potential members—can identify a problem, propose a strategy, and mobilize individuals is empirically dubious and begs the question of political practice and coordination within a social movement. It is impossible to assign intention to a process. In other words, a frame, which is a concept, cannot assign meanings or make interpretations.

However, according to Gramsci's 1917 discussion of the Turin Factory Council Movement (1977), his 1918 article on the Russian Revolution (1977), and his 1920 article on Lenin's role in the revolution (1977), as well as his study of intellectuals (1971, 1995a), movement participants assign meaning to a problem and interpret events. Intellectuals and leaders mobilize members, garner support, and demobilize antagonists. This contradicts the criticism of the Marxist concept of ideology in social movements, which either "masks" social relationships or has an opposing, "remedial" function

(Snow 2004: 381). In fact, ideology can serve a theoretical, scientific, and pedagogic function (Augelli and Murphy 1988; Gramsci 1995a; Sassoon 1987; Thomas 2013). Movement participants coordinate the ideological standpoint of a specific social movement for both members and antagonists.

Intellectuals and Frame Alignment

Frame alignment is a concept that categorizes modifications and changes within the framing process. Frame alignment signals a process whereby a frame "could be modified or aligned in various ways so as to better fit the beliefs and sentiments of those to whom they were directed" (Westby 2002: 288).[14] These alterations to frames are viewed as tactical. Snow, Rochford, Worden, and Benford (1986) describe four tactics that are active in the process of aligning frames: frame bridging, frame amplification, frame extension, and frame transformation. Although these categories that describe tactical practices are demonstrated in a handful of cases, these cases demonstrate the existing theory but fail to add substantively to the theory.[15] Questions remain with regard to testing how frame alignment processes work, when and how they may not work, or when and where they may not be necessary. Questions also remain as to what types of political practices modify and align frames and when these tactics are necessary. This is an empirical question requiring an investigation of these tactics. Gramsci's analyses of ideological processes and his study of the role of the intellectual in Italy offer insights not explored in the literature on frame alignment processes (1971; see also Augelli and Murphy 1988).

Gramsci's discussion of intellectuals' roles in fostering an ideology and his training movement members to be active participants in the construction of movement ideology—in other words, his teaching the "rank and file" how to analyze events, or how to be intellectuals—contributes an analytical perspective not offered in the frame perspective. I have noted, in this chapter, how Gramsci's concept of ideology as "historically organic" contributes directly to the concept of ideological contention, since it explains how ideology affects the organizational patterns and strategic thrust of mobilizations. Gramsci's broader conception of "organic" forces and the link between the agents of change and their ideational framework illustrates the broad variety of actions, mediations, and outcomes of mobilization efforts that go beyond a frame and into organizational structures, expressive politics, and contexts.

Substantively, historically organic ideology expresses structural aspects of *contemporary* society from a vantage point within class relations. It refers

to both public and private institutions and organizations that play a fundamental contemporary role constituting the lived social relations that mediate
the ways individuals are connected to the world. Ideological contention
develops Gramsci's concept of historically organic ideology so that it pertains to social movement organizations that are responsive to and emerge
from contemporary social forces. By way of a brief example, historically
organic ideology could include the concretely grounded rhetorical mediations that an entrepreneur uses to connect financiers to industry, or it could
include the role that a new political party plays mediating its members' relationship to their occupational fields. Like framing, it offers a neutral conception of mobilization.

Although various institutions and organizations, taken together, represent a part of the ensemble of social relations in society at a given historical
moment, the ways that they are made intelligible depends upon *agents* that
are embedded within groups in that structure and that express the most
salient characteristics that connect individuals to society. These agents are
"organic intellectuals." Gramsci states:

> Every social group, coming into existence on the original terrain of an
> essential function in the world of economic production, creates together
> with itself, organically, one or more strata of intellectuals which give it
> homogeneity and an awareness of its own function not only in the eco-
> nomic but also in the social and political fields. (Notebook 12, §1; 1971: 5)

As discussed in this chapter, Gramsci attributes the role of an organic intellectual to any participant in the contemporaneous organizational structure
of economic production as long as they meet certain conditions: 1) Organic
intellectuals reflect on and elaborate their position in the structure (relative
to others), 2) the position of others in the structure at a general level, 3) all
of these roles for a broader public by explaining (social field) and legitimating
(political field) their organization's role within a hegemonic framework.
However, at this point it is important to specify the following: Gramsci's
definition encompasses many different potential occupational roles and
strata—technical, operational, administrative, and organizational—within
those roles, Gramsci's definition limits occupations to those that are fundamental to economic production. To sharpen this point again, both the category of historically organic ideology and the organic intellectual are neutral
categories for the purpose of analysis. However, the difference between
an entrepreneur who is legitimating and justifying the role of a firm that

produces software essential to organizations and individuals but is forcing society to rethink the legal limits to privacy every time anyone signs up to use the application and a hacker who is a member of a political organization that is intervening in software markets to create and distribute productive implements that enable the free development and distribution of software are anything but neutral. Both challenge what we understand as property relations but for very different reasons and with very different ends. Both, however, fit the definition of an organic intellectual.

One's class location, or location within the structure of economic production, however, is not a limitation upon broader political activity. Revolutionary political activity requires a deeper, long-term, and self-conscious embeddedness in working-class productive strata or in the most organic aspects of objective class places. This is demonstrated through the discussion, in the second chapter, of Gramsci's efforts to "fully proletarianize" himself. Gramsci states:

> The relationship between the intellectuals and the world of production is not as direct as it is with the fundamental social groups but is, in varying degrees, 'mediated' by the whole fabric of society and by the complex of superstructures, of which the intellectuals are, precisely, the 'functionaries.' It should be possible . . . to establish a gradation of their functions and of the superstructures from the bottom to the top (from the structural base upwards). (Notebook 12, §1; Gramsci 1971: 12)

Gramsci is describing the relations of production and the development of productive forces in an analytically specified historical context. The level of complexity is central to his analysis. The preceding quotation demonstrates that with increasing societal complexity comes increased distance from the "fronts" of working-class struggles. As Gramsci begins to describe the extraordinary complexity of contemporary societal strata, his immediate example is on the side of capital. He notes:

> The capitalist entrepreneur creates alongside himself the industrial technician, the specialist in political economy, the organizers of a new culture, of a new legal system, etc. It should be noted that the entrepreneur himself represents a higher level of social elaboration, already characterized by a certain directive . . . and technical (i.e., intellectual) capacity: he must have a certain technical capacity, not only in the limited sphere of his activity and initiative but in other spheres as well, at least in those which are closest

to economic production. He must be an organizer of masses of men; he must be an organizer of the 'confidence' of investors in his business, of the customers for his product, etc. . . . If not all entrepreneurs, at least an *élite* amongst them must have the capacity to be an organizer of society in general, including all its complex organism of services, right up to the state organism, because of the need to create the conditions most favorable to the expansion of their own class; or at the least they must possess the capacity to choose the deputies (specialized employees) to whom to entrust this activity of organizing the general system of relationships external to the business itself. (Gramsci 1971: 5–6)

However, he also gives an example for labor. He states:

Indeed the worker or proletarian, for example, is not specifically characterized by his manual or instrumental work, but by performing this work in specific conditions and in specific social relations. . . . (I)n any physical work, even the most degraded and mechanical, there exists a minimum of technical qualification, that is, a minimum of creative intellectual activity. (1971: 8)

The entrepreneur described earlier organizes capital (differentiating entrepreneurial positions based on the entrepreneurial function at specific levels of social strata). The paramount activity of the entrepreneur entails a broad body of administrative knowledge beyond private industry. Most significantly, it entails understanding the relationship between state institutions and private industry (as well as industry and finance) as it benefits the entrepreneur's class fraction. Entrepreneurs also identify other intellectuals that can effectively mediate these relationships. From the perspective of labor, however, developing intellectual capacity is specified organically with another social-institutional process. Gramsci explains:

School is the instrument through which intellectuals of various levels are elaborated. The complexity of the intellectual function in different states can be measured objectively by the number and gradation of specialized schools: the more extensive the "area" covered by education and the more numerous the "vertical" "levels" of schooling, the more complex is the cultural world, the civilization, of a particular state. A point of comparison can be found in the sphere of industrial technology: the industrialization of a country can be measured by how well equipped it is in the production of machines with which to produce machines, and in the manufacture of ever more accurate instruments for making both machines and further instruments for making machines, etc. The country which is best equipped in the construction of instruments for experimental scientific laboratories and in the construction of instruments with which to test the first instruments, can be regarded as the most complex in the technical-industrial field, with the highest level of civilization, etc. (Notebook 12, §1, §3; 1971: 10–11)

The theoretical quality of organic is linked to the *degree* and *kind* of structural embeddedness (of people) and, at the same time, the societal and political potential to articulate an ideology. At this point, it is important to indicate that the term "organic" is, in my argument, signifying precisely the degree and kind of structural embeddedness of people and also the linkage between ideological expression and the organic quality—the degree and type—of ideological expression, obvious rhetorical and strategic mediations notwithstanding. A note on translation makes this linkage possible. In *Selections from the Prison Notebooks*, *organicità* is translated as "organic quality." Gramsci defines this term as follows, "It should be possible both to measure the 'organic quality' [*organicità*] of the various intellectual strata and their degree of connection with a fundamental social group, and to establish a gradation of their functions and of the superstructures . . ." (Notebook 12, §1; 1971: 12).

As is the case with the concept of ideological contention, ideology is not the fairly stable basis through which a frame is imposed upon tactical forms of political communication. Rather, it is an expression of the social formation and the changing context of a political organization's relationship to society, to itself, its members, and other organizations. The mechanics of contention—outwardly directed and internal to the movement and its successive struggles—change the articulation of an ideology (concerning the parameters of external and internal forms of embeddedness) and effect *movement organization, the process of ideological elaboration, strategic choices, and tactical repertoires.*

Gramsci's insights refer to the social fomentation from which emerge revolutionary political organizations; they also indicate an extraordinary complexity that the relations of production, in the framework of industrial capitalism, imposes on labor. The political struggles of labor against capital change, in both quality and quantity, with the complexities of the technical division of labor. These technical divisions, viewed from the perspective of labor, become the basis for potentially innovative forms of organization, tactical action, and, eventually, transformation as labor struggles against capital. These tactics, then, are subject to persistent revision if they are to be successful in the broader framework of waves of mobilizations and protest actions. Gramsci's historical case studies demonstrate and explain when these tactics are necessary and for whom they are necessary and why. For example, during the Turin strike of 1917 Gramsci observed that ideological statements during the protest failed to mobilize allies in the city center as well as they did for managers and engineers sympathetic to the Italian Socialist Party. Rigorous dichotomies, structured as class difference as opposed to the common interests of all workers—including foremen—damaged the strike's longevity (Fiori 1971; Gramsci 1971; Sassoon 1987). In this example, ideological justifications for the strike demonstrated problems with cohesion among potential allies. Framing often fails to account for both the positive and negative effects of debating ideological positions. However, Gramsci was directly sensitive to the tactical and ideological limitations that often could falter in the face of external political forces. If the structural, ideological, organizational, strategic, and tactical frameworks through which mobilizations could be effective were not viewed through a positional and contentious framework, and if they were not understood through the expression of ideologies organic to specific strata in specific ways, then the analytical acuity necessary to maintain mobilizations would ultimately falter.

Conclusion

Framing implies cohesion. However, Miller (1999) has asserted that ideology is a factor in movement structures, and when ideology is absent, movements risk dissolution (Freeman 1972). Westby notes that ideology can produce tensions, or worse, within movements:

> Although a single movement ideology from which frames are derived sometimes seems implicit in the ideology/framing commentaries, a moment's reflection reveals the limitations of this: (1) movements frequently have internal schismatic struggles over ideology; (2) the various forms of collaboration in movements often engender contentious ideological variants; (3) there may be differences regarding the primacy of particular aspects of the ideology; or (4) the movement may march under an eclectic banner of more than a single distinct ideology.... [D]espite an absence of systematic treatment in the literature, there is at least some

reason to think that ideological diversity can be important in framing. (Westby 2002, 290–291)

It has been demonstrated through an analysis of peace movements, the farmworkers' movement in the United States, and the women's movement in Chile that ideological fissures affect framing (Benford 1993; Mooney 1995; Noonan 1997). Where framing verges toward a seamless structure of interpretation for a social movement, the preceding examples indicate that ideology could explain how frames are formed, how and why they transform, and in what way they are salient cases. Westby (2002) points out that though little work has been done to theorize the role of ideology for social movement framing processes, these examples "do seem to support the intuition that ideological diversity is an important condition of movement framing" (2002, 291).

Gramsci approaches ideological diversity as a certainty in his attempt to mobilize workers, veterans, and peasants in the early twentieth century. He gives shape to his mobilization efforts through innovative tactical practices, the development of a strategic program, the construction of organizational frameworks that reflect shifting social and economic circumstances, and finally, through lengthy political analyses of contexts. Up to this point and across the first three chapters of this book, I have tried to demonstrate these, and other, facets of Gramsci's mobilization efforts. Specifically, I have attempted to capture the interaction of race, class, and mobilization by introducing a new theoretical framework, "ideological contention," which describes the dynamism internal to social movement organizations, a dynamism also engendered by the external political forces that act upon organizations and through which organizations engage in tactical interventions. The tactical practices of social movement organizations and their relationship to the ideational structures that are expressed ideologically become the target of the next chapter. In "Expanding Ideological Contention Theory" I am interested principally in exploring the relationship between ideas and action in Marxist theories of ideology and social movement studies analysis of the role of ideology in organizational frameworks and in the context of political mobilizations. I situate the discussion of ideological contention in these two approaches that have tried to come to grips with how ideas are expressed and their relationship to what happens when tactical practices attempt to establish concrete groundwork. The chapter explains the expression of political ideologies in a new way and sets the stage for a complex discussion of the relationship between race and ideology in the last chapter of the book.

CHAPTER THREE

Expanding Ideological Contention Theory

Social Movement Organizations and the Political Mobilization of Ideas

The critique from the preceding chapter discussed how social movement theories of framing focus on the integration of ideas and actions, but they fail to address other outcomes like fractionalization and demobilization because framing, as a concept, is neither connected to organizational structures nor actively connected to a concept of ideology. Alternatively, I posit an approach to the interrelation of ideas and actions that is connected to organizational structures through a specific conception of ideology or through ideological contention theory (ICT). Specifically, ICT describes the interrelation of ideas and actions and their effects upon organizational frameworks. A departure from the frame approach and based in Marxist theory, ICT addresses the relationship between social movement organizational composition, strategic choices, tactical actions (protest), and ideology whereby organization and ideology form a dialectical relationship. Specifically, ICT addresses the mediation of organizational forms and the interrelation of ideas and actions in 1) organizational strategies, 2) the selection of tactics and organizational change, and 3) intragroup conflict. Through my conception of ICT, I am able to describe how strategies impact the relationship between ideology, organizational structures, and tactical choices over time, through patterns of collective memory. Through ICT we can analyze how organizational patterns are affected by political struggles as these struggles are remembered and expressed by movement participants. ICT takes its departure point from Marxist ideology theory, specifically a lineage within Marxism that I describe as "organizational-relational"; it views ideology as both a necessary and fundamental aspect of any social organizational form. In this chapter, I establish the theoretical foundations for my concept of ideological contention in the previous chapter. The importance of ideology to the analysis of racialization processes, racism, and antiracism is explored in the remainder of the book. This chapter is an attempt to expand upon and clarify the relationship between the conceptualization of tactics, ideological contention, and the theoretical and conceptual foundations for both; as a result, it is dependent on the case study methodology from the previous chapters, but it is both theoretical and explicatory in nature. In specific, this chapter is essential to establishing a specific theoretical perspective on ideology as a process that not only renders social forces concretely but is also dependent on the presence of social forces in a specific social arrangement or ensemble. Specifying the arrangement or ensemble of social forces (in, for example, a specific conjuncture) illuminates the concrete force of ideological powers that effectively maintain more than merely a representation of reality but an operative and concrete reality.

An Organizational-Relational Approach

In a recent book, *Theories of Ideology: The Powers of Alienation and Subjection* (2013), Jan Rehmann demonstrates that the Marxist perspective on ideology has generated effective analytical tools to understand the interrelation between ideas, organization, and action. Apart from this, in the context of social movement studies, the discussion of social movement mobilizations— where commentators have noted that only a narrow definition of ideology has been expressed[1]—Rehmann's Marxist interpretation of ideology theory can be understood, in part, as introducing possibilities for recasting the relationship between *ideas, organization, and action.*[2] Rehmann's analysis of ideology makes it possible for the status of each of these three terms and the relationship between them to be transformed.

In the chapter on Marx and Engels, Rehmann organizes their contribution to ideology theory into three categories from questions and conceptions that can be traced from very early work—the *Introduction to the Contribution to the Critique of Hegel's Philosophy of Law* (1843–1844) through to the third volume of *Capital* (1894). The first of these three categories he refers to as *ideology-critical.* He attributes it mainly to "Lukács and the Frankfurt School," who "interpreted ideology as 'inverted' or 'reified' consciousness" (Rehmann 2013: 21). The second is *neutral*: "formulated in particular by Lenin and predominant in 'Marxism-Leninism,'" the neutral approach is "a class-specific conception of the world" and includes Marxism (Rehmann 2013: 21). And the third, which he does not name, I will refer to as *organizational-relational*. Although Rehmann does not give this conception of ideology an explicit name, he states that it "ranged from Antonio Gramsci to Louis Althusser and from Stuart Hall to the PIT" (2013: 21–22).[3] In this conception ideology is "the ensemble of apparatuses and forms of *praxis* that *organize the relation of individuals to the self and to the world*" (Rehmann 2013: 22; see also Koivisto and Pietilä 1996). In other words, in a lineage of ideology theory issuing from Gramsci's work, it is possible to produce a theory of ideology that links the conscious, collective, and communicative work of social movement participants to the organizational and structural frameworks that they produce as fundamentally relational. These relations constitute links between individual participants, the organizational frameworks that they build collectively, the political community that is maintained within the organization and, most significantly, the process through which they articulate these relationships to themselves, to others, and to a broader concept of belonging to the world. Ideology binds and separates; it produces groups and identities; it frames issues; it challenges orthodoxies and maintains some of its own. But, most importantly, it is both the collective product of its members and interpreted and realized by each person through what they do, remember, and experience. Hence, it is essentially contentious. ICT is an organizational-relational and essentially contentious theory of ideology, organizational structure, and political action.

I begin this chapter with a discussion of Rehmann's book, in particular, because of the *organizational-relational* approach, and because he demonstrates both categorically and substantively the role that the concept of ideology plays within the traditions of Marxist thought. First, Rehmann's book demonstrates that a common set of inquiries and responses occur within the framework of a persistent Marxist concern that, although it appears within different categories, concepts, and theories (such as commodities, money, fetishism, "objective thought forms," reification, social formation, contradiction and overdetermination, isolation effect, instrumentalism, culture, etc.) is tantamount to aspects of ideology or what may be considered *the ideological*. Second, Rehmann demonstrates that within the normative descriptions of this concept, what are perceived as beliefs, values, or "merely" political or cultural forms of expression not only have a concrete organizational basis but also demonstrate a specific lineage within Marxist theory. The conversation on ideology within Marxism is introduced in Marx and Engels's work in 1845. The role of bourgeois ideology as a form of domination and the positioning of ideology in the superstructure—in other words, both in relation to the state and civil society—is taken up and addressed centrally by Lenin, Gramsci, Lukács, and members of the Frankfurt School. In the latter half of the twentieth century, the conversation is renewed and reinterpreted by Althusser and his students; addressed, also, by István Mészáros and Stuart Hall and members of the Center for Contemporary Cultural Studies in Birmingham, UK; and, most substantively and recently by Terry Eagleton, Frederic Jameson, W. F. Haug, and Jan Rehmann. These frameworks of ideology theory and ideology analysis reproduced, as necessary, descriptions or conceptual frames needed for specific analytical points, or reinterpreted these points as persistent and concrete historical, social, and cultural inquiries about the interrelationship of, most broadly, the structural and juridical, political, societal, and cultural aspects of capitalism or, in short, ideas, institutions, and action. Ideological contention theory demonstrates, in part, the selection of a specific Marxist lineage (Engels—Gramsci—Haug and PIT) and its transformation to address a central question for the study of social movements.

This chapter offers a theoretical expression of how we might understand that transformation, in the form of a Gramsci-based approach to organization and ideology in social movements: *ideological contention*.[4] It also describes the ways in which such an approach may intervene, positively, in the social science literature on social movements. The analytical guidelines that I develop in this theory are based, primarily, on a specific interpretation of Gramsci's concept of historically organic ideology in Notebook 7, §19, page 21, his conception of intellectuals in Notebook 4, §49, as well as through an interpretation of PIT. In short, this chapter offers a transdisciplinary approach to ideology taking insights from across the Marxist tradition as well as from deconstruction, theories of gender, cultural anthropology, and classical texts as an organizational power: a concept introduced through PIT and based on Engels's conception of "ideological powers" from *The German Ideology*.[5]

ICT, based on the theoretical perspectives discussed earlier, focuses expressly on the role that ideology plays in shaping social movement organizations. It addresses how organizational forms mediate (form a relationship or a set of relationships between) the interrelation of ideas and actions. It explores the idea that there is something distinctive about the dynamic between social movement organizations (SMOs) and ideology. Subsidiary points illustrate issues pertaining to organizational strategies, the relationship between the selection of tactics and organizational shifts, and intragroup conflict. Specifically, ICT focuses on how strategies—when implemented and extended tactically—impact the relationship between ideology, organizational structures, and tactical choices over time. It explores what the implementation and effect of implementing strategies through tactical practices tell us about the political-organizational character of movements and how organizations maintain themselves and change.

By looking at ideology as a whole way of conflict, competition, or challenge *within* (or as a general or at least repeatable instance of) a SMO or coalition and *against* external political, social, or economic forces, ideology takes on a dynamism that demonstrates how ideas about a movement's goals in relationship to broader forces change. Most importantly, understanding the key organizational-relational components of ideology, which are explored time and again in Marxist theory, specifically, that it contains *both* "the ensemble of apparatuses and forms of praxis" that work to "organize the *relation* of *individuals* to the *self* and to the *world*," it becomes possible to explain the linkage between organizational frameworks, political subjectivity, and ideology (Rehmann 2013: 22). Through ICT, we can come to a more complex, robust, and concrete conceptualization of the dynamic aspects of SMOs as these dynamic relationships within a SMO pertain to the interrelations of ideas and action. We can understand the role of tactical practices (from the first chapter) in contentious and racist environments (from the second chapter) through a theoretical lens that is focused, in total, on the contributions of individual movement participants—with their own perspectives, memories, and experiences—as they contribute to a collective interpretation and realization of the social reality that they are working to engender.

This chapter is broken into two halves. The first discusses the literature in the area of social movement studies, including the adoption of theories in semiotics, cultural semiotics, and symbolic interactionism, to help explain the interrelation of ideas and action. The second half of the chapter is focused on developing a theory of ideology based in the work of Friedrich Engels, Antonio Gramsci, Wolfgang Fritz Haug, and PIT as well as other Marxist contributors. These two sections, taken together, establish the critical theoretical basis for ICT.

Interpretation, Framing, and Ideology: Culture, Cognition, and Intention

The most consistent and concise definition of framing across the social movement literature is attributable to Rucht and Neidhardt. Framing is defined as "collective patterns of interpretation with which certain definitions of problems, causal attributions, demands, justifications and value-orientations are brought together in a more or less consistent framework for the purpose of explaining facts, substantiating criticism and legitimating claims" (2002: 11). This definition is derived from Erving Goffman in *Frame Analysis* (1974), where "frames" are described as "schemata of interpretation" that "locate, perceive, identify, and label a seemingly infinite number of concrete occurrences defined in its terms" (21). The primary difference, however, between these two definitions is the unit of analysis. The study of social movements is a subset of the sociology of collective behavior; Goffman's frame analysis is written for the individual's participation in small units of interaction. Specifically, where the contemporary social movement theories of frames encompass "collective patterns of interpretation" or are attributed to groups of people, Goffman's frame represents cognitive organizational characteristics of an individual person producing interpretations and meanings. Despite obvious differences between groups and individuals, the description of how both the group and the individual mediate or interpret their relationship to events and produce information remains, more or less, the same.

Presumably, collective interpretations produce communication: speech and writing or texts. In "A Methodology for Frame Analysis" (1995) Hank Johnston refers to these as printed and stated information. However, it would seem that there is no need for an individual to externalize or objectify cognitive processes; it is more likely that individual interpretations produce or contribute to an internal dialog. The production of an interpretation and its (written or stated) dissemination would be qualitatively and substantively different in collective and individual settings.

Regardless, a way around the problem of collective attribution of interpretation has been to start from the individual, not the group, as the unit of analysis, and explain, describe, or impute group relations. It is absolutely consonant with Goffman's *Frame Analysis* (1974), then, to state that "the 'true location' of a frame is in the mind of the social movement participant" (Johnston 1995: 218), and, as such, the frame itself provides the point of

contact between collective meaning and individual cognition. This, also, is
not without its problems. Johnston's cognitive approach identifies linguistic
behaviors as texts (speech and writing) and as products of cognition. His
method requires "an ongoing empirical dialogue between linguistic behavior
and the mental processes they are said to manifest" (Johnston 1995: 219).
He states that we work backward from text to frame, or from language or
speech to cognitive schema. However, the link between cognition, on the
one hand, and speech and writing as intentional acts, on the other, is analytically problematic. This is especially so when analysis begins with an
object—a text—that willy-nilly contains no intentionality.

Johnston makes a distinction between macro-discourse analysis
(which he attributes to poststructuralism and "textual decomposition") and
micro-discourse analysis. A micro approach is "a more intensive approach
that takes a specific example of written text or bounded speech and seeks to
explain why the words, sentences, and concepts are put together the way they
are" (Johnston 1995: 219). This conceptual distinction falls flat when the
explanation for how text or speech is produced depends upon an intentional
cognitive act. Jacques Derrida (1980, 1982) has analyzed the interrelation
of speech, writing, and intention across various levels. According to him, all
language works upon human cognition and consciousness through a chain
of supplementary and differential meanings: through difference (between
words) and deferral (adding words to qualify a meaning, thereby producing a
more symbolic distance between a single utterance or word and a single corresponding meaning) (Derrida 1982). Further written or spoken acts operate
through supplements (attempts to qualify meaning by adding text and func-
tionally producing deferrals), which have the persistent effect of never fully
capturing intended meanings. Derrida goes on to suggest that there is no
original place from which meaning is issued; the spontaneity of producing
meaning vocally (*phonocentrism*) does not make it any more authentic than
when it is symbolic (*logocentrism*) (Derrida 1980). Elsewhere, Derrida states
that in the Western epistemological tradition, ascribing a special status to
speech or spontaneous contexts as more bounded to true intention ignores
the rules of language, meaning, and intentionality.

Language and speech always exceed the contexts in which and through
which they operate, regardless of how intensive or bounded a context may
be. This would mean, then, that cognition—which works through language—is privy to the same exact effects. In other words, the substantive
matter (language and speech) upon which cognition works can neither be
entirely fixed objectively (lexically, external to speaker and context, and

noninterpretive) or subjectively (cognitively). In this schema, meaning and intention, between thought and speech, may not be completely fixed. Gillan (2008) makes a similar criticism—regarding the relationship between thought and act—where he states that the effects of a frame on cognition cannot be observed. They "are indirect, rather than resulting from conscious knowledge. One cannot become, as it were, part of that individual to learn the frame *as one can become* part of an organization that utilizes a collective action frame" (Gillan 2008: 251). This suggests that the analytical approach to understanding how issues are framed resides more strongly in the realm of organizations, the collective acquisition of meaning, and the role of the individual in interpretation and organizational participation.

What Johnston and others have illustrated is that *the traffic in content* between the frame and the individual has to be explained (Gillan hints that collectives and organizations are, at least, more empirical). How do groups cordon off or corral the cultural contents of speech and language into an interactive stream? How do SMOs frame? Theories regarding the dynamic interaction between individual behavior and frames identify the substantive cultural and political contents of that particular group (values, beliefs, narratives, symbols) as ideology. The two are set off from one another such that frame processes are dynamic, and ideology is best conceived of as a repository of cultural resources (in the form of symbols, narratives, ideas, etc.) from which frames derive meaning. This is congruent with various approaches to the study of the cultural aspects of social movements, especially *semiotics* and *symbolic interactionist* approaches (i.e., symbols) as well as *cultural semiotics* (i.e., narratives), all of which place these expressions of ideology into an interpretive or meaning community (not unlike a framing dynamic), providing a grounding and analytical basis for the *traffic in content* within a SMO or coalition.[6]

However, the approach to how meanings traffic between groups and individuals who are culturally embedded, on the one hand, and forms of collective behavior and action, on the other, rely more strongly on classical models.[7] These models—symbolic interactionism, semiotics, and cultural semiotics (including cultural studies)—describe the exchange of texts or meanings between members of a group in a context that is limited by shared sets of beliefs, values, commitments, and so forth, a dynamic that includes individuals, groups, signification or meaning, and, at least, implies an organizational form. Ideology takes a role such that it limits what is either significant in the framework of a social movement group, or ideology forms the parameters of available meanings—it works either by limiting the potential "signifieds" of a meaning community (symbolic interactionism) or limiting the community-meaning relation (semiotics). Ideology is the set of predominant meanings attached to contexts, which produce significations and signs and, thus, a meaning-based community. In both cases, framing is the dynamic interaction of meanings and ideology limits the range or scope of those meanings.[8]

What Frames Do and What They Don't Do—What Ideology Does and What It Doesn't Do

Frames are described as aligning an individual perspective with the work that a SMO does. That individual, ideally, is anyone: the "bystander public" as well as activists who already participate in the organization. As discussed in the second chapter, this process is called frame alignment. The task of frame alignment is to facilitate "the linkage of . . . interpretive orientations, such that some set of individual interests, values and beliefs and . . . activities, goals, and ideology are congruent and complementary" (Snow et al. 1986: 464). This definition is organized so that "interests, values, and beliefs" belong to the individual, whereas "activities, goals, and ideology" belong to the organizational or group level. Between these two levels, a frame is generated; it allies the activities' goals and, ultimately, the ideology of the group with individuals who are or may become a part of the movement organization. More importantly, both external political events (which introduce a problem to the organization) and internal planning leading into an event (e.g., a protest action) trigger frame alignment. Irrespective of the size or significance of the event, when frames perform a strategic-interpretive function they seek to ally individuals and movement organizations through diagnostic, prognostic, and motivational techniques or means. Briefly, there are three aspects: 1) the diagnostic aspects of a frame—identify a problem and assign blame; 2) the prognostic aspects—suggest solutions (i.e., strategies and tactics); 3) motivational aspects—legitimate and drive action.

These techniques or means vary across different contexts, which may introduce specific problems that require strategic redress to include others. Snow and colleagues (1986) introduce four concepts that describe these strategic shifts: frame bridging, or "the linkage of two or more ideologically congruent but structurally unconnected frames regarding a particular issue or problem" (1986: 467); frame amplification, or "the clarification and invigoration of an interpretive frame that bears on a particular issue, problem, or set of events" (1986: 469); frame extensions, or the "exten[sion of] the boundaries of its primary framework so as to encompass interests or points of view that are incidental to its primary objectives but of considerable salience to potential adherents" (1986: 472). The final concept, frame transformation, describes instances where proposed frames "may not resonate with, and on occasion may even appear antithetical to, conventional lifestyles or rituals and extant interpretive frames" (1986: 473).

Up to this point, ideology that has been defined as values that are either influential or informative seems to lack the analytical acuity or methodological guidelines to describe how ideas expressive of a particular political standpoint can be mobilized and transformed into strategic plans or protest actions. Although others have noted that framing provides greater analytical precision appropriate to the scope and size of SMOs,[9] there have also been dissenters that connect ideology with behavior as a political or religious concept.[10] Still others note that conceptions of ideology better explain empirical aspects of cultural expression and organizational structure[11] and the relationship between ideas, beliefs, and values (Oliver and Johnston 2000a, 2000b) regarding protest events (Westby 2002). As I point out in the second chapter but will discuss in greater depth in this chapter, David L. Westby, for instance, cites studies that demonstrate how ideology seems to have different effects on communication, strategy, and organization.[12] Most importantly, Westby finds that ideological diversity has the effect of both unifying and fractionalizing movement organizations.

The empirical effects of ideology on social movements, movement organizations, and individual and potential members, fellow travelers, and bystander publics have been described and theorized in identitarian, organizational, and behavioral terms. Though all important and relevant contributions when separated from one another, they offer partial perspectives on the role of ideology within the framework of a SMO. A debate in the pages of the journal *Mobilization* between David Snow and Robert Benford, on the one side, and Pamela Oliver and Hank Johnston, on the other, settled on the idea that ideology constrains movement participation through a kind of solid identitarian framework. Movement participants' located continuity with other struggles—the movement connected them to a history, which impacts the way that they identify their movement and their role in it both politically and culturally. Ideology is the glue that connects these elements together. Mayer N. Zald provides insights as they pertain to the relationship between ideology, SMOs, and individual participants. In particular, Zald views ideology in social movements as a complex and logical system of belief through which individuals challenge the sociopolitical order and provide political interpretation of the world (1996). Consonant with his earlier research, Zald introduces the concept of "ideologically structured action" (2000). Zald demonstrates how ideology functions as a complex logical system whereby individual prognostic and diagnostic acts militate between individuals' political perspectives and strategic plans. He states, "If your goal is to describe and analyze specific movements or families of movements, then it is highly likely that you must take into account the ideological diagnoses and prognoses that shape movement adherents' world view and programs of action" (2000a: 5). Zald bypasses the frame, seeing many of its characteristics in extant political definitions of ideology.

In all of the aforementioned studies (with the exception of Zald [2000]), both those that focus on behavior and cognition as well as those concerned with the interrelation of ideology and framing at the organizational level, there is no substantive review of ideology independent of framing (or ideology as a potentially dependent variable in the study of social movements). David L. Westby (2002) is interested in discerning the aspects of ideology that are particularly important for framing. He cites studies that describe how ideology, within a single movement, produces a range of distinct empirical effects on movement messages, strategies, and organization. After reviewing each of the studies that attempt to explain how frames unify movement activity by, in part, drawing on either an explicit or implicit ideological perspective, he finds, first:

> Although a single movement ideology from which frames are derived sometimes seems implicit in the ideology/framing commentaries, a moment's reflection reveals the limitations of this: (1) movements frequently have internal schismatic struggles over ideology; (2) the various forms of collaboration in movements often engender contentious ideological variants; (3) there may be differences regarding the primacy of particular aspects of the ideology; or (4) the movement may march under an eclectic banner of more than a single distinct ideology. (Westby 2002: 290–291)

This leads to a second, or concluding statement where Westby asserts, "Despite an absence of systematic treatment in the literature, there is at least some reason to think that ideological diversity can be important in framing" (2002: 291). These observations lead to an obvious set of questions:

1. What is *the reason* for SMO internal struggle over ideology? What is "the nature" of the struggle? What are the outcomes?

2. Westby suggests that "the various forms of collaboration" (unification) often result in "contentious ideological variants" (fractionalization). How does this occur?

3. For Westby, there are internal differences that develop in a SMO regarding what is most ideologically salient for participants and there are often different ideologies contained within a single movement/SMO. What, however, is responsible for differences of interpretation establishing a more salient ideological position and how do organizations/movements remain unified despite ideological differences?

Both the questions posed here and Westby's discussion of the interrelation of ideology and framing are focused on group relationships mediated by collaborative strategy making, agreements and disagreements in the context of fractionalization or SMO coalitions, or fundamental or interpretive disagreements about a political organization's ideology. The combination of group relationships and structural mediations, such as ideological and organizational features of the social movement, suggest an organizational-level view to understanding how organizations are still able to mobilize ideas politically, not only despite differences, disagreements, and so forth, but, rather, in what seems like an environment where these dynamics are persistent. Perhaps, more importantly, both the observations and questions require organizational analysis that would depend, specifically, upon a theory that demonstrates how ideology and SMOs (possibly political organizations more generally) are necessarily interrelated while maintaining some analytical distinction between the two. Such a perspective would have to capture both the (group) organizational level and the dynamic relational aspects (i.e., dynamics that require collective participation) of social movements. ICT offers a theoretical framework that explains the dynamic relationship between ideology, a SMO, and the movement community that strategizes and participates in protest actions.

Ideological Contention Theory

ICT describes the collaborative dynamism (relationships) within a social movement or SMO whereby ideology is a central organizational component of a SMO. By analogy, Clifford Geertz singularly captures both the fundamental and the dynamic aspects of the relationship between ideology and political organization when he describes how the development of our central nervous system, specifically the neocortex, was not merely shaped by but was, rather, required by our interaction with culture.

> As our central nervous system—and most particularly its crowing curse and glory, the neocortex—grew up in part in interaction with culture, it is incapable of directing our behavior or organizing our experience without the guidance provided by systems of significant symbols. . . . To supply the additional information necessary to be able to act, we were forced, in turn, to rely more and more heavily on cultural sources—the accumulated fund of significant symbols. Such symbols are thus not mere expressions, instrumentalities, or correlates of our biological, psychological, and social existence; they are prerequisites of it. (Geertz 1973: 49)

In short, Geertz posits that these two distinct spheres of human experience, and objects of study or inquiry, *are deeply interdependent* in our understanding of human existence. He states, "Without men, [there is] no culture, certainly; but equally, and more significantly, without culture, [there are] no men" (Geertz 1973: 49). I posit that the arrangement of structure or organizations and ideas in the context of a theory of ideological context is unique, such that *without organization, no ideology, certainly; but equally, and more significantly, without ideology, no organization.*

The dynamic or collaborative dynamism within the movement organization is essentially contentious. This is important because although framing explains a process whereby a perspective becomes shared, the reality of SMOs is that within it there are disagreeable exchanges at the least, and experiences of volatility at the most. This dynamic is not exclusive to the SMO; external political forces (EPFs) affect social movements/SMOs. Both the organizational and ideological character of SMOs are such that events do not produce reactions but, rather, set movements in motion; dynamics, then, are responsive, adaptive, strategic opportunities, and so on. Resultantly, EPFs influence *movement organization, strategic choices, and collective memory*; finally, recognizing the interrelation of *organization, strategy (and tactical implementation), and memory—taken altogether with my conception of IC in the subsequent chapter—helps us understand the process of organizational cohesion and organizational change.*

ICT describes the interrelation of ideas and actions, how this relationship impacts and is, in turn, impacted by the SMO—both in a given instance and over time, and the multiple potential effects that this relationship may have on an organization, including fractionalizations and dissolution. ICT maintains that ideology is the most dynamic mediator between participants and a SMO. Ideology, in the framework of ICT, represents the sets of ideas that emerge within as well as alongside of it and that change it as the movement organization engages in various protest actions. For example, as I discussed in the first chapter when Aldon Morris describes the role of militants in the broader framework of the civil rights movement, their insights shape protest strategy and the adoption of specific tactical practices. Also, they remain within the movement while, simultaneously, threatening the implicit tactical perspectives that bind it together as a political community. Significantly, Kathleen Cleaver recounts how when she participated in the Student Nonviolent Coordinating Committee (SNCC) it had just begun to articulate the concept of black power as an ideological position internal to SNCC. That ideological position, adopted within SNCC, effected its organizational structure in several ways (one, in particular, limited the resources it received from donors due since black power was perceived as militant). The Black Panther Party, according to Cleaver, formed a new organization—which pulled participants away from SNCC—that reflected the ideology of black power (which could not be easily reconciled with the predominant ideologies in SNCC). She states:

> [W]hat appealed to me about the Black Panther Party *was that it took that position of self-determination and articulated it* in a local community *structure*, had a *program*, had a platform and an *implementation through the statement* of how *blacks should exercise community control* over education, housing, business, military service. (PBS 1997, emphasis mine)

In short, the *operative and active* basis for the Black Panther Party, allowed it to "articulate" an ideology that was more consonant with Cleaver's perspective than the SNCC. It was both the position of the organization and the way that the organization's position was realized structurally, strategically, and through tactical practices. The basis for ICT, as we will see, comes from Gramsci's definition of ideology as historically (and organizationally) organic, as well as Miller's discussion of "adaptive responses." ICT derives further legitimacy as structuring and constraining communities in specific ways from Engels's notion of "ideological powers" and PIT's concept of *Vergesellschaftung* or "societalization." Ideology provides a social or organizational constraint, whereby the SMO's internal dynamism (as it pertains to strategic choices and the implementation of tactics, primarily) is driven by ideological disputes (consonant with the point that Pamela Oliver and Hank Johnston make but that act upon organizations and not individuals). By way of an example, we might say that the structure of an organization is the material realization of its ideology. What it stands for shapes its organizational form. For example, the Occupy! movement, which was purported to be a mass movement of the people, the 99 percent, responded to challenges, crises, and organizational concerns through a medium of communication that has been described as horizontalism (Sitrin 2006) or, more empirically, as "stacked" (Dean 2014). Further, a SMO's means for acquiring resources are linked to its strategies (civil disobedience, property damage, etc.). ICT connects tactical practices, strategic programs, organizational structure, organizational resources, and ideology into a holistic conception of social movement dynamics.

If ideology is organic to (not imposed upon) an organizational structure, then any event that threatens its explicit organizational parameters requires a response. Acquisition or exchange of resources of all kinds— alliances and nonalliances, separations, protest actions, and so on—if not planned, agreed upon, or done in a programmatic manner, invite contention. Accepting needed resources or choosing not to ally with another organization, whether a major or minor event, necessarily changes the organizational dynamics and the perception of the organization to its members, bystander publics, the media. Anything that is added or removed or any event that the movement participates in is mediated by the SMO ideology. These mediations are essentially contentious; organizational patterns are affected (fractionalized, disrupted, or strengthened) by outcomes as they are remembered and expressed by movement participants as, for example, successful strategies.

In fact, in Notebook 13, §36, Gramsci, in a footnote, argues for a democratic dynamic within the organizational structure of a party. He is attempting to make a case (he here is posing his position against both Amadeo Bordiga and Joseph Stalin) for the political party structure as collective, persistently organic, and taking its cues from the tactical successes of the progressive members directly engaged in struggle. Gramsci's concept of organic democratic centralism describes an organization as a participatory collective where members are affected by the organizational form in which they participate and, more importantly, develop and drive the organization through their collective, tactical, efforts. Their ability to determine and experience their concrete and collective role through participation is at the core, or rather, is the proof, of what is in the context of Gramsci's quotation, a democratized party structure. Put plainly, he gives more than a mere measure of autonomy to "rank-and-file" members of the party. He states:

> 'Organicity' can only be found in democratic centralism, which is so to speak a 'centralism' in movement—i.e. a continual adaptation of the organization to the real movement, a matching of thrusts from below with orders from above, a continuous insertion of elements thrown up from the depths of the rank and file into the solid framework of the leadership apparatus which ensures continuity and the regular accumulation of experience. Democratic centralism is 'organic' because on the one hand it takes account of movement, which is the organic mode in which historical reality reveals itself, and does not solidify mechanically into bureaucracy.... In parties which represent socially subaltern classes, the element of stability is necessary to ensure that hegemony will be exercised not by privileged groups but by the progressive elements—organically progressive in relation to other forces which, though related and allied, are heterogeneous and wavering. (Notebook 13, §36; Gramsci 1971: 188–189).

The real movement of the subaltern elements that are actively engaged, day to day, in class struggle is, according to Gramsci, its "progressive elements." He means, in a literal sense, that their direct daily engagement with class struggle (i.e., forces) pull in, drive, and direct the middle strata and inform or generate the strategies "from above" that seek to both stabilize and serve the subaltern groups who are daily and directly engaged in class struggle. The party, in Gramsci's case, provides a support framework, resources, and a broader strategic and political direction for its organic subaltern elements; holding the organization together and developing its capacity. The most organic elements—those who are most deeply embedded in and affected by social, economic, cultural, and political relations exercise the most progressive responsive potential for tactical creativity and autonomy in the context of social struggles. All are organic to—a part of and not outside of— the party structure; all serve an intellectual function for the party.

Intellectuals: How Ideology Is Organizational and Organizations Are Ideological

In the second chapter, I have provided some detail about the role of intellectuals in Gramsci's notebooks and preprison writings. I want to describe how certain details from Gramsci's concept of intellectuals make specific contributions to ICT. In short, Gramsci's contribution to the concept of ideology is unique. It is primarily historical but also organizational or con-

crete in the sense that, for him, ideologies necessarily emerge in contexts alongside organizations and endure as indispensable to civil and state-based needs. It should be noted that, in both cases, organizations and institutions that are organic to a context are only organic if they create or address a new need (civil society) or a new circumstance (rights and privileges, states, parties, etc.).[13]

In the case of organic intellectuals, the groups attached to these organizations not only enjoy preeminence but, importantly, they become memorialized or symbolized as great leaders, geniuses, and rebels, that is, figures of great importance. Already, as in the preceding examples (e.g., Kathleen Cleaver), individual contributors are singled out as examples. They play a specific role for predominant ideological frameworks providing continuity between the past and the present even if their role was disruptive during the time that they live. They are "traditional intellectuals." However, at the national level, (in the context of national ideology) very often traditional intellectuals become memorialized whether their contributions were private or public, for example, as heads of state or fighting for recognition (e.g., rights) of marginalized or oppressed groups. First, these figures embody what has come to be the colloquial understandings of "intellectual" as a uniquely expressive figure; their persistence is linked to a narrative authority like a national ideology. One can think of the Martin Luther King Jr. memorialized by the United States and the historical man in an almost radical contradistinction. One can think of the Gandhi of passive resistance and the Gandhi of the Hind Swaraj again in radical contradistinction. In both cases, the former is symbolized as a simple, two-dimensional ideological representation. Or, the individual is summarized through a catchphrase (Zald 2000a): "nonviolent or passive resistance." These historical figures, each led complex lives, movements, and organizations, were organic to a context—they were both products of it and produced it (Carley 2019a). Their struggle depended on actual forces and actual responses to those forces in the form of counterforces, alliances, agreements, strategies, and tactics, and so on. Organic to a past moment, the traditional intellectual provides continuity between present-day values through a mythologized or selectively organized past broadcasting of a sensibility of historical continuity and stability, making it difficult to even imagine historical transformation and occluding the organizational and societal basis for change. This figure of the intellectual often represents the co-optation by an external predominant narrative in an attempt to legitimate historical events for the predominant narrative. However, traditional intellectuals (whether oppositional or not) are embedded in historical, social, political, ideological, and organizational contexts. ICT is concerned with how intellectuals are embedded within organizational frameworks and develop ideological frameworks through contention, a contention that is often ignored when these figures are reinterpreted through predominant ideological frameworks.

Marxism, Communism, and Political Organizations: Lenin, Luxemburg, Gramsci, and Jodi Dean

The concept of the intellectual must also be placed in the context of the institutional formations—consonant with Gramsci's discussion of organic intellectuals—that are responsible for their production. The Southern intellectual in this context (Gramsci 1971, [1926] 1995b) is both a "social fact" (as discussed in Notebooks 4, §49; 12, §1; 25, §1, and "Some Aspects Concerning the Southern Question") and a possibility based on struggles, institutional nexuses, and transformations in civil society. For example, the juridical transformations that Lenin explains are a result of Nations' Rights to Self-Determination (1902, [1914] 1927)—in dialog with Rosa Luxemburg (1909)—are an argument about the interrelationship between changing conditions, institutional-legal possibilities, and new formations that rise out of them. The argument between Lenin and Luxemburg is an argument about strategy, tactics, and, most specifically, the most appropriate social location of their application (e.g., class conflict, in Luxemburg's case and law enshrining the development of economic and political forces in Lenin's case).

The issues of political strategy in the Marxist framework of Communist Party building are addressed by Gramsci in his notebooks. Taken in abstraction, the relations that constitute "The New Prince" (the Communist Party) are neither simply the Communist Party—in a purely abstract and functional way—nor are they the preeminence of a specific member. Rather, what "The New Prince" describes is the party process—the only process by which a structural transformation can occur in the framework of vast, integrated nexus of public and private social institutions. This nexus allows for the transfer of state power to political cadres *only* in the form of parties and coalitions of parties, on the one hand, and locks the state into relationships with the class representatives in civil society, on the other. The latter, however, must have the collective legal, economic, and financial—in short, the organizational—means to challenge if not cripple the state, as it were, and at the cost of disintegrating the society. This is why hegemony cannot be understood without both the war of position and the war of maneuver or the requisite capacity and consensus to seize state power. It is here that the gravity of Poulantzas's conception of the "isolation effect" (1973a) (i.e., how class place requires an effective political class positioning) reminds us that the enormous struggle in civil society is also, and primarily, a struggle against ideology and the foundations that materialize it. *It is a struggle to elaborate an ideology in both word and deed; both organizationally and tactically.* Intellectuals cannot link word and deed unless they possess organizational-relational means in the form of an institution. For Gramsci and Poulantzas, that institution is a party and not a factory council, trade union, or trade union coalition.

Gramsci's interdiction (the party is the laboratory of the state) in revolutionary communist theory is his conception of the role of the party as opposed to factory councils. Although civil society is certainly the basis for revolutionary struggle, the political sphere is the terrain where the revolutionary intellectual plies his or her trade. In short, the preeminent organizational-relational characteristics exist in party and state. It is through the party form that intellectuals can begin to connect the vast array of civil (private) institutional forms that have already collected and organized (in complex organizational forms) a vast array of occupational, specialized, and educated trade personnel—political, cultural, managerial (of all kinds), and religious—that will be needed for the reorganization of society. Gramsci's concept of intellectual groups—as both organic to their institutional locations and organic or traditional within a historical bloc—exhibit the motivating force behind the unifications and fractionalizations that occur in political society, with their attached civil interests. In the early waves of Gramsci scholarship Jacques Texier (1979) interprets details of Gramsci's theory of the party in an argument with Norberto Bobbio. He states:

> The new social group *must be revolutionary in economic terms*, that is, *it must be capable of transforming the economic base and establishing such production relations as will permit the new development of productive forces*. Its political hegemony will therefore have an economic base and content. . . . *It would be a grave error* on the part of the new ruling class *to consider that, since the essential task is the transformation of the economic infrastructure and the development of the apparatus of production, "the superstructural facts can be ignored," "left to themselves" and "to develop spontaneously."* (Texier 1979: 64, 69, emphasis mine)

Texier describes the relationship between organizational change and ideological articulations; you can't have one without the other. Regarding organizational forms, for Gramsci, the limitations of the factory councils (which was mentioned in the first and second chapters) was their level and scope of activity.[14] Although in a concrete and immediate sense it would seem that demonstrating not only that the workers could seize the productive forces and govern their operation autonomously was of paramount importance, the factory councils failed precisely in that out of the factory floor a limited potential for alliances (class corporatism and hegemony) beyond it existed. At the micro level, the demonstration of autonomy seemed sufficient to revolution, but the conditions necessary to facilitate the hegemony of the working class could only be met through the ascendency of a revolutionary party who could connect the civil and political elements together both broadly and substantively through state and party. This perspective is echoed in the spirit and in some cases the letter of Jodi Dean's new theories of communism and the role of the party (Dean 2014, 2015; see also Biebricher and Celikates 2012). Not only is there a precedent for "reimagining" the role of intellectuals (as a category) or leaders, organizational forms, or dynamics but, more importantly, contemporary work on ideology as a necessary organizational basis for social dynamics—as described earlier by Rehmann—has been developed in some detail by PIT through the concept of societalization (*Vergesellschaftung*). Up to this point, I have attempted to demonstrate the complex arrangement between organizations, participants, and ideology. Intellectuals produce a dynamic articulation of these elements intervening into social and political forces transforming them. But, there is an even more fundamental understanding of the interconnection between people, ideas, and organization. Societalization illustrates the necessity of an ideology to forms of social organization that strongly supports the position, in ICT, that ideology is necessary to an organization and an organizational form necessarily produces an ideology. Implied in this framework is the communication and elaboration of social interaction. As such, participation in an organizational form and, at the same time, an ideology demonstrates Gramsci's famous claim that everyone has the capacity to be an intellectual and, in fact, is, regardless of his or her social function. More importantly, the intellectual contribution of every member of a group, within an organizational form, constitutes both the social structure and the corresponding ideological frameworks in rich and organic ways. Societalization captures these relations and provides strong legitimacy for ICTs foundational perspective on ideology.

In the work of PIT, W. F. Haug's *Vergesellschaftung*, which translates as "societalization," is used to describe the means by which relationships between members of a society are organized; the form of organization is based upon "competencies." It is necessary to understand what "competencies" mean to begin to see how ICT is connected to Gramsci's conception of ideology as historically organic and also to intellectual roles both traditional and organic. More significantly in the framework of ICT, a competency—a socially developed repertoire of abilities—links concrete organizational forms to broader sets of ideas through the participants in an organizational form. To be competent is to be able and to understand what one is abled for or how one is oriented within a large framework. The degree to which one participates in the broader organization of one's own abilities and ideas, or the extent to which one is the purveyor of one's own competencies, is central to the concept of societalization.

First, competencies are the "organizational-relational" basis in ICT. Competencies connect Marx's conception of "species being" to the historical (or accumulated and developed) and current ensemble of social relations (Marx [1844] 1971). In short, the *anthropological* meeting of needs and the production of new needs through labor are a part of a broader framework that represents the *social* nexus of human relations. Social relations express both aggregate need and aggregate labor skill that produces (historically) variable forms of management or administration. These vary between the more-or-less equal and collective attribution of administration and the external administration of a structure by a group that is classed as separate and only serves an administrative function. This is the departure point for understanding the ideological: competencies and how they are expressed socially and realized politically. The ideological, understood within this paradigm, is not primarily something mental but represents a modification and a specific organizational form of the "ensemble of the social relations' and of the individuals' participation in controlling these relations, or at least their integration within them" (Haug 1987: 60). W. F. Haug makes the point, echoing Engels, that the state is merely one of these forms of administration. It would follow that a SMO is another.

The formation of the state—echoed in cultural and economic anthropology as well as in eighteenth-century European philosophy—is that it provides a specific framework whereby the interrelation between social practices and institutions requires a population or group that accepts formal (e.g., legal) guidelines for behavior. In so doing, individuals, elements of the population, become *"subject to" their own competencies as alienated and superordinate forms of their own group coordination.* ICT and social movements—which often place aspects of this group coordination in question—not only reintroduce antagonism into society through political forces but, more specifically, demonstrate through their own organizational framework various (e.g., horizontal) aspects of governance as it pertains to the mobilization of resources, the agreement on a strategic platform, the participation in tactical practices, and the goals and purpose of the movement. ICT brings social antagonisms into the center of the theoretical picture not only as a concrete organizational feature but also to both demonstrate and explain the connection between these organizational features, modes of governance, decisions regarding collective forms of action (strategies), the coordinated implementation of these actions in specific contexts (tactics), and the long-term effects of this process (collective memory). Haug points out that the organizational basis for the state was the placation of social antagonism: "Social antagonisms which transcend that which can be inner-societally settled in 'horizontal' processes of building a consensus are a prerequisite for the formation of state power" (1987: 61). ICT describes these antagonisms in the framework of a SMO. Since these SMOs find themselves in (often operating against and sometimes with) the context of state power and, also, since they are neither states nor political parties, organizationally, this would suggest that SMO ideology requires an independent form of theorizing.[15] How effective a social movement is at transforming relations of domination and exploitation depends both on its ideology, organizational form, and the EPFs that constitute the constraints and possibilities of a specific context.

In *Unravelling Gramsci* (2007) Adam David Morton addresses this precise problem as he seeks to understand Gramsci's analytical purchase on present-day political-organizational forms like the Zapatista National Liberation Army (Ejército Zapatista de Liberación, EZLN). The EZLN poses a particular problem to connecting Gramsci's concept of hegemony to a movement that is both modern and indigenous and that seeks to build its own society apart from the existing polity. It, in essence, is not a party but a society. It only defends its autonomy (a socially, politically, and socially separate sphere) against the repressive forces of the state without any inclination toward a hegemonic struggle to seize the Mexican nation-state. In his interest in both retaining and extending Gramsci's ideas in this context, Morton states that "the co-ordination of popular movements through organic intellectuals is linked to a postmodern collective prince" (Morton 2007: 208). A postmodern collective prince, as Morton describes it, "binds together intellectual and political leaders with a mass base" in the style of Gramsci's concept of the political party whether or not the EZLN represents "the relationship between a 'party' and fundamental social-class forces" in a Gramscian way (Morton 2007: 208). For Morton, the example of the EZLN not only raises questions about whether Gramsci was focused on an organizational form that is no longer relevant—that is, it raises questions about Gramsci's concept of the party as it relates to the stages of hegemony, wars of maneuver and position, the concept of the integral state, and the historical bloc—but, moreover may require "going beyond the notion of the party as creator of a new state" (Morton 2007: 208). First, Morton implies that the organizational form of the EZLN has neither the ideology nor the goal of forming a state and, as such, requires a "going beyond," a rethinking Gramsci's theory of the party as the revolutionary "subject of" hegemonic struggle. Second, or as such, this would imply that aspects of a, or Gramsci's, theory of power would require raising the question of theorizing new organizational forms with distinctive dynamics. SMOs, especially organizations contending with state forces but not seeking state power, would require a reimagining of the role of ideology, its organizational function, and the practical aspects of forming and implementing strategies. To view the EZLN as a process of societalization and, moreover, to understand its specific ideological iteration of autonomy or libertarian socialism in indigenous frameworks provides both a functional and extreme example of ICT where EPFs are *antithetical* (modernity vs. indigeneity) to both the ideology and the organizational structure of the EZLN in the territory of Chiapas. Or, put differently, the EZLN represents the alterglobalization movement; it is an articulation of the "anti-thesis" of the Mexican state in the framework of global forces.

In the context of the previous discussion and ICT, the organizational form of the SMO requires some conception of an active adaptation to implement strategy and to cope with EPFs as well as internal forms of contest. Even in the case of the EZLN, it takes a posture of self-defense against the Mexican state. Koivisto and Pietilä writing on Haug's contributions to PIT develop his notion of *Vergesellschaftung*, or societalization, to reflect its connotation of *making socialism* or a process of "making socialist" through political struggles. Making socialism is, in this case, a process of society building. Their insight points to the concept of "adaptation" and "active self-adaptation" through the concept of competencies. They state:

'[S]ocialization' is the direct translation of *Vergesellschaftung* since it normally means either 'making socialist' or adapting individuals to the social order. *Vergesellschaftung* has the wider meaning of 'making society'; besides the adaptation of individuals to society (which can never happen purely passively, but always incorporates a moment of active self-adaptation) it refers to 'the shaping and realization of social relations on all levels.' (Koivisto and Pietilä 1996: 47)

This process of "shaping, realizing, and organizing" the world around oneself and one's group in such a way that participants adapt to it is the dynamic upon which ICT is most focused. Since this process is most fundamentally mediated by societal, political, and cultural forces that persistently confound SMOs goals in the short and long term, it is worth discussing some of the empirical effects that are explained through consonant theoretical perspectives from the social movement literature, specifically, the effects of or the relationship between adaptation ideology and SMO members to reconnect the concept of societalization to SMOs. By grounding societalization into contemporary empirical studies of ideology, organizational structures, strategy, and their expression in tactical practices, the dissensus, disagreement, and potential fractionalization can be understood alongside the collective and political-communal aspects of a SMO that, taken all together, comprise the central dynamics of ICT.

The Interrelation of Organizations, Strategy, Tactics, and Collective Memory: Miller, Raboy, and Gramsci

Frederick D. Miller (1999) studies the relationship between SMO's structure and ideology. He describes social movement members' "adaptive responses" as central to the relationship between the structure of a SMO and the movement's ideology. Miller makes two points. First, that external forces (including repression, which may hamper a SMO's ability to get resources), ideology (which influences tactics and organizational structure), and organizational structure (which influences tactics and how resources are mobilized) are interrelated across several historical cases and may not be studied in isolation from one another. He states, "Both movement ideology and structure, which shape each other, are created by the members' adaptive responses to external forces. Once created, neither ideology nor structure is static; both influence strategic choices that organizations make" (304). Second, when an organizational core is no longer maintained in a movement or SMO, and when there is no support from others, the movement often comes undone. This point echoes Freeman's (1972) discussion of the outcomes of movements that lack strong organizational cores.

The dynamic aspects of Miller's study—when placed against the discussion of societalization—help demonstrate that "adaptive responses" can be understood as expressive of the democratized formations of socialization in the context that I describe here. Adaptation does not preclude contention. Whether contention is present between movement actors and external forces, internal to the movement, or both, it is necessary to understand that the process of horizontal socialization is often contentious. It is further possible to see social movements as a laboratory of societalization, especially in instances where the ideology, tactics, or militant stance of the movement is radical, revolutionary, or both. In other words, the theoretical description of "horizontal socialization" is an ideal, a category. Empirically, horizontal management would be expressive of conflict. How the conflict is mitigated requires "cycles," so to speak, of decision-based processes (agreeing upon strategies) and, also, placing the movement organization into circumstances where members act on behalf of the organization and experience the successes and failures associated with their acts and the actions of the group.

The successes and failures are or become a part of the collective memory of the movement or the history of the movement as it is experienced by its participants and, also, rearticulated through them. This memory is, and has been, analyzed in its expressive aspects by both Raboy (1984) and Legaré (1980). Verta Taylor (1989) describes this aspect of maintaining movement integrity as abeyance structures. Though similar, Taylor's concept marks a movement's retreat from contentious politics. It describes how a social movement manages to remain both relevant, even contentious, by other means prior to future expectant mobilizations (Taylor 1989).

Raboy's research focused on contending forms of political communication in the mainstream and alternative political press in Quebec during the 1960s and '70s. Articles that Raboy analyzed as data focused on the analytical perspectives taken by group members. In this case, not only was ideology expressive or, more significantly, took on characteristics that could drive empirical analysis, but, substantively, the writing of movement members—which was analytical work—looked at the proposals, strategies, and protest actions of the movements and demonstrated internal interpretations of "reformist" and "revisionist" perspectives on these aspects of the movements' trajectory over time. Though not captured at committee meetings or in public spaces during protests, Raboy points out that an analysis of this kind points to the highly contentious ideological work that largely goes unnoticed by observers. Citing similarly focused research by Legaré (1980), Raboy describes "how important and relevant a *group of articles on class analysis can be to a collectivity's political memory*" (1984: 147).

Gramsci's discussion of the "Sassari Brigade" and its role in the Biennio Rosso, contains many of the same elements of Raboy's (1984) analysis of tactics that emerged alongside the "October Crisis" in the early 1970s, the subsequent general strike, and the emergence of the Marxist-Leninist movement there. Gramsci's discussion demonstrates the interrelation between mobilization and collective memory. Specifically, it describes "pathways" or outcomes that occur after successful mobilizations, which include fractionalizations, new organizational forms, as well as substantive aspects of movement participation beyond just participation in mobilizations and protest actions. In a quotation that has appeared in chapters 1 and 2 and bears repeating here, Gramsci states that the events of 1917

> have had *results which still subsist to this day* and continue.... *They illuminated, for an instant, brains which had never thought in that way, and which remained marked by them, radically modified*.... We can recall dozens and indeed hundreds of letters sent from Sardinia to the *Avanti!* Editorial offices in Turin; letters which were *frequently collective*, signed by all the Sassari Brigade veterans in a particular village. By *uncontrolled and uncontrollable paths*, the political attitude which we supported was disseminated ... and it would be possible to recall in this respect episodes that are *rich in content and significance*. ([1926] 1995b: 26–27)

In both the first and second chapters and, now, in the context of this chapter, it is important to reinterpret this quotation. The radical modification of participants in the repertoire of tactical practices during the Biennio Rosso was a product of Gramsci's articulation of racialized peasant groups into the broader framework of industrial workers' struggles. Certainly, the peasants came to view their relationship with society differently. Certainly, the inclusion of diverse elements into a workers' struggle that was contained within the walls of the factory changed the organizational framework of class-based industrial struggles and the perspective of the industrial workers toward peasants participating in these struggles and the veterans that came to challenge them but, instead, became their allies. More significantly, the organizational framework also changed to reflect the transformation of the workers' movement into a mass movement. Many different brains had been radically modified. The context in which they struggled had been radically modified. The experience and how it is recalled becomes a concrete marker, a turning point, that makes it possible to imagine future struggles as a radical modification of history itself. But, most significantly, these groups needed to articulate or produce a common ground out of what was perceived as internal and, in some cases, insurmountable differences. That common ground reflects a process of societalization. As demonstrated in the first chapter of this book, the ideology of the workers' struggle produced radically modified organizational forms that made that struggle concrete, made it grow. None of this was seamless and none of it was produced through automatic agreement. It was the contention among peasants, trade unionists, and within the socialist party that Gramsci attempted to articulate into the postwar class struggle. That same contention led to a split within the socialist party that produced a communist party that fractionalized only years later. ICT captures the dynamism of transformation, fractionalization, mobilization, and demobilization by focusing on the episodes that, rich in content and significance, shape the practices and consciousness of collective participation in the framework of social movements and the organizational bodies they build.

Conclusion

The goal of this chapter was to introduce my concept of ICT into the discussion of the interrelation of ideas and action in the context of political organizations, specifically SMOs. In it, I recast some of the examples from the theoretical framework and case study in the previous chapter to situate them more strongly in the theoretical literature in both Marxism and social movement studies. ICT is a Marxist-based theory that I have elaborated, here, to further explain the interrelations between organizations and ideas and their relational patterns over time, placing the dynamism of collective agency at the theory's center. ICT articulates how organizational forms mediate the interrelation of ideas and actions. It demonstrates the role of ideology in a SMO as organizationally distinctive in consort with strategic and tactical outcomes. By including a specifically Marxist lineage, ICT provides a lens on the dynamics of social movement organizations that is consistent with the existing social movement literature but that addresses important questions pertaining to both theory and analysis, specifically to the connections between tactical practices, ideological expression, and organizational structure. Rehmann's discussion of what I have termed the "organizational-relational" aspects of ideology theory help establish the need for the kind of intervention that ICT makes in addressing the role of ideology within the frame perspective.

In this chapter, organization and social structure are firmly linked to a concept of ideology demonstrating the constructive interrelation between these two concepts as a collective expression of social subjectivity. As a more intensive inquiry into the cultural basis for explaining the dynamics of social movement framing, ideological contention can be conceived of as a political process through which groups attempt to determine social forms that make concrete interventions into and against stolid civil and social expressions of exploitation and domination. The remainder of this book will focus on contemporary theoretical frameworks that focus on the forces of exploitation and, more significantly, domination through race, racialization, and racism. In the next two chapters, I place Gramsci's thought into relationship with cultural theoretical approaches to the analysis of racism and aspects of critical race theory especially as they pertain to the state and contemporary ideology. Placing my analysis of some of Gramsci's insights about the intersection of race, mobilization, tactics, political organization, and ideological frameworks in conversation with contemporary theories of race, racism, and racialization, I will demonstrate how my conception of tactical practices and ideological contention contribute to contemporary inquiries into ideology, the state, race, and class.

CHAPTER 4

Agile Materialisms

The Gramscian Foundations
of Racial Analysis in Cultural Studies

Each of the previous chapters has stressed the connections between tactical practices, ideological expression, and organizational structure taking both race and mobilization to be central and dynamic mediators. The previous chapter explores the theory of ideological contention. The second chapter establishes the framework for and introduces the theory of ideological contention; it stresses the national, ideological, and pseudoscientific context through which a racist framework legitimated a political stance toward Southern Italian peasants and veterans (building on work in the first chapter). This chapter and the following one express theoretical linkages and new concepts that bring together some of the insights about race and mobilization into contemporary theoretical discourses that focus on race, racialization, and racism specifically in the areas of cultural studies and critical race theory. This chapter, in particular, contributes to theories or perspectives on race through an investigation of Gramsci's and Stuart Hall's theoretical frameworks, how those frameworks are interrelated, as well as the historical contexts in which they developed. Specifically, this chapter investigates why Gramsci's theories and concepts have a discrete relevance to the study of race and ethnicity in contemporary contexts. I claim that, during the time he lived, Gramsci's writing (scholarly, journalistic, and personal letters) demonstrates that he did not enter into the positivist and modernist discursive framework on race (and nationalism) that looked to biological features for evidence to explain and interpret the cultural and sociological expressions of racial difference. For Gramsci, race and difference can and should be linked to a modified historical materialist framework that I refer to as "agile materialism." A theoretically driven strategy, agile materialism is linked closely to cultural and political transformations with regard to race. It depends upon Gramsci's concepts or methodological guidelines for the concept of conjuncture. Stuart Hall's work, specifically that of the period between 1980 and 1986, then takes up these concepts to develop a conception of racialization and racial domination that is significant across the twentieth century.[1]

I argue that Gramsci's conception of history, culture, society, and economy as well as his attitudes toward race, racialization, and politics demonstrate and make possible Hall's affirmative reading of Gramsci's work. To demonstrate the connection between Gramsci's conceptual framework and race and his connection to Hall's work, I analyze Hall's adaptation of Gramsci's concepts of the conjuncture and hegemony. I also read Gramsci's essays, correspondences, and discuss mobilizations that Gramsci was involved in that are substantively different from material considered in previous chapters. The examples discussed in this chapter focus on peasant mobilizations in Southern regions that occur in the framework of the Catholic modernism and popularism movements.

By developing these and other examples into a limited-depth case study framework, I am able to show through these contexts and, also, through a discussion of Gramsci's perspectives on religious humanism, nationalism, race, and political mobilizations that Gramsci understood race and difference as embedded in questions concerning the historical and political transformations that inform "praxis" (or questions pertaining to both mobilization and organization). I show how the concept of articulation connects structure and culture at an abstract level. As such, the method in this chapter is directly intended to illustrate the framework for agile materialism, to explain the process of development of this concept between Gramsci's and Hall's work, specifically to explore uncharted issues as they pertain to the conceptual relationship between structure and culture in the context of understanding race, and, finally, to pose provocative questions (Reinharz 1992: 167). Consequently, this chapter considers other ways that race and difference do inform Gramsci's theoretical perspective. Evidence for this is rooted in his transformation from an Italian socialist "Southernist" perspective to a communist (also a constructivist and culturalist) perspective and, furthermore, is linked to his various roles as a scholar, journalist, socialist organizer and activist, and communist parliamentarian and party leader. In short, the shift from socialist to communist forced Gramsci to consider, more centrally, the role of racial difference in cultural and political contexts (Verdicchio 1995).

Gramsci's questions concerning the application of historical materialism to mobilization—or, broadly speaking, political action—result in his criticism and disavowal of modernist and positivist biological perspectives on race. More specifically, the link between race and nationalism, which was instrumental in configuring fascist and modernist Italian, as well as similar European and American, discourses on race, criminality, and nationalism, presented a singular problem for Gramsci's politics (Gibson 1998; Horn 1994). As I discussed in the first chapter, a significant detail regarding Gramsci's politics and the racialization processes that informed "racial science" in Europe, the United States, and elsewhere was that Gramsci's experience with subaltern groups absolutely flew in the face of the so-called findings of "racial science." Every political party, including the Italian Socialist Party, expressed a perspective on Southern Italians that was allied with or informed by (as in the case of Enrico Ferri, a criminal anthropologist and prominent socialist) the findings of "racial science." Gramsci analyzed and understood how both race and difference are configured at the political level, in specific ways and at specific moments, as instrumental to the state in determining national belonging. As Stuart Hall points out, Gramsci's work resists homogenizing tendencies in theoretical discourses on race (Hall 1986a). Gramsci's work also shows how the configurations of racial and ethnic difference and the pseudoscientific and, therefore, ideological justifications for these differences affect class formations (Augelli and Murphy 1988; Hall 1986a). The constellation of race, ethnicity, conceptions of nature, and their ideological positioning represents a complex formation of issues that I address in the next chapter. However, specifically regarding class, it is important to note that Gramsci persistently analyzes class in his work. It is both a concept and a concrete empirical category. Gramsci demonstrates the need to understand and develop a political, cultural, and pedagogical process through which workers and peasants from different regions in Italy can be unified and mobilized in the face of "scientific" justifications for racial ideologies (Borg, Buttigieg, and Mayo 2002; Notebook 11, §12; Gramsci 1971: 330–331; Thomas 2013; Verdicchio 1995).[2]

By investigating fragments of Gramsci's writing on race—in his notebooks, letters, and journalism—and the politics surrounding the process of racialization in Italy, especially in the south of Italy, I demonstrate why Gramsci's discourse on race challenges and exceeds the biologically based paradigm prevalent (throughout modern, industrial Western countries) in modernist and positivist discourses on race and nation in the early part of the twentieth century. I argue that this may have had ramifications for Stuart Hall's adaptation of a "cultural hegemony" framework for his analysis of contemporary racism. I am interested in *why* and not *how*, as in the case of Stuart Hall it is that Gramsci's work informs contemporary analyses of race, given that during the period in which he wrote, most scholarly conceptions of race were rooted in biological, sociobiological, and criminological approaches.[3] Understanding the special perspective that Gramsci held, especially in light of his organizing, strategic, and tactical efforts discussed in the previous chapter is important to the broader discussion of the racialization of contemporary ideological forms through which racism is expressed in the next chapter.

This chapter makes two theoretical points with regard to race, class, labor, and mobilization. First, through Gramsci's work, Hall's approach to the structural/cultural theory problem provides a connection point for cultural and structural approaches to race. Using Gramsci's methodological guidelines and focusing principally on the concept of the conjuncture (and also the analyses of the situation and the historical bloc) and taking the category of class to be analytically salient along with race, Hall demonstrates that throughout the course of the twentieth century, capitalism depended both on (free) market relations as well as compulsory relations regarding labor. He further demonstrates that the racialization of labor and the coercion of workers in colonial and neocolonial contexts, with regard to the "Global South," was the rule and not the exception (Hall 1980). Through Gramsci's methodological guidelines, Hall makes conceptual connections that become necessary to the study of race. Race, then, becomes indispensable to any and all analyses of the material bases of power in the twentieth century, given the extensive exercise of power and domination that depended or depends, in some way, on racial (racist) categories or racial (racist) sense-making (Escobar 1994; Marx 1998; Mills 1997; Said 1978, 1993). Through Gramsci, Hall demonstrates that throughout the twentieth century—from, for example, the early phases of mass industrialization to globalization, from late colonialism to postcolonial independence movements, and from modernity through to current neoliberal perspectives—the cultural phenomenology of race becomes a de facto social and political-economic category.

Second, through an analysis of a discourse on race located across Gramsci's writing, and framed historically, I demonstrate that Gramsci's discussion of race or racial categories was connected empirically to politics.

Specifically, Gramsci's understanding of race was linked to the tactics and strategies of trade union and party-based mobilization. In what follows, I build on the context provided in both the first and second chapters and I provide more historical context through essays by Gramsci, his correspondences, and secondary historiographical sources. From Gramsci's discussion of the counterinsurgent role of the Brigata Sassari in 1917 preceding the beginning of the Biennio Rosso (1919–1920) to the additional context for the counterinsurgent (as well as antifascist) role of the radical and oppositional elements born from the Catholic "white unions" in the South, politics, mobilization, and racialization are all central to Gramsci's theoretical, analytical, and strategic concerns. It is through these investigations, I argue, that Gramsci's Marxist-materialism demonstrates an agility (an ability to move amongst the analytically determined levels of reality, discussed in the first chapter) that becomes attractive to Hall in his discussions of the politics of race in the latter half of the twentieth century.

I begin with Stuart Hall's description of how Gramsci's theories and concepts are relevant to the study of race and ethnicity. I will then link Hall's description—through an investigation of specific aspects of Hall's research and writing on race (Hall et al. 1978; Hall 1980, 1986a; Hall and Back 2009)—to an exploration of the specific concepts in Gramsci's work that contribute to Hall's assumptions.

Contextualizing Stuart Hall, the Politics of Race, and the Problem of Cultural and Structural Analyses

Stuart Hall (1986a) discusses a specific theoretical problem that is central to his studies of race and racism: How can one link structural (economic-based) theories of racism to cultural theories of racism? Though this problem is not unique to Hall, it has been central to his thought from his earliest studies of national racial formations in *Policing the Crisis* (1978) through to his reflections on the role that culture, representation, and identification play in the politics of structural transformation (Hall and Back 2009). "Gramsci's Relevance for the Study of Race and Ethnicity" (1986a, hereafter "Gramsci's Relevance") is a significant article precisely because it introduces avenues through which to explore the connections between structural and cultural explanations of racism. Hall had explored these avenues in previous studies using Gramsci's work as a theoretical and methodological guideline (Hall 1978; Hall et al. 1978; Hall 1980). So, as the title suggests,

"Gramsci's Relevance" poses a meta-theoretical question, requiring a separate consideration, which arises from Hall's prior work: How is Gramsci relevant to the study of race and ethnicity? In this specific article, Hall seeks to move between both structural and cultural models of race theory without allowing one model to supersede the other. "Gramsci's Relevance" then is an attempt to "sketch," as Hall states, the ways in which his work fits these multiple approaches to race within a single framework.

In a study of race and labor in South Africa, Hall introduces the nature of the problem as he sees it:

> If the first tendency (structural) is broadly correct, then what is often experienced and analyzed as ethnic or racial conflicts are really manifestations of deeper, economic contradictions. It is, therefore, to the latter that the politics of transformations must essentially be addressed. The second tendency (cultural) draws attention to the actual forms and dynamics of political conflict and social tension in such societies—which frequently assume a racial or ethnic character. It points to the empirical difficulty of subsuming these directly into more classical economic conflicts. But if ethnic relations are not reducible to economic relations, then the former will not necessarily change if and when the latter do. (Hall 1980: 18–19)

Following this passage, Hall makes the point that the nature of this problem is strategic more than theoretical. But one could also argue that the problem is theoretical. The potential point of contact between structural theories of race and cultural theories of race is inherently distant due, primarily, to how one conceives of the empirical basis for each of the theories. Although both theories look at forms of racial and ethnic conflict, the scope of each— the structural and the cultural—cannot be joined at the conceptual level without compromising the analysis and explanation of either one. Put succinctly: One may believe that racial discrimination can best be understood as a result of socioeconomic status, education, occupational compartmentalization, structural mobility, geographical segregation, and a host of other variables. Or, one may believe that racial discrimination is best understood by interviewing people about their experiences with racism. The object of both analyses is race; the presumptions and data that inform these studies are inherently different. More to the point, this problem is endemic in the social sciences. In this vein, McKee (1993) offers an interesting discussion of the history of the politics of race and class, caste and economics in sociological analysis.

As Hall states, the problem remains strategic for two reasons: because reducing cultural theories of race into more classical economic frameworks begs the question of why it is necessary to analyze the cultural aspects of racial and ethnic conflict, since the presumption is that the ultimate determinant lies within the economic structure; and because the economic structure tells us nothing about the content of these racial and ethnic conflicts, since it requires recourse to another logic of conflict altogether. That is to say, one must choose between either the structural or the cultural approach, and that choice is based on a belief (presumption) that the seat of these conflicts (relations) is best explored through culture rather than structure, or vice versa.

In "Gramsci's Relevance," Hall finds a partial solution to bridge the theoretical and conceptual distance between both approaches. This, in no small part, is how Gramsci's theories and concepts are relevant to the analysis of race and ethnicity. In the final section of "Gramsci's Relevance," Hall describes eight specific ways that Gramsci can make a solid contribution to the analysis of race and ethnicity. These eight points offer what Hall describes, earlier in the essay, as theoretically sophisticated ways to mediate the conceptual distance between structure and culture: 1) historical specificity; 2) national characteristics; 3) the interrelationship between class and race; 4) the "class subject"; 5) the (lack) of correspondence between structure and class, political, and ideological dimensions; 6) the state; 7) culture; and 8) ideology. In each of these sections, Hall describes Gramsci's theoretical sophistication, which arises from Gramsci's attention to empirical details. A large part of what Hall means by sophistication, then, refers to Gramsci's ability to describe historical detail and political impacts in relation to the flexibility of his theoretical approach.

According to Hall, this flexibility is rooted in a Marxist framework (Hall [1974] 2003). In his 2009 interview with Les Back, Hall links the methodological framework explored in Karl Marx's *Grundrisse* ([1857] 1973) to Gramsci's ability to discern and interpret events with a broad theoretical approach. Hall refers to Gramsci's ability to analyze discrete events as "conjunctural understanding" (Hall and Back 2009: 664).[4] The power of Gramsci's analysis, for Hall, is rooted in the modifications that Gramsci makes to a general "historical materialist" approach. These modifications are necessary to explain transformations in both Italian history and Italian politics—Gramsci's object of analysis. Hall's overarching argument is that a historical materialist framework, upon closer inspection and taking account of its theoretical and methodological goals (as laid out in the *Grundrisse*) must be fundamentally open to transformation in ways that differentiate it from classical philosophical and social science modes of analysis. Regarding the Marxist method and its epistemological foundations as a departure from both philosophical and social scientific approaches, Hall states that

> [i]t remains an "open" epistemology, not a self-generating or self-sufficient one, because its "scientificity" is guaranteed only by that "fit" between thought and reality—each in its own mode—which produces a knowledge which "appropriates" reality in the only way that it can (in the head): and yet delivers a critical method capable of penetrating behind the phenomenal forms of society to the hidden movements, the deep-structure "real relations" which lie behind them. This "scientific" appropriation of the laws and tendencies of the structure of a social formation is, then, also the law and tendency of its "passing away": the possibility, not of the proof, but of the realization of knowledge in practice, in its practical resolution—and thus, the self-conscious overthrow of those relations in a class struggle which moves along the axis of society's contradictory tendencies, and which is something more than "merely speculative," more than a theoretical speculation. Here ... we are no longer dealing with "the relationship 'thought-being' within thought, but rather with the relation between thought and reality." (Hall [1974] 2003: 137)[5]

On the one hand, unlike certain aspects of idealism and moralism (Kant) or historicism (Hegel) with regard to philosophical justifications and imperatives regarding reality, for Hall, a historical materialist framework is open to transformations in reality so that it can generate knowledge. This does not mean that those other approaches are not valuable. However, philosophical systems, when geared toward explaining events, cannot be self-sufficient or they risk replacing analysis with platitudes.

On the other hand, where social science focuses upon proving and explaining either the existence or function of specific types of relations in a societal context, the scientific and empirical aspects of a historical materialist approach offer recourse to a deeper and more differentiated form of empiricism. One could argue that historical materialism is not a "science" in the sense that its very raison d'etre is based in a value judgment with regard to class and, more broadly, to oppression, exploitation, equality, and freedom. However, social sciences, which both precede and follow this form of analysis and explanation, presume these values, although it is often the case that they remain both hidden in and inherent to the overall reason for constituting a research question. Also, it is precisely because inferences about the current state of society are disconnected from method (if not rendered entirely invisible) in the genesis of questions and, subsequently, theories and methods that—during the time in which Gramsci lived—positivism contributed to scientific justifications for racism and fascism. Whether we are referring to Lombroso or Ferri (regarding criminology and racism), Mosca or Pareto (regarding fascism and the social sciences), their sociological and criminological analyses were based in an inquiry that presumed specific historically embedded valuations about what constituted deviance and politics. In the previous chapter, I discussed the historical context in which early positivism and social-scientific forms of investigation contributed to racism, politically and at the national level. For now, however, I continue to unpack Hall's relationship to Gramsci's Marxist materialism.

Hall demonstrates that the impetus for historical materialism is an analysis of class relations as well as all facets of social organization that contribute to a full understanding of class. This is because the principle of societal organization and differentiation that is central to the current historical formation, according to historical materialism, is class (Hall [1974] 2003; Hall and Back 2009). By analyzing the key contradictions that produce the central dissonance between what a society purports to be and what it is (i.e., "penetrating behind the phenomenal forms of society to the hidden movements, the deep-structure 'real relations' which lie behind them"), historical materialism represents the path often not taken or the hard road between theory and empiricism (Burawoy 1989; Therborn 1985). In short, this route represents theory's ability to mediate between historical, cultural, and political events and their structural contexts, which both make these events possible and prevent other events from occurring. This brings us back to the problem of explaining the significance of racism and the structures that facilitate racial oppression.

It is precisely because Hall takes this approach seriously that he refuses to consign historical materialism to an eschatological and teleological determinism; rather, he seeks to include another category that introduces central societal contradictions: race. According to Hall, among the insights that Gramsci's work provides is his attention to transformations at both the cultural and historical levels. Transformation is thematic to the eight points that, according to Hall, emerge from Gramsci's work. Gramsci's analysis enables multiple points of transformation. He connects historical and cultural frameworks to structural transformations by analyzing discrete events that he refers to as "conjunctures" (Notebook 13, §17; Gramsci 1971:

177; Hall and Back 2009). At the level of the conjuncture, both cultural (including political and historical) and structural transformations can be analyzed and explained in relation to one another. In other words, for Hall, the concept of the conjuncture provides a way to breach the structural and cultural divide by developing a concept that provides a methodological guideline for placing structural and cultural analysis in relation to one another.

In brief, the conjuncture is a concept that pinpoints the historical, social, cultural, and economic forces—at a given moment in time—that give expression to what may be perceived as an anomaly or, as Gramsci puts it, "movements . . . which appear as occasional, immediate, almost accidental" (Notebook 13, §2, 17; 1971: 177). The conjuncture is the locus of potential transformation. The transformation is potential, because "the political forces which are struggling to conserve and defend the existing structure itself are making every effort to cure them, within certain limits, and to overcome them" (Notebook 13, §17; 1971: 178). Now, what is important to understand, in this context, is whether social change is produced (e.g., "incessant and persistent efforts [since no social formation will ever admit that it has been superseded] form the terrain of the 'conjunctural,' and it is upon this terrain that the forces of opposition organize" [Notebook 13, §17; 1971: 178]). The continuity sought by those who are in power, whose interest is in maintaining the extant political forces, that is, the status quo, leads to a "modification" in the social forces that, in the conjuncture, disrupt—but are necessary to maintain—continuity. This leads Hall to specify how structure can be placed in a relationship to culture in such a way that both can be understood as linked, not causally, but asymmetrically, since the conjuncture results in either continuity (in the form of modifications of social forces) or change, since structural change produces the conditions through which culture is expressed and mobilized as independent from the structure. The following chapter will demonstrate how aspects of a conjuncture are manifest through shifting terrains of cultural discourse and ideological expression. Also, significantly, the concept of the conjuncture has been illustrated in both the first and second chapters of this book. To clarify, Gramsci's organizational efforts, beginning in 1916, should be understood as fomenting the subjective elements of potential transformation (through organizational forms and waves of mobilizations) over and against the existing structures' efforts to maintain and build capitalist industry. Also, In chapter 2, in specific, I illustrate the incessant and persistent efforts of Sardinian and Italian elites to maintain their sociostructural position through appeals to a common Sardinian lineage, on the one hand, and through the use of force, on the other. In 1919, the meeting of the Giovane Sardegna (Young Sardinia) group demonstrated how an appeal to a common cultural lineage marked an attempt to steer a regional political bloc into supporting the elite's status quo. The failure of elites to mobilize Sardinians in their interests was due, largely, to the successful mobilizations that Gramsci had participated in, the transformation of a fraction of Sardinian peasants into veterans, and the rapid postwar industrialization in the north of Italy. These examples also illustrate how Hall's insights about how the connection between culture (in this case, expressed racially) and structure can be articulated. These insights are explored, in depth, in Hall's essay "Gramsci's Relevance" (1986a).

In "Gramsci's Relevance" (1986a) Hall demonstrates how Gramsci's insights change the way that we understand the relationship between structures that maintain racism through power but also allow for modifications to it. The issue is the specificity of analyses and what analyses tell us about social change and power. In the context of history, Hall explains:

> These general features [of racism] are modified and transformed by the historical specificity of the contexts and environments in which they become active.... [W]e would do well to operate at a more concrete, historicized level of abstraction (i.e., not racism in general but racisms).... It is often little more than a gestural stance which persuades us to the misleading view that, because racism is everywhere a deeply anti-human and anti-social practice, that therefore it is everywhere the same—either in its forms, its relations to other structures and processes, or its effects. Gramsci does, I believe, help us to interrupt decisively this homogenization. (Hall 1986a: 23)

Most antiracist theories of race, whether philosophical and phenomenological (e.g., Frantz Fanon, Charles Mills, or Cornel West) or sociostructural, necessarily link the impetus or cause to a singular historical event or a chain of events as in, for example, the emergence of "civilization" in Europe and its many forms of cultural contact, or to a cognitive imperative as in, for example, the deep structure of consciousness as negation or violence (e.g., "othering"). Racialization and racism, in this discursive context, is rooted in asymmetries of power relations, and expressions of racial power become rooted and stolid. This is not an incorrect perspective; however, it does not explain the transformations in the way that racism persistently reframes itself and the mechanics for this reframing. Culture produces surprising articulations of structural racism like, for example, "colorblindness," which I will discuss, in detail, in the following chapter. Moreover, it fails to perceive the structure as, itself, changing to maintain some continuity with power in the interrelation between the state and civil society as Gramsci's concept of hegemony expresses it. The continuity with power is taken for granted: in this context, racism is racism. The historical, societal, and political forces that produce these combinations become the object of investigation and discussion in chapter 5. Through the concept of aporetic governmentality, introduced in the next chapter, the complexity of the multiple historical, societal, political, and cultural dynamics that contribute to racialization; the process and expressions of racism; and how this dynamic arrangement of forces and their transformations work will require or demonstrate a more intensive analysis of the various manifestations and optics of power. As I will demonstrate, an analysis of the historical and structural factors contributing to contemporary discourses of racialization requires an analysis of the broader context through which the contemporary racial conjuncture is manifest. Regardless, what is useful in Gramsci's perspective is that while he acknowledges the antihuman and antisocial basis for racism (see especially his correspondences on Judaism [Gramsci 1975: 212–217]), he is able to analyze and explain the specific determinants and modifications to racist practices with a greater acuity and agility than both structural and phenomenological approaches that seek a root impetus or, in some cases, cause.

At this point, "Gramsci's Relevance" (1986a) shifts to a focus on the relationship between race and class; this is the root of the problematic Hall raises in his study of labor rationalization in South Africa in "Race, Articulation, and Societies Structured in Dominance" (1980). Hall focuses, specifically, on the conceptual distance between class and race (based in the divide between structural and cultural approaches), racial differentiation within the category of class, and on the problem of theoretical correspondence in analyzing both class and race. This represents both the centrality of Gramsci's relevance to the analysis of race and the importance of Gramsci's concept of the conjuncture, which appears as anomalous in the framework of contemporary society but, as Gramsci points out, introduces the departure point for a cultural articulation of a potentially new politics alongside of struggles to maintain the status quo. As I have demonstrated, this is the central problematic for Hall: he reminds us that "the interrelationship between class and race ... has proved to be one of the most complex and difficult theoretical problems to address, and it has frequently led to the adoption of one or another extreme positions" (1986a: 24); he also restates the nature of the relationship between structural and cultural analysis more succinctly:

> Either one "privileges" the underlying class relationships, emphasizing that all ethnically and racially differentiated labor forces are subject to the same exploitative relationships within capital; or one emphasizes the centrality of ethnic and racial categories and divisions at the expense of the fundamental class structuring of society. Though these two extremes appear to be the polar opposites of one another, in fact, they are inverse, mirror-images of each other, in the sense that both feel required to produce a single and exclusive determining principle of articulation—class or race even if they disagree as to which should be accorded the privileged sign. I believe the fact that Gramsci adopts a non-reductive approach to questions of class, coupled with his understanding of the profoundly historical shaping to any specific social formation, does help to point the way towards a non-reductionist approach to the race/class question. (Hall 1986a: 24)

To better illustrate what Hall describes as Gramsci's nonreductionist approach, in "Race, Articulation, and Societies Structured in Dominance" (1980) Hall analyzes labor rationalization in South Africa. His findings raise significant issues in relation to the specific problem of how different approaches to race give rise to different and separate determinations. He finds that though South Africa meets the conditions of an advanced capitalist society, the forms of labor rationalization it depends upon require the presence of "unfree" or "forced" labor in combination with "free" labor. The assumption, of course, is that the fundamental requirement of capitalism and its juridical forms is that labor is "free" so that the laborer can alienate his or her labor power, that is, he or she is free to sell it as a commodity. This is not only the basis for most Marxist perspectives, but the juridical issue regarding the transformation of labor into the commodity form also marks the beginnings of theories of the state.[6] Hall states, "Whatever is the specific legal form with which capitalist development 'corresponds,' it must be one in which the concept of the juridical 'contract' between 'free persons' appears, which can legally regulate the forms of contract which 'free labor' requires" (Hall 1980: 44). The persistence of unfree labor, despite the enormous disadvantages to the societal context within which capital accumulation occurs in South Africa, is based in a racial economy whereby race is the central determinant for social organization in an advanced capitalist society, not class. Hall says that although there is proof that this affects the economy within

South Africa negatively, he also points out that this case introduces a socio-logical question that requires more concerted theorization. More impor-tantly, he indicates that the dissolution of Western colonial enterprises and the long duration of revolutions and declarations of postcolonial, national independence are producing formations of racially differentiated labor across the globe that are the rule and not the exception. As a result, the materialist premise regarding the indispensability of free labor to a fully functioning capitalist economy is not wrong; however, Hall explains further:

> [T]his does not mean that the tendency to combine capitalism with "free labor" cannot, under specific historical conditions, be cross-cut or coun-termanded by a counteracting tendency: namely, the possibility of certain of the conditions of existence of capitalism being effectively secured by combining "free labor" with certain forms of "unfree" or "forced" labor. Once we move away from European to post-Conquest or post-colonial societies, this combination—free and "unfree" labor, on the basis of a com-bination of different modes of production—becomes more and more the paradigm case. (Hall 1980: 44)

Hall is fundamentally in agreement with the Marxist materialist premise that the conditions most favorable to the accumulation of capital, realized by increasing its capacity for concentration and centralization with the aid of the nation-state, remain unchanged. However, also central to the materi-alist premise is the commodification of all goods and services including labor power. Finally, though, and in this case, securing the conditions for capital accumulation relies on an uneven combination of "free" and "unfree" or "forced" labor. In short, the level of highest abstraction in Marx's economic theory enters a "conjuncture" where a counteracting historical tendency (the introduction of forms of labor that do not benefit capital accumulation—in theory) are necessary to ensure the continuity of capital accumulation at the nation-state level. As we will see in the following chapter, the content of a conjuncture expresses race relations through changing material conditions and discursive expressions (e.g., liberal policy perspectives that dispropor-tionately affect racial groups but are coded as equal alongside "colorblind" ideologies of race) that find an affinity within broader ideological frame-works such as neoliberal variants of abstract liberalism. However, more to the point here, "unfree" and "forced" labor is precisely the labor of groups, in the modern nation-state, that have been racialized in changing nation-al-social formations. The challenge that is posed here has to do with the uniformity (free labor) of labor power as a condition necessary to the general law of value within Marxist frameworks.[7]

This raises issues of the correspondence between theory and reality as well as the explanation of historical contingencies that do not fit neatly within theoretical frameworks (Marxism) that retain explanatory power despite the seeming anomaly of "unfree" or "forced" labor. Contingency, of course, is designed to address these anomalies. Specifically, regarding the composition of classes within modern capitalist frameworks, the interrelation between race and class, and the correspondence between theory and reality, Hall finds affinity with Gramsci's perspective.

> He never makes the mistake of believing, that, because the general law of value has the tendency to homogenize labor power across the capitalist epoch, that therefore, in any concrete society, this homogenization can be assumed to exist. Indeed, I believe Gramsci's whole approach leads us to question the validity of this general law in its traditional form, since, precisely, it has encouraged us to neglect the ways in which the law of value, operating on a global as opposed to a merely domestic scale, operates through and because of the culturally specific character of labor power, rather than—as the classical theory would have us believe—by systematically eroding those distinctions as an inevitable part of a world-wide, epochal historical tendency.... Capital can preserve, adapt to its fundamental trajectory, harness and exploit these particularistic qualities of labor power, building them into its regimes. The ethnic and racial structuration of the labor force, like its gendered composition, may provide an inhibition to the rationalistically conceived "global" tendencies of capitalist development. And yet, these distinctions have been maintained, and indeed developed and refined, in the global expansion of the capitalist mode. (Hall 1986a: 24)

In the context of Hall's previous study, "Race, Articulation, and Societies Structured in Dominance" (1980), the problem of classes representing units of analysis linked to the value form as free labor—as commodities—is disrupted by the reality of what Hall refers to as labor rendered through culturally specific forms (which include race, class, and nationalism). In these instances, it is the forces of capital accumulation that adjust the social structure to exploit these cultural differences. These differences categorize labor power in the interest of exploitation. This maintains the Marxist materialist premise, with regard to the law of value and the rate of exploitation specifically; however, these modifications to regimes of accumulations signal a conjuncture. Hall analyzes the conjuncture on the national level, but he is able to raise this example to a greater level of abstraction in a postcolonial and emergent global context, where the racialization of labor and cultural differences become the sine qua non of historical transformations with regard to the maintenance of power and social structure in the context of modern capitalist states. The issue of empiricism in relationship to abstract levels of theory is addressed, through Gramsci's work, by conceptualizing this "conjuncture" as an attempt to modify transformations in the global landscape of capital accumulation in the context of postcolonial and (in the context of modernization and development in Latin America) postimperial nation-states.

Finally, understanding transformations within labor rationalization and regimes of accumulation in an emergent global context depend upon differentiating the correctness of the materialist perspective from the structural fact of the differentiation of forms of labor. Hall finds that it is through Gramsci's conceptualization of conjunctures as both seemingly anomalous but as producing structural stabilization and (societal and historical) continuity that we can understand the interrelation of culture, race, and structure in new and important ways. These conjunctures or moments, not captured in the separation between structural and cultural frameworks, actually form a perspective that enables theorists to understand the importance of cultural and racial differentiation to the modifications and transformations within structures that enable the continuity of national power. Cultural studies target the mediations between social structure and culture.

We might do well to claim, further, that the conjuncture is potentially disruptive to the structure; through political power, the structural elements seek to transform existing conditions and incorporate or eliminate racial groups—a dynamic that is precisely related to the concept of aporetic governmentality in the next chapter. To the extent that a conjuncture is seized upon politically and counterforces assert themselves into social reality (for however limited a time), the process through which that rupture is explained away and continuity is established results in the demobilization of the oppositional political forces that mobilize and organize in the framework of the conjuncture. Also, as continuity between periods of political power is reestablished, the historical significance of oppositional groups is abrogated significantly or is only a trace in a broader and authoritative history that, in turn, is also a legitimation of the continuity of the political and social status quo.

Hall reminds us that Gramsci's original conception of hegemony is not about the solidity and endurance of power through the formation of stolid structures, but that it is about placing cultural difference and cultural meaning and mobilization into a relationship with power and justifications for the continuity of power. Hall writes:

> Even the "hegemonic" moment is no longer conceptualized as a moment of simple unity, but as a process of unification (never totally achieved), founded on strategic alliances between different sectors, not on their pre-given identity. . . . [T]here is no automatic identity or correspondence between economic, political and ideological practices. This begins to explain how ethnic and racial difference can be constructed as a set of economic, political or ideological antagonisms, within a class which is subject to roughly similar forms of exploitation with respect to ownership of and expropriation from the "means of production." (Hall 1986a: 25)

To conclude, it is this fundamental instability—which is rooted in the empirical instances of class formations as inherently nonhomogeneous—that Gramsci attempts to explain while remaining within the highest levels of abstraction afforded through a historical materialist standpoint. By developing a way to militate between the centrality of racial and cultural difference within a structural framework, Gramsci provides, for Hall, an enduring relevance especially since race and cultural nonhomogeneity seem to be the rule, and not the exception, that is reintroduced as the forces of capital accumulation become more global in character. These same forces that find the hallmark for this modification in the structure of capitalism in the name of globalism or globalization, are actually operating in a paradigm where the shift from colonial and imperialist frameworks to a brief period of independence, postcolonialism, and postimperialism—and, finally, to postindependence, neoliberalism, and neoimperialism—can be leaped over willy-nilly. Each represents discrete modifications to structure and power in the form of necessary racializations or forms of reidentification that never maintain themselves for very long.

By understanding these modifications as a conjuncture within a stream of structural modifications to capitalism, Hall builds a new relationship between culture and structure that is rooted in Gramsci's theories and concepts, necessary modifications that are put in place to account for the analysis of events located at the empirical level. What remains to be explained, however, is *why*, for Hall, Gramsci has anything relevant to offer to an analysis of race. In the following section, I want to explore, in part, Gramsci's perspective on race, racism, and racialization. In the 1980s and 1990s, Hall, with the exception of Verdicchio (1995), is the only person to write about Gramsci and race in any detail. However, the question as to why, in a context where race is primarily understood as the racialization of people and cultures due to appearances, Gramsci could provide a way to understand racial differences as cultural, national, ideological, and discursive constructs—as well as race and culture as sites of identity that endure through transformations in both meanings and traditions—remains an open one.

Why Gramsci Is Relevant: Catholicism, Humanistic Rationalizing Discourses, and Worker and Peasant Mobilizations

Gramsci's centrality to contemporary cultural and structural approaches to race is due to his resistance to racist discourses of criminality issuing from social scientists during the time that he wrote. This can and should be interpreted as a significant, not merely contingent, part of his larger perspective on culture, power, and politics. The significance of Gramsci's conception of race is due largely to the connection between Gramsci's resistance to conceptions informing racial pseudoscience and Gramsci's attentiveness to how cultural differences emerge from the societal structuration of racial and ethnic difference precisely around the mobilization and demobilization of racialized groups in Italy.

It is possible to weld aspects of Gramsci's perspective on race into a counterdiscourse that offers an alternative to modernist-positivistic based "scientific" discourses of race—discourses that inform biologically based racist perspectives that contemporary cultural theories of race have worked to debunk. Hall derives the coordinates of this discourse not from Gramsci's letters, as I do in this chapter, but from Gramsci's sensitivity to history, class, race, culture, and ideology. My goal here is to link Gramsci's perspective on race—which I derive from his correspondences, the sections of his notebooks (specifically Notebook 10II, §54; Notebook 7, §55; and Notebook 19, §24) that discuss the logical, conceptual, and historical importance of religious and humanistic concepts in framing approaches to difference and the attempts to realize these concepts politically, and his essays: "The Southern Question," "The Revolution against

'Capital' "—to contemporary cultural perspectives on race and mobilization and to demonstrate the ways in which this linkage helps to explain why Gramsci is relevant to the study of race.

Gramsci's discourse on race represents a departure from the predominant positivist perspective that influenced Italian discourses on race and criminality. What contributed to Gramsci's perspective on race, and why? To help address this question I rely on historical data derived from Gramsci's personal correspondences as well as from essays that explicitly discuss both race and difference.[8] I've organized these writings not in historical sequence but, rather, to develop my discussion that links Catholic humanism to racialization in Gramsci's writing to further illustrate how the broad framework in which presuppositions about the study of Southern regions—whether by criminological or population "science"—is embedded in preconceptions around "human studies." I then pursue the link between Catholicism and social and political mobilizations in the south of Italy, looking at Gramsci's studies of the role of the Catholic modernization movement and the role of the Popular Party in demobilizing Southern peasants. I conclude the section by taking a critical approach to Gramsci's reflections on broad-based mobilizations in and around the Biennio Rosso. I have already described how the richness of Gramsci's perspective on race makes it possible for other aspects of his more systematic theoretical framework to be adopted by Stuart Hall to establish a cultural basis for thinking about race in post-Marxist and postcolonial frameworks, especially in relation to the separation of cultural and structural approaches. Hall in "Race, Articulation, and Societies Structured in Dominance" (1980) and "Gramsci's Relevance for the Study of Race and Ethnicity" (1986a) demonstrates that Gramsci's work is central to contemporary cultural and structural approaches (both analytical and theoretical, respectively) to race.[9]

The following excerpts come from letters written by Gramsci to his sister-in-law during the first year of his incarceration, as the Italian authorities, in anticipation of his trial, repeatedly relocated him.

> I realized how difficult it is to understand the true nature of men from outward signs. At Ancona ... a kind old man who seemed to be of humble, provincial origin asked me to let him have some soup. . . . I gave it to him . . . taken with the serenity in his eyes and his modest gestures. Immediately afterward, I learned that this repellent beast had raped his own daughter. (Gramsci, corresponding with Tania Schucht, February 12, 1927)

Naples: I began to recognize a series of highly interesting types, whereas before the only southerns I had known at close quarters were Sardinians. (Gramsci, corresponding with Tania Schucht, April 11, 1927)

At first glance, the two quotations are anecdotal; they describe encounters Gramsci had with other prisoners as he traveled between the Regina Coeli prison in Rome, the Carmine prison in Naples, a penal institution in Palermo, then to a period of confinement on the island of Ustica. Subsequent to his stay on Ustica, he made several other stops to prisons in Cajanello, Isernia, Sulmona, Castellammare, Adriatico, Ancona, and Bologna. He then arrived at the prison of San Vittore in Milan where he stayed until right before his trial.[10] In May of 1928, Gramsci returned to the Regina Coeli prison in Rome, to be in the city where his trial would take place. As is well known, Gramsci's final stop on this extensive tour of Italy's penal institutions and quasi-exilic geographies—which contributed to ill health that plagued him throughout the course of his twenty-years-plus sentence—is the prison at Turi, where he writes his "prison notebooks."

The preceding quotations record encounters that he had with other prisoners, mostly Southern Italians, as he traveled the circuitous route between Regina Coeli in Rome and San Vittore in Milan between November 1926 and February 1927 (Buttigieg 2010). They also demonstrate a context: the *pervasiveness* of racial discourse in Italy as it pertained to Southern Italians (since each of these quotations are literally speaking both within and against it) and, more specifically, that Gramsci was thinking critically about race as he was moved across the south of Italy. In short, these brief quotations are inextricably embedded in racial discourse since this was the means and measure through which Southern Italy had been constructed by Italian criminologists of the positivist school, such as Lombroso, Ferri, Sergi, Niceforo, and Orano, as discussed in the second chapter.

Gramsci was not in agreement with the positivists, and both quotations demonstrate that. Niceforo's famous claim from *Crime in Sardinia* (1897) that criminal intent can be discerned, or read, from physical deformities or "atavisms" (i.e., outward signs) is explicitly referred to in the first sentence of the first quotation. The man with whom Gramsci shares his soup exhibits only kindness and humility despite the nature of his crime; an implicit refutation of Niceforo's claim regarding his study of Southerners—specifically Sardinians, the population that Niceforo studied and Gramsci's own origin. The second quotation represents an attempt to separate the category of "Southerner" into groups that exhibit differences or are nonhomogeneous:

his reference to his own Southern Sardinian origins imports him into the discourse both directly and as a bearer of a distinctive regional culture; it can be surmised from the content of these quotations that differences refer to cultural distinctions or types and not, obviously, to biological types.[11]

In these instances, Gramsci's correspondences can be seen as countermanding the predominant discourse on race (and especially criminality—these are his letters about his encounters with prisoners) in Italy during the time that he lived. Quite literally, Gramsci is pointing out that the theoretical premises for criminology—rooted in a "biologicalization" (i.e., the ability to read race on the surface of the body and from behaviors)—are factually incorrect; they contradict his actual experience with Southern Italians. I want to discuss how some epistemological issues that Gramsci raises in his studies in the early 1930s expose a constructivist and cultural orientation toward understanding race. Of all of the instances of discourses on race from Gramsci's writing, these are the most explicitly descriptive and conceptual. They require the "working out" of categories as they pertain to conceptions of humanism within the transformations introduced through modernity.

To provide some context for the following analysis, I would argue that Gramsci's framework for the discussion of race seems a "feint" of sorts. He introduces his conception of race not through sociological or anthropological frames but, rather, through philosophical, theological, and humanistic frames—specifically through Catholicism. An important frame of issues of race, racial politics, and mobilization in and across Gramsci's work, Catholicism is central to the historical and political context through which Gramsci thought and in which the fragments from his work are steeped. As Gramsci's analyses of history and culture have political goals, my analysis connects race to politics through historical context. In Gramsci's analysis of politics, Catholicism—more so than race—is connected to his thoughts on the political party, mobilization, and modernity. Hence it is more specified and developed in Gramsci's writing. However, by connecting these categories together I want to demonstrate that the discourse on race and racialization was never far, conceptually, from an inventory of political concepts. As Gramsci interprets specific aspects of Italy's cultural landscape, the seeds of a materialism that Stuart Hall was keen to notice in his thinking about the modernist cultural politics of race, racism, and racialization (or in international, global, and cosmopolitan contexts) become clear.

The text that contains race in the 1971 edition of Gramsci's *Prison Notebooks*—which is organized both thematically and historically (like passages are linked across periods of historical time)—begins with a discussion of Catholicism. Gramsci discusses the historical duration of Catholicism's impact in Europe, the specific historical and ecumenical developments, and the relationship between the church and politics in modernity in the context of Italy. Hence, he is extensive in his study of Catholicism, especially its relationship to politics in Italy, and notes the different intellectual variations, forms of political expression, and cultural and intellectual developments.[12]

The function, however, of my beginning a discussion of race with Catholicism is to demonstrate that the intellectual trend in the West has been to determine a set of "universal" characteristics that comprise a common definition of people, and then to substitute these characteristics for an ideology of humanism that is historical, institutional (ecumenical), and therefore religious. The attempt to constitute an essential, in this case, metaphysical, definition of the human person and then the subsequent typologies that are cleaved to a fundamental position are mirrored in the logic of the criminal anthropology school and the description of regions and populations discussed in the second chapter. It is precisely this kind of generalization that Gramsci's materialist methodological approach would cast as spurious from a sociological, religious, and humanistic perspective (Buttigieg 1990). Finally, and more specifically, it is worth pointing out, at this juncture, that in the second chapter I develop this racial dynamic through a discussion of the role of racial pseudoscience, early Italian social science, and how that knowledge informs the admission and exclusions of groups at the national-political level after Italian unification. More broadly, this dynamic of racialization, further, is rooted at the beginning of nation-state consolidation across the West.

To demonstrate, in the 1971 edition of Gramsci's *Prison Notebooks*, the text is headed by the question "What Is Man?" (which originally appears in Notebook 10II, §54, and Notebook 7, §55) It contains a discussion of several discursive standpoints: philosophical ethics, religion—specifically Catholicism—anthropology, biology, ideology, historical materialism, science, positivism, history, and the philosophy of history and politics, specifically the state and issues pertaining to inequality. Gramsci moves through these different positions. His goal is to demonstrate that, contained within specific dominant discursive frames like criminal anthropology, the scientific study of populations by region, and the political-ideological posture toward the south of Italy, configuring people as concepts (through whatever means) is and can only ever be tantamount to a religious-style perspective. In the case of contemporary pseudoscience, all variants of cultural expression across the modern Italian nation become subsets of the contemporary "imaginary" of the modern Italian citizen (Mazzini 1912).[13] The "master discourse" or central frame for the concept of race—whether as the "human race" or as a marker of difference therein—is always organized back into a categorical hierarchy. Hence, the use of data to derive a human "phenotype" from a "genotype" (based on humanistic presumptions) is an ideological use of science based on metaphysical remnants. This precise dynamic finds further specifications in the final chapter with the discussion of the discursive process (racial talk) of inclusion and exclusion that inform ideologies of "colorblind racism" and "abstract liberalism" in Bonilla-Silva's work.

Gramsci, then, effectively knots together philosophy, biology, and anthropology as discourses trapped within a crude premodern racialist empiricism. Gramsci's rhetoric indicates that it is as though everything is pointing at a move to a "heliocentric" model (as far as understanding race is concerned), but still the notion that the earth is the center of the universe is retained. Gramsci states: "But is the 'human' a starting-point or a point of arrival, as a concept and as a unitary fact? Or might not the whole attempt, in so far as it posits the human as a starting-point, be a 'theological' or 'metaphysical' residue? Philosophy cannot be reduced to a naturalistic 'anthropology': the nature of the human species is not given by the biological nature of man" (Notebook 7, §35; Gramsci 1971: 356).

This quotation indicates, first, that, for Gramsci, the question of race is not the domain of a single epistemological standpoint—a point that Hall develops in his mediations between structural and cultural approaches to racism. Secondly, it indicates that any perspective that forms its question based on the presumption of a unitary conception of humanity (a starting-point assumption) is starting from both an empirically and conceptually wrong spot. In short, the question with regard to the development of the human species, the question that it seeks to answer departs, already, from a false assumption: the unitary conception of humanity—the very object of its inquiry. And, finally, the biological sciences, no more than any metaphysical standpoint (e.g., theology and philosophy) can neither capture the cultural and sociological complexity of humanity, on the one hand, nor determine its political futures, on the other.[14] Similarly, Pizza (2012), who also locates Gramsci's direct comments on race and nature in his correspondences, argues that in the field of medical anthropology, Gramsci's "anti-essentialist approach to reasoning about 'nature' " and his recourse to a discussion of social and historical relations in determining the meaning of the term "nature" facilitate ethnographic investigations of politics in the fields of health management (2012: 96).

Gramsci's discussion of Catholicism and its deterministic legacy toward conceptions of what constitutes humanity did not only serve as a convenient framework through which to illustrate the connection between a materialist perspective and the analysis of racial and ethnic differences that manifest culturally and socially. Rather, Catholicism becomes the basis for a political movement that worked to demobilize Southern Italian peasants whose radical activity surged alongside the Biennio Rosso. Both Cammett (1967) and, more recently, Foot (1996, 1997) discuss the network of strong relations established through the Church's institutions, which included various Catholic associations, leagues, and, more concretely, "mutual aid-societies, cooperatives, and rural banks" (Foot 1997: 415). Foot also mentions that "[c]enturies of assiduous work by local priests, catholic organizations, and church-backed newspapers and cultural bodies had constructed a 'catholic world' of great strength and power" (1997: 416). However, the Biennio Rosso and the radicalization of elements of the peasantry following the war (and discussed in the first chapter) created an environment of contention between the "red" unions, conservative elements within the Popular Party, the left-Catholic "extremists" (Estremisti) within the "white" Catholic unions, the socialists that were fought out, in the South, through the Popular Party platform.

In brief, in his "Notes on Italian History" (the portion discussed here originally appears in Notebook 19, §24) Gramsci discusses the "modernism" and "popularism" movements. The popularism movement becomes the Popular Party in Italy in 1919. Both modernism and popularism, Gramsci tells us in a footnote, were "intellectual movements which developed among Catholics in the late nineteenth and early twentieth centuries" (Notebook 19, §24; Gramsci 1971: 62, note 14). Their purpose, he goes on, was "to bring the Church into harmony with the culture and society of the contemporary world—especially with new developments in scientific and sociological thinking" (Notebook 19, §24; Gramsci 1971: 62). Though these movements were entirely demobilized through papal decree, they later find their political legs in the form of the Popular Party and, in the latter half of the twentieth century, as the Christian Democratic Party.

The Popular Party is founded in 1919, in part as a reaction to the Biennio Rosso. Directed outward (based not on church reform but social reform), the party's base grew in agricultural areas. Though Gramsci does not discuss the party's composition, according to Cotta and Verzichelli (2007), the party enjoyed electoral successes until it was demobilized by the fascists in 1925. Gramsci notes that the Popular Party served two significant roles: First, it was an attempt to co-opt the socialists and eradicate the communist base through a counterstrategy. Second, and in this vein, it introduced "white unions" to co-opt the "red" communist trade unions and their attempt to mobilize Southern peasants during the same time. It must be noted, however, that from within the "white unions" an extreme Catholic left (Estremisti) still emerge and with shocking ferocity and a strong record of successes. Regardless, their "interclass" platform, propproperty stance, disfavor among socialists, and late alliance with the "red" unions in the regions where they were strong prove fatal for their movement, overall (Foot 1997). The charismatic presence and questionable political-intellectual stances of their leading figure, Guido Miglioli, led Gramsci to establish a slow alliance with the radical-left elements of the "white" unions, over time. Gramsci was critical of the alliances that Miglioli formed, his political perspectives on interclass relations and private property, and his perspective on socialism and the "red" unions. Gramsci, however, also remained critical of perspectives that demonized Southerners especially when the discussion of politics was elided or replaced with discussions of a single protagonist. For example, Gramsci discussed how Italian intellectuals misinterpreted David Lazzaretti's messianic view of "southern liberation," not taking into consideration the forces that Lazzaretti had mobilized against to build an effective agrarian peasant movement (Green 2013: 120). Regardless, it is over four years after the successful wave of contention attributable to Miglioli that Gramsci, in the "Minutes of the Political Commission Nominated by the Central Committee (of the PCI) to Finalize the Lyons Congress Documents" (January 1926), offers unqualified support of the necessary relation between the PCI and Miglioli (Gramsci 1978: 277, 316). Almost one year prior to Gramsci's support of Miglioli, Gramsci mentions in his "Report to the Central Committee" (February 1925) that the PCI will fund Miglioli's paper, that Miglioli will agree to accept an editorial board that represents Gramsci's line in the PCI, and Miglioli will join the Red Peasants International, also accepting organizational elements from Gramsci's line within the party. Foot (1997) also notes that Gramsci's position toward the radical elements of the peasants (Estremisti) associated with the "white" unions and the Popular Party was significantly different from the prevailing position on the left (which was, in the main, against them in 1919 and 1920). And, although Gramsci's interventions steered elements of the left toward a more favorable evaluation of the peasant movement in the South, according to Foot, the crucial moment when the Estremisti were the most active and effective, during the Biennio Rosso, was, regretfully, missed (Foot 1997: 431–433).

However, it remains true that the Popular Party proffered a significant, if contended, challenge to the energy generated through the successes of the Biennio Rosso. More to the point, the Catholic interaction with modernity was a tactic, turned outward, to use the peasants as an instrument to keep both "unification" and the left at bay by granting them a seeming measure of political participation. Gramsci notes that "modernism and popularism were a result of—and aimed to counteract—the influence of Croce and Gentile on the one hand, and socialism on the other" (Notebook 19, §24; Gramsci 1971: 62). What is significant, here, however, is that the development of the ideologies of both popularism and modernism were craven attempts to gain access to a large and seemingly disorganized peasant population in the south of Italy through a Catholic, humanistic political rhetoric where modernization, mediated through the "white unions," represented a recognition of labor solidarity in an agricultural industrializing context (especially in the case of dairy and textile workers). Implicit in these ideological perspectives was the incorporation of the Southern population into a contemporary and modernizing Italy. These ideological frameworks seemed to offer to Southern Italian peasants membership in Mazzini's idealistic identitarian construct: "The Italian Working Men" (1912), transforming peasants into Italians. Gramsci's "The Southern Question," based in his specification of race through culture, was an attempt at theorizing a lasting strategy to challenge the Southern intellectuals (gentry) and cultivate an organic intellectual class from the peasantry (Gramsci [1926] 1995b).

Intellectuals are both a concept and social fact and are central to political strategy (Gramsci 1971, [1926] 1995b). This, in no small way, was significant to Gramsci's interest in Guido Miglioli as a potential point of articulation between the Catholic elements of the peasantry and the Italian Left. In this same vein, in "The Southern Question," Gramsci discusses the Brigata Sassari (Sardinian Peasant Brigade) in detail as well as the role of Sardinian intellectuals in the Northern industrial regions of Italy. Discussed, in part, at the end of the first chapter, the Italian Communists, the FIOM (La Federazione Impiegati Operai Metallurgici, or Federation of Italian Metal Workers and Employees), and other militant groups made use of informal polling procedures to establish some basis through which to predict the potential success of workers' mobilizations during the Biennio Rosso (Cammett 1967; Gramsci [1926] 1995b: 26). Gramsci states that the communists had discovered that the Brigata Sassari lacked the will to fire on striking workers, demonstrating the ongoing effectiveness of the workers' mobilization. What Gramsci makes clear in "The Southern Question" is that the (strike-busting) strategy described earlier was tried on Italy's industrial North, without success. Described in detail in the second chapter, Gramsci frames his discussion of the Brigata Sassari with a discussion of the success of a small and committed band of Sardinian Communist intellectuals (who had been in the north of Italy and who were, at the time, a part of the Left mobilizations in Turin) who, prior to the Biennio Rosso and, of course, the Brigata Sassari strike-busting efforts, were able to explain to the peasants— in a contentious political environment—that neither ethnic regionalism nor nationalism should be the basis for their politics. Here, Gramsci is demonstrating a larger theme in "The Southern Question" about the careful articulatory function of intellectuals in unifying classes across regional, racial, and cultural differences. The strategy of the text is to demonstrate that Gramsci's (and the PCI's) perspective on the question of Italy's South can be applied strategically to good effect, even when the PCI and its allies have a small presence. The discussion of the Popular Party is, in many ways, a cautionary tale for the PCI (see Cammett, 1967: 79–81; Urbinati 1998a: 385).

Both Gramsci's discussion of race in the fragments from his notebooks as well as his perspectives on his encounters with prisoners find their basis in experiences that he had, and attempted to explain, during the heyday of his activism during the Biennio Rosso, when workers participated in a general strike in Turin at Fiat. In what follows I want to end by discussing, in the context of "The Southern Question," two occasional essays as well as reflections on the Biennio Rosso that appear in the notebooks. My interpretation is that Gramsci develops his perspective on race in coming to terms with ideological differences and unities witnessed through his participation during the Biennio Rosso (which he reflects on later). These perspectives on race develop, substantially, across his polemical work between 1920 and 1926 (demonstrated, for example, in his essays "Workers and Peasants" and "The Southern Question"). It is from the standpoint of communism—and a more theoretical embrace of historical materialism—that there is an explicit linkage between racial difference and real political action, a connection that Hall is able to perceive and that, I believe, allows for Gramsci's work to fit both the spirit and the letter of Hall's perspective on Gramsci's theoretical importance for the study of race and ethnicity.

I've established that Gramsci's level of awareness pertaining to the "scientific" discourse of the positivist school, a self-identified group of "criminal anthropologists" who seeded the cultural ground for the "Southern question." In turn, "the school" provided scientific support for the continued administrative domination over the Southern regions; in fact, their information made Sardinia out to be an island of "barbarians" to rival Sicily (Gibson 1998; Gramsci [1926] 1995b).[15] This predominant discourse on race informed Gramsci early in his life and before the general strike in Turin in August of 1917.[16] He held a "Southernist" position that was common to socialist perspectives during that time, and that he describes, in reflection (in 1926), as follows: "[T]he South is the ball and chain that prevents a more rapid progress in the civil development of Italy; Southerners are biologically inferior beings, either semi-barbarians, or full out barbarians, by natural destiny. . . . The Socialist Party was in great part the vehicle of this bourgeois ideology" (Gramsci [1926] 1995b: 20).[17] Here Gramsci argues that the South should be of central importance to the Italian Communist Party (PCI). The polemical import of this essay, firstly, is to distinguish the PCI's position from that of the Italian Socialist Party (Hall 1986a; Gramsci [1926] 1995b; Pozzolini 1970; Sassoon 1987). Second, Gramsci describes a tripartite linkage between criminological discourse, discourses of development—which were of central concern to both bourgeois and socialist ideology alike (discussed in chapter 1)—and national racial ideology (explored, more deeply, in chapter 2). This link will be explored, in depth, in the subsequent chapter. Given the oppositional politics of the socialists and the political fractions of the bourgeois classes, Gramsci demonstrates that, at least in the first decade of the twentieth century in Italy, this discourse was near universal within a national context. However, Gramsci's experiences with workers from across Italy, well before his incarceration, demonstrate the means through which he distanced himself from a "Southernist" stance. This, in no large part, was the impetus for his essay "The Southern Question." In an affirmative sense, this essay introduced a polemic of unity that would form the groundwork for coalition building for the PCI. Also, as is already discussed in chapter 1, this polemic is based on organizational, strategic, and mobilization-based experiences that comprised an intensive political period in Gramsci's life between 1916 and 1920.

In an essay that represents the first theoretical statement regarding the importance of coalition building and precedes "The Southern Question" by almost a decade, Gramsci reckons with the affirmative role that regional, ethnic, racial, and ideological diversity plays in the framework of workers' mobilizations. Following the Fiat strike of August 1917, in which Gramsci was a participant, in December of that same year, he published "The Revolution against 'Capital,'" where he stated that "the Bolshevik revolution had triumphed in Russia against all the Marxian schemas," and that the "Revolution had been victorious by contradicting Marx's *Capital* or, rather, the Marxian Theory of socialism as something that can be brought about only by, and in, an advanced industrial society. Instead, the Revolution had won in a backward country composed predominantly of illiterate masses of peasants of hardly any political experience; it had won because of Lenin's anti-positivist, non-evolutionist doctrines" (Pozzolini 1970: 29). Pozzolini explains that this article, as well as Gramsci's other work from this period, caused great controversy among the Italian socialists, and as a result of its publication, Gramsci was accused of supporting "voluntarism" (*particularly for the passage that I cite later in this chapter*) and deviating from the principles of (what was, at the time, the Italian socialists' rather mechanical interpretation of) historical materialism (Pozzolini 1970). Regardless, Gramsci does, in fact, retract his position in this article. But, an important point remains.

Gramsci's initial experiences with militant protest actions, strategies, and tactics enabled him to conceive of the role of the party vanguard and party intellectual in a way that is distinct from other Marxist perspectives. The discussion of tactics across chapters 1 and 2 demonstrates this point. Although the category of the intellectual in Gramsci's work is of signal importance to the dialectical movement of history, to his conception of praxis, and later to his detailed discussion of the state and civil society in the notebooks, it does not exclude rank-and-file trade unionists, political radicals, and others on any basis, including race. In fact, it is precisely the broad and differentiated composition of the strikers upon which Gramsci takes a strong and, at the time, politically problematic position—but an important and revealing position. However elaborated, the position in "The Revolution against 'Capital' " I believe represents the expression of Gramsci's direct experience of participation in a protest action with laborers from "social worlds" beyond Northern industrialized Italy.[18] In the position of organizer and as a leading intellectual in a strike in Northern Italy, it is during this time that Gramsci begins to establish his position regarding the South, or Southerners of Italy after this strike (see Fiori 1971 and Cammett 1967). The effects of this protest action mark the beginning of a broad contravention in the positivist discussion of the concept of race and its incorporation into national ideology predominant at the time, the basis for what is theorized in the second chapter.

Turning to Gramsci's recollections of the Turin movement, there is evidence of a perspective on mobilization and what we might call the determinants of an important racial composition. He writes:

[The movement] was accused at the same time of being "spontaneist" and "voluntarist." . . . Once the contradictory accusation is analyzed it shows instead the fruitfulness and the justness of the leadership given to that movement. The leadership was not "abstract." It did not consist in mechanically repeating some scientific or theoretical formula; it did not confuse politics, the real action, with theoretical dissertations. It applied itself to real men, who had been formed in particular historical relations, with particular feelings, ways of looking at things and fragments of conceptions of the world, etc. which were the result of the "spontaneous" combinations of a given environment of material production, with the "accidental" agglomeration in it of disparate social elements. This element of "spontaneity" was not neglected and even less despised. . . . This unity of "spontaneity" and of "conscious direction," that is of "discipline," is precisely the real political action of the subordinated classes. (Notebook 3, §48; Gramsci 1971: 198)

Despite the controversy surrounding this passage and Gramsci's disavowal of this particular article, I think that this piece has to be looked at across the trajectory of activism that Gramsci engaged in between 1916 and 1920—the political work I describe at the end of chapter 1. Gramsci had been interested in understanding the organizational framework that would unify and direct the Turin working-class toward mass revolutionary action. We know that he understood the differences that separated, even opposed, various subaltern groups active in Turin at the time. So, placed in historical context, the members of the movement that contributed to the strike—a lead up to the events surrounding the Sassari Brigade and the Biennio Rosso—were attached to cultural and historical forces within and beyond Italy. This is captured in the preceding quotation. More importantly, these same groups would be players on the societal and political stage leading into the two red years, despite there being a fundamentally different scene. Southerners and islanders—attached, generationally, to peasant communities and regional and oral dialects (often not literate)—were linguistically, culturally, and historically differentiated from both the Northerners as well as one another. Only a year later Gramsci would begin his struggle to unify these groups, as I discussed in chapter 1: Southerners but also Northerners, members of the urban proletariat, some more attached to Europeans from the Northern Alpine region, others who descended from urban artisans, and still others who had gone to the North from the South generations before. Italy's involvement in World War I, specifically the battles fought for Trieste and the Trentino, as well as the rapid rise of the industrial North, provided a new context for the participants in these waves of strikes and protests beginning in 1916 and culminating in 1920.[19]

It is within this context that Gramsci was first able to analyze the effect of cultural, linguistic, and traditional (or formative) historical differences on class-based forms of protest. This period of Gramsci's thought has been described as his "idealist" period, but also the period within which he formed his concept of "factory councils" (influenced by the Soviet example) as the basis for a worker's democracy (Boggs 1984; Hall 1986a; Sassoon 1987). Others have indicated that the tactical flaws inherent in Gramsci's position were abandoned, later, due to historical changes (Felice 1982). Finally, some see Gramsci's experience with the factory councils as enabling a more intensive consideration—in Gramsci's work after 1930—of the conceptual connection between "organic" and "conjuncture" (Caceres 1986). In short, in the period of Gramsci's political journalism, race, racialization, and difference were central to his understanding of protest, antagonism, and the potential for a political unity that gave the lie to the predominant discourses of racialization in Italy during the time that he lived. I have tried to analyze, historically, the determinants of racial discourse in the context of the early twentieth century in Italy and Gramsci's position within this discourse (as counterdiscourse and not as an explicit systematic theoretical stance on race, racialization, and racism) to demonstrate why it is that Gramsci is relevant to contemporary theories and analyses of race and ethnicity. I want to also point out that it is in the work of Gramsci that we can begin to perceive a counterdiscourse on racialization and modernization that finds its roots in analyses and that modifies (through empirical and analytical specification) classical conceptions of historical materialism.

Conclusion

This chapter demonstrates that there is a conceptual and historical basis upon which Stuart Hall can base Gramsci's relevance for the study of race and ethnicity. Gramsci's analysis of historical and political patterns in Italy (via "conjunctures" and "historical blocs"), which lead to mass movements (and the unraveling of these movements), discussed cultural differences manifest regionally, socially, and culturally as a salient determinant in movement mobilization. Gramsci wrote about and discussed race on several occasions between 1917 and 1930 (in and through multiple discursive markers). In other words, race emerges as a discussion point throughout his long career as an intellectual, activist, socialist, and communist. Finally, I have attempted to demonstrate, in this chapter, that Gramsci's discourse on race countermands the predominant discourses of racialization and criminality in Italy (and arguably, by extension, Europe and the United States). His perspective is what enables aspects of Gramsci's theoretical framework to make their way into contemporary theories of culture, race, and power as exhibited in the work of Stuart Hall, a pioneer in the field of cultural theories of race.

As Hall demonstrates in his diacritics, theoretical work, and analysis, Gramsci's concept of the conjuncture represents a nexus that connects the theoretical impasse between structural and cultural theories of race and offers guidelines to understand the political mobilization of culture as racist or against racism. The notion of political and structural modifications to discourses of racialization is, really, a cultural studies–based perspective—one that Hall deploys, especially in work subsequent to "Gramsci's Relevance" (see Hall 1987, 1990, 1992a, 1992b)—but which has not been worked out in any great detail, in this context, until now. By providing the conceptual and epistemological basis to Gramsci's relevance for the study of race and ethnicity and, also, by demonstrating the context through which this relevance is, or becomes, possible, we can challenge the epistemological limitations placed on historicist, sociological, or cultural perspectives on race and racialization, especially as it pertains to the framework of historical materialism, which often is viewed as deterministic and inattentive to race, ethnicity, and culture. Gramsci's and Hall's work demonstrates that it is not only possible to place these theoretical and conceptual categories into correspondence with one another but, more to the point, that doing so helps to link theoretical approaches that have been thought of as incommensurable. The agility of materialist approaches to the analysis of exploitation and domination requires a conceptual framework through which to articulate seemingly disparate structurations of class exploitation with the cultural frameworks that either legitimate ideologies of racial domination or, conversely, express grievances and demands that inform political struggles where class conflict may be represented through myriad forms. As I've demonstrated here, Hall's analysis of race depends on a conjunctural analysis of class, demonstrating both the centrality of cultural formations in positioning and articulating class struggles and the role of culture in producing racialized class positions and market relations that maintain the core premises of a Marxist materialist standpoint and, at the same time, argue for the broad centrality of racial domination to class exploitation. Working within a

Marxist materialist framework, Gramsci's persistent efforts toward peasant mobilization demonstrate a studied approach to articulating regional, ethnic, and racial differences with effective political mobilization over and against humanistic, pseudoscientific, and nationally sanctioned discourses of racial domination, class exploitation, and political exclusion.

Race and political exclusion remain salient to the analysis of contemporary society. Despite the successes of the civil rights movement in the US, for example, new modes of "racial talk," as described by Eduardo Bonilla-Silva, and the extraordinarily violent posture of US police toward black people (and other racial and ethnic groups) demonstrate new means of political exclusion. In the next chapter I extend a materialist approach to the analysis of race by arguing, similarly to Hall in "Race, Articulation, and Societies Structured in Dominance" (1980), that the analysis of a historical context and the modes through which it produces (and reproduces) forms of racial domination require theoretical and conceptual interventions to link racist pasts to racist presents.

CHAPTER 5

Conceptualizing *Aporetic Governmentality*

Rethinking Practice through Structural Marxism, Colorblind Racism, and Abstract Liberalism

This chapter uses Eduardo Bonilla-Silva's (2013) concept of colorblind racism to expose some of the limits of the concept of institutional racism, specifically, how race and power work at the level of the state and governance. In the United States, we have recently witnessed the application of state power to the collective and individual black body to a degree that mirrors crackdowns on social protest in more repressive states (e.g., Turkey's 2015 response to Gezi Park—including the use of armored tactical vehicles and tear gas—appears very similar to events in 2014, in Ferguson, Missouri). Though not new, these "states of emergency" raise questions, not about the degree and extent of repression leveled against legitimate black protest, but about the state, its institutions, and its limits.[1] If repression is directed disproportionately at the collective black body, if the state's policy of "strategic," limited, or nonengagement with largely or entirely white celebrations of sporting victories in the form of looting, property destruction, and mob violence, as well as the government's shocking response to the Bundys' (first Cliven, then Ammon) show of arms and illegal use and seizure of public lands, then it is difficult to deny that there continues to be something rotten about how the state responds to legitimate black protest.

I argue that states exercise power visibly and institutionally, but when states exercise power over black people and other racialized groups, a nonvisible history—still embedded in the state and its ensemble of institutions and practices—emerges, reproducing a broad range of structured racist responses and racist practices. I call these nonvisible historical and institutional arrangements aporetic governmentality. I further argue that the institutional and historical blindness to race contributes directly to ideologies of colorblindness. Colorblind ideology reorganizes racist signification in public discourse where overt expressions of resentment are masked in a pseudoscientific language or so-called "facts" emerging from immediate experiential observations. For example, the simultaneous historical, sociostructural, and geographical fact of segregation is described as a natural phenomenon of all cultural groups (e.g., both white and black) preferring to associate with those similar to themselves. Despite the legal fact of desegregation, schools and neighborhoods remain segregated. Moreover, the target of racial resentment is no longer focused on a particular group of people but mediators, such as affirmative action, welfare, and, more broadly, government intervention, masking racism or making racism seem indirect (Bonilla-Silva and Forman 2000). Here, we might reconsider Anthony Marx's insight from the beginning of the second chapter. Once race is no longer encoded into the states' discourse as racial domination, issues and conflicts with regard to race become "diluted," setting the stage for "colorblindness." Racism, in general, and racial resentment, in particular, is hidden behind a discourse of liberalism or ideas regarding governance and conceptions of fairness that are asocial and ahistorical.

Colorblind ideology is configured against overt post-antebellum racial antagonism that reaches a fever pitch just prior to, during, and subsequent to the struggle for civil rights in the United States. The theorization of colorblind ideology (by Bonilla-Silva) is of signal importance because it both names and frames the expressive manifestation of contemporary racism in the United States today. Colorblind racism, then, is obviously not the evolution of antiracist consciousness in the United States (it does not mean a blindness to racism) but, rather, another expressive manifestation of racism that shifts direct antagonism over to the public and institutional sphere targeting policies that benefit black, brown, and red people under the guise of an antiprogressive yet liberal ideology. It is a blindness to history. These "epochs" of racist consciousness, like Althusser's conception of ideology, have no history; they produce no historical consciousness of institutional racism and racist practices. They mask the current of racism that is a part of the United States' identity and history. But more significantly and in the long run, they produce disconnection and asymmetry between periods of racist expression and antiracist struggle. In short, they mirror the discussion of how power maintains status quo politics across various conjunctures through which groups may mobilize to change hegemonic conditions as, in this case, they pertain to race. Black people only become a party to political representation, and only partially, after slavery ends. Slavery, however, sits at the origin of the constitution of racial discourse in America. And, during slavery, no social process, no institutional configuration, allowed black people access to a foundation for subjecthood. Aporetic governmentality represents a conceptual connection between the period of colorblind racism and postracialism and the period of black enslavement. If the history of racial consciousness that produces our contemporary racial context has no history, is an ideology—a persistent masking of the slavery that lies at the root of racial relations in the United States—then aporetic governmentality is a concept that explains why the most vicious forms of racist practice (e.g., like in Charlottesville, Virginia) can coincide with declarations of colorblindness and postracialism. What, for example, does "black subjectivity" mean today when we can literally see that Walter Scott *was not even afforded the privilege of interpolation* by the state? Scott, a fifty-year-old black man, was shot in the back, multiple times, on the morning of April 4, 2015, in North Charleston, South Carolina, by police officer Michael Slager while fleeing from a traffic stop for a nonfunctioning brake light. Eyewitness reports and a video show Slager shouting at Scott *after* delivering a fatal volley of what appear to be eight gunshots into the back of Scott's body as he ran away. Cornel West describes this phenomenon, in *Keeping Faith* (1993),as "extermination with insignificance" (268). Scott did not enjoy the privilege of an interpolated subjecthood—that dynamic was not afforded to him by the state and its agents; it was absent, socially. And, yet, somehow, we've entered a period of postracialism from a colorblind ideology.

I argue that the ideology of colorblindness is a symptom of aporetic governmentality. The term "aporia" refers to a hole and a puzzle, a persistent absence of something—in this case subjectivity—for racialized groups. Governmentality signifies a productive relationality whereby social subjectivity comes with requirements about self-conduct in society. The modes of self-conduct that governmentality offer are predominantly white. (A glimpse of this is captured by the practice of banning locked [natural!] hair as unprofessional in the workplace, forcing black people to pay for extensions or straightening or pressing hair, which is physically damaging.) In slavery, there was no subjectivity offered to black people based on a productive form of exchange, either social or economic, only domination. Following slavery, strategies of containment were exercised by the state and private enterprise and these strategies produced separate spheres of subjectivity; they bolstered violent practices of racial resentment leading into the struggle for civil rights, the period of black militancy, and, also, black entrepreneurship, and higher education (Ferguson 2012). As discussed by several scholars, the practice of colorblind racism paints a shiny semiotic gloss over a very recent history of the most antihuman forms of racist practice. There is, however, a social, cultural, and historical depth to racism that is linked, directly, to the manifestations of racist violence we witness today and that can be explained by the concept of aporetic governmentality. In this arrangement, the state masks racial relations as it has done with class relations.

For example, in the structural Marxist tradition—whether we are dealing with Antonio Gramsci's (1971, 1995a) conception of hegemony, Louis Althusser's (1971) conception of the subject (that can be interpolated), Nicos Poulantzas's conception of class positions/places and isolation effects (1973b), or Bob Jessop's "relational orientation" (1982)—states have an interest in maintaining (in some cases increasing) rates of exploitation while maintaining *some kind of* compact between capital and labor. As relations between state and civil society change, the expressions of predominant ideologies also change. The state is interested in maintaining favorable relations between itself and fractions of the capitalist class as well as mediating the capital and labor compact (to either maintain or increase rates of exploitation). The structural Marxist tradition theorizes the role of the state's intervention in the economy to maintain favorable conditions for capital accumulation—a socially "productive" paradigm for capital.

In Michel Foucault's conception of power as disciplinary (1975), and his conception of governmentality as conducting the conduct of others ([1979] 2000), the state and institutional power subject, isolate, infect, even break the body down so that it can become useful, capable, increase its own power, and even become self-directed is also a productive paradigm. In comparison to the structural Marxist tradition, it is directed at individual bodies. However, black, brown, and indigenous peoples do not share *that same relationship* to power, institutions, and the state in the West, in general, and the United States in particular. They are prey to the same institutions and have been so, historically. Theories of power and governance speak of institutions and the power they exercise independent of "other" institutions—manifest destiny, settler colonialism, slavery, Jim Crow, and so on—as though the latter belong to some other social world. In fact, the state and its institutions (along with sets of actors, agents, and practices) produced these "other" institutions directly and through the same "democratic" frameworks and liberal perspectives. The productive schema of institutional power, largely attributable to Foucault (1975, [1976] 1990, 1978, [1979] 2000, 1987, 1997), has another side as well: this marks the departure point for aporetic governmentality.

As we trace Foucault's conceptions of power to their apotheosis—governmentality—we cannot ignore a history of institutional arrangements and networks of power relations that work by breaking the body to bits; using the body up, discarding it, and replacing it with another; working bodies "wholesale" and not "retail"; and punishing with no disciplinary goal. These bodies are objects, which can never be made docile or are only ever docile but, fundamentally, reside outside of schemas and orders that perceive individual bodies as potentialities. The concept of aporetic governmentality marks this exterior. In what follows I will discuss what this concept is and how it emerges from an interconnected reading of structural Marxism, Foucault's theories of power as applied in various institutional settings, and colorblind racism.

Race, State, Power, and Ideology: Antonio Gramsci and Raymond Williams

State power has been theorized in relation to racial oppression, successfully, through the imputation, and transformation, of the framework through which specific aspects of state power are emphasized in connection to racism. In particular, Gramsci's theory of hegemony (particularly, the interaction of state and civil society in the context of political forces) has directly influenced theoretical lenses that contribute to our collective understanding of racism, as it is both structurally organized and both politically and culturally expressed. For example, in *Racial Formation in the United States* (1994) Omi and Winant relate racial formations to the polity through Gramsci's concept of hegemony to explain racial domination. They note, "Ruling groups must elaborate and maintain a popular system of ideas and practices—through education, the media, religion, folk wisdom, etc." (1994: 66–67).

Gramsci, who stands at the beginning of the structural Marxist tradition, is able to connect ideology and actions as a system of ideas and practices that, as the preceding quotation describes, incorporates groups of people but also separates out others who are either potentially revolutionary or who are targeted as instruments of the state (e.g., military conscription) or civil society (e.g., peasants, labor rationalization, forms of agricultural organization). The relationship between racism and politics through Gramsci's insights appears in Omi and Winant's "racial formation theory" as well as Stuart Hall's sociological investigations of race in the context of Thatcher's England (1971, 1978), his early–mid career analysis of racism, culture, and socioeconomic structure, ethnicity, and identity (1980, 1986a, 1986b, 1987). As I have demonstrated in the previous chapter, Hall's relationship to Gramsci was more than merely a conceptual or theoretical one. Hall saw in Gramsci's work an important mediation between both structural and cultural aspects of racism. The analysis of race in the framework of cultural studies, through Gramsci, makes it possible to link sociological articulations of racism to cultural expressions of race and racism. As such, this chapter and the previous one mark an attempt to bring critical race theory together with cultural studies investigations of racialization and racism into an alliance. Notably, Glenn E. Bracey II has artfully read the state into critical race theory, potentially reorienting analyses of structural racism as it relates to politics, social movements, and law (Bracey 2015). In each of these approaches the state is positioned as a substantial, if—in the case of Bracey—inaccessible, nodal point in the dissemination of *power* determining aspects and instances of structural racism (Bracey 2016).

As Bracey (2016) adroitly surmises, it is the lack of accessibility that black movements have to the polity, through political opportunities and the political process, which must be linked to the question of historical analysis; the role of social structure, in particular, states; distinct institutions in maintaining historical continuity, for some and not for others; and, finally, the continuance or emergence of specific forms of racism, like colorblindness—all factors that David Theo Goldberg notes as significant in his research, despite his having a different scope (Goldberg 2002: 235). More recent work on racism and the state has demonstrated how liberalism became and remains hegemonic and, also, theorizes how an ideology that expresses a fully inclusive polity maintains racist practices. Mills (2011) argues (in a similar fashion to my work) that the modern state is transparent, but not in the case of race. Rather, it takes a "principled anti-transparency on matters related to race"; he refers to this as "racial opacity" (33). Rodríguez (2011) makes a compelling case and provides analytical guidelines to understand white supremacy as more than merely a logic or a discourse but, rather, as sets of practices that are materially and institutionally contiguous across historical time and, as a result, reproducible. Both Mills (2011) and Rodríguez (2011) share similarities with the perspective I take on the racist state. My conception of aporetic governmentality, however, is an attempt to articulate, theoretically, how racist practices are materially, historically, and institutionally contiguous. In my conceptual framework, the reproduction of racism is connected to the fundamentally limited or absent production of viable subjective space for black and other ethnic and racial minorities. Colorblind ideology, in turn, places greater distance between race and power, adding an important dimension to the link between abstract or neoliberal ideologies of race and my conception of race as a historical and social aporia.

Gramsci links the lack of political opportunity (and the ready availability of it to others) to the question of historical analysis and the relative stability of social structures, but he does so by focusing on the uses of tradition and culture in the framework of his broader theory of hegemony. Addressing the cultural dissemination of hegemony—including "residual" aspects of tradition—Raymond Williams makes the important point that, as we consider the interrelation of history, tradition, and hegemony,

[w]hat we have to see is not just "a tradition" but a selective tradition: an intentionally selective version of a shaping past and a pre-shaped present, which is then powerfully operative in the process of social and cultural definition and identification.

It is usually not difficult to show this empirically. Most versions of "tradition" can be quickly shown to be radically selective. From a whole possible area of past and present, in a particular culture, certain meanings and practices are selected for emphasis and certain other meanings and practices are neglected or excluded. Yet, within a particular hegemony, and as one of its decisive processes, this selection is presented and usually successfully passed off as "the tradition," "the significant past." (Williams 1977: 115)

Williams's discussion of "selective tradition" within a hegemonic framework, especially as it pertains to the preceding Omi and Winant quotation, demonstrates that entire groups of people may be left behind (not selected) or incorporated (transformed and included).[2] Transformation, as such, may not be complete or total, and certain groups of people may be prone to exclusionary practices dependent upon context. This dynamic is important: as necessary and indispensable as the variegated approaches are to structural racism, we need to address a racist dynamic that permits the simultaneous phenomena of colorblindness, along with liberal political ideologies that promote so-called tolerance or racial inclusion, and also extreme forms of state and state-sanctioned violence directed, individually and collectively, at the black body. The idea of selective tradition—which pulls "residual" culture into the present—actually raises a question about how selection works when it pertains to race and historical context. Traditions, institutions, and the historical continuity that allow for the reproduction of racism at the social and cultural level need to be explained. We need a theory of structural racism that can account for the deep antihuman continuity of racism along with the various new cultural "fronts" of racist practice. To be clearer, we need to address aspects of cultural and social reproduction that pull what Bonilla-Silva describes as "crude and vulgar antiminority sentiment and actions" into present-day colorblind racism and the abstract liberalist ideologies that bolster it. Although certain racist practices may seem to disappear (or be disparaged when they reappear), the historical continuity that maintains racism as a deep, antihuman, social, cultural, and political current and an ensemble of practices depends, to some extent, on a repetition of old ideas and practices.[3] Aporetic governmentality demonstrates how there is a link between "vulgar" or "residual" antiminority sentiment and blindness, how it is mediated both publicly and through state power.

Gramsci and the theoretical contributions from structural Marxism have demonstrated that *state power* depends upon *ideology*, specifically its extension through public *institutions* and, also, civil society as well as the *practices* that these institutions foment and engender (Althusser 1971). Specifically, state power, in the framework of structural Marxism, is described by many as the *ideological* balance of forces—political, societal, and economic—that maintain the relations of production for capitalism or class domination (Althusser 1971: 128–134). Relying principally on the state to mitigate the objective and uneven place of class in capitalist society, some have theorized, albeit somewhat differently, that the state plays an active role in the class struggle by concealing it (Miliband 1969; Poulantzas 1973a). Instrumental to the concealment of class power is the ideological expression of abstract liberalism. It is the "master frame" of state power; it regards each person as an individuated monad having equal opportunity in exercising choices abstracted from any and all institutional contexts. Abstract liberalism—liberal ideologies that are related to the state and its institutions—both masks the class relation *and, also, constitutes one of the four frames of colorblind racism.* How well, however, does abstract liberalism do with regard to concealing racism?

This brings us to a more specific question regarding analysis. *If the ideological work of the state is largely successful at balancing, to the point of nonviolent domination, the political forces well within its purview, why is such extraordinary repressive violence directed at the individual and collective black body?* In other words, if there is either a real or analytical distinction to be made between the ideological function of institutions and their repressive function, and, moreover, if their ideological function has proven successful at "conducting the conduct" of individuals (contemporary abstract liberalism or neoliberalism—see Foucault [1979] 2000), why do the repressive aspects of these institutions persistently exercise symbolic but, more to the point, real violence against individual and collective black bodies? The larger question, then, is not "are institutions colorblind" or, even, "how are institutions colorblind" but, more pointedly: *How does colorblindness work at the institutional level and, also, why does it manifest, often and repeatedly, as repression and violence?* Why does there seem to be a blindness toward these very public instances of collective structural racism?

Concerning State and Civil Society: History, Racism, Antiracism, and Their Limits

In suggesting an answer, I go a step further in this chapter. Following themes of absence, erasure, and exclusion in radical and theoretical antiracist traditions, it becomes reasonable to claim that the historical blindness to race (especially in the United States) has deep institutional roots. Those roots—whether we are reviewing structural, poststructural or institutionalist, postcolonial, and some critical race perspectives—describe neither a process or act of "overlooking" nor an "ignorance" (as colorblindness is so often associated with) but, rather, a kind of abjection, a vicious invisibilizing or a process of erasure (what West [1993] describes as "extermination with insignificance" [268]). For example, in "Race and Social Theory" (1993) and *The Racial Contract* (1997) both Cornel West and Charles Mills, respectively, point out (Western) humanism depends upon racism. Mills (1997) squarely roots this logic in the genesis of social contract theories, proto-nationalistic and modernistic. In *Keeping Faith* (1993), West sees a tripartite logic of white racial supremacy emanating from civilizational *ur-texts* (e.g., Old and New Testaments), micro-institutional practices (discourses, common sense, including the repetition and dissemination of platitudes rhetorically linked to *ur-texts*), and macro-social structures (e.g., economic institutions, ideologies, and practices). Racism resides at the distinction between, specifically, nature and culture in the period of "exploration and discovery" and, later, "colonialism and nationalism" (Dussel 1998). Jackson (2012) demonstrates how it replicates itself across the various ideological and institutional frameworks through a persistent and absent discourse of discovery shaped, repeatedly, by forms of racial (indigenous) exclusion. This line of inquiry is also powerfully articulated by anticolonial writers.[4]

Most importantly, this observation appears across subaltern studies, most prominently in "Can the Subaltern Speak" (1988). Gayatri Spivak demonstrates that the subject of racial domination can only be heard through organizational and societal categories emerging from the enlightenment that subsume or erase race; acceptance of these categories legitimates both real (Fanon 1964) and symbolic (Bourdieu 1989) violence—a fact of slavery and colonialism and *a necessary condition of modernity, the nation-state, and capital accumulation* (Carley 2016; Goldberg 2002; Marx 1998). This, of course, is why, outlined here in the first chapter, Gramsci articulating a connection between racialized groups and Northern Italian industrial workers is so significant. This is also why it is important to understand the racial context and racial characteristics of Italian struggles against the liberal ideologies that promote a "unified" Italian nation-state. Without these struggles and mass movements, *the subaltern cannot speak; when she does, she is erased. Humanism, whatever its political-ideological expression may be, cannot hear her; it can only hear itself reflected in her speech.* Contemporary challenges to continued institutional racism that, in the contemporary ideological framework of abstract liberalism, are more perniciously blind are based on forgetting that, historically, race has been relegated to shifting sets of negative, especially negation-based, categories. These categories have manifested in history and have never been addressed structurally. Rather, they have only been entreated to the persistent assertions of an antiracism based on the supposed enlightened attitudes ever-present in American ideologies of contemporary liberalism. This requires the expression of a more profound blindness—both historical and institutional—and one that is intimately linked to specific forms of racial-institutional violence (e.g., settler colonialism, colonial administration, antebellum slavery, Jim Crow, apartheid, etc.) that appear as the "flip" or "B-side" of *visible and celebrated* Western institutions. Williams (1977) explains how tradition reproduces itself selectively. West (1993), Mills (1997), Dussel (1998), Jackson (2012), and others demonstrate that humanism is a powerful transhistorical bedrock undergirding exploration, discovery, modernity, nationalism, and the formation of the state. Finally, Spivak (1988) explains that to speak in a way that can be heard is to speak only through these traditions; it is to speak oneself and one's history out of existence.

Regarding contemporary liberalism and colorblindness, Bonilla-Silva states in the preface to the updated and revised fourth edition of *Racism without Racists* (2013) that the persistence of old and new racisms with one another is the "[c]oexistence in America of crude and vulgar antiminority sentiment and actions alongside the ideology (and its corresponding behaviors) [that] I label in this book as color-blind racism. . . . Racial orders are never 'pure,' as elements of the past (and even of the future) often coexist with the dominant ways of conducting racial business" (2013: xiv). In other words, Bonilla-Silva's colorblind ideology fits within this tradition in theorizing race. Recently, Marlese Durr (2015), comparing police behavior to antebellum slave patrols, states, "Slavery was part of the U.S. legal system—sanctioned through and by the Congressional passage of Fugitive Slave Laws (1789, 1850). . . . Virginia . . . enacted more than 130 slave statutes between 1689 and 1865, while Connecticut and New York, alongside other colonies promulgated laws to criminalize and control slaves" (2015: 874–875). Durr's research question, more than merely valid, is precisely correct in scope and depth. More to the point, as Durr begins to address state-based and, most often, sanctioned racial violence, she provides an important clue to help us conceive of the "impure" nature of "racial orders," to restate Bonilla-Silva, the "coexistence in America of crude and vulgar antiminority sentiment and actions alongside the ideology . . . of color-blind racism" (2013: xiv).

Durr renders racist state and institutional history visible through a stark comparison between two institutional practices. The "institution" of slavery is an analytically distinct set of relationships that are legal, symbolic, but no less concrete than other institutions that are, at the same time, a product of the modern democratic nation-state—a concrete location for liberalism. One institution is visible; the other is not or, at least, not as an inseparable from the modern democratic nation-state and its law-making institutional frameworks. *Durr's comparison between contemporary U.S. policing and slave patrols demonstrates the need for a theory that holds the modern democratic nation-state in connection with the institution of slavery and that theorizes the two in combination.*

Trafficking Racism Institutionally through History

With regard to the persistence of racism, both West and Mills' perspectives depend upon what West refers to as "fears of '*extinction with insignificance*'" (West 1993: 268). To be clear, West is not calling for a transhistorical and transcultural theory of racist *practice* but, rather, "a radically historical investigation into the emergence, development, and sustenance of white supremacist *logics* operative in various epochs in the modern Western (Eastern or African) civilization" (West 1993: 268). In other words, racist practices may not ultimately be reduced to abjection or absence but, rather, must be analyzed through the presence of those logics in some form (e.g., discourse).

I want to suggest that the continuity of racist *practices* that share a *logic* rooted in fears related to "*extinction with insignificance*" are *trafficked through history institutionally*. My investigation will claim that racism emerges, is developed, and sustains itself, again and again, through the same institutions that support and promote freedom in the form of abstract liberalism. These institutions render only some aspects of the social structure visible for some people (or for those who are able to mask themselves—only ever temporarily or contextually) while, simultaneously, concealing vicious pasts and violent and destructive practices. The ideology of colorblindness framed through abstract liberalism is grounded in an institutional history that is only partially visible. Hence, our social structure reinforces colorblindness as it does with other ideological perspectives.

If ideology in general but also colorblind ideology, in particular, is understood to be more than merely a symptom of race or racism but, rather, the concrete basis through which practices and behaviors are either legitimated or reinforced, or both, then the conjoined and mutually constitutive set of relationships that consist of institutions, ideologies, practices, and behaviors are addressed in the structural Marxist literature.[5] The continuity of these institutionally durable social formations can be measured by looking at the expression of political forces, which ideologies are most prominent, or what ideology is prominent.

However, the explanation for the historical continuity of institutions—which are, in part, sites that reproduce and distribute ideology (or from which ideologies emanate [Althusser 1971; Foucault 1979]) is attributable to both Raymond Williams's conception of selective tradition and residual cultural forces (1963, 1977) as well as Antonio Gramsci's conception of "traditional intellectuals" and "historical blocs" (1971, 1995a). Williams explains the dynamic by which only a part of history is told and retold. Gramsci, however, explains how political power (in the form of hegemony) persists across historical time and, further, how new political and civil institutions—that produce their own army of defenders, "legitimators," and standard-bearers (organic intellectuals)—depend on these same people from the past to provide an immediate historical continuity between "old" and "new" forms of power (traditional intellectuals). This intellectual and institutional alliance represents these forms of power to everyone ideologically, coded as normal, continuous, linear, progressive, mutually beneficial, and so forth (Katznelson 2005).

Finally, the contents of colorblind ideology that depend upon an abstract liberalism and its expressive variants can be linked to Michel Foucault's theory of governmentality. Governmentality represents a least-qualified freedom. It is the neoliberal realization of abstract liberalism—general forms of conduct are internalized and repeated *without a sense* that power is being applied in some way (as opposed to discipline). Governmentality does two things: It provides categories for and explains how power and domination have been disseminated through institutions, occupations, and roles—formal and informal—historically, and it exposes race as outside of this schema and brings us to its own limit. In the framework of liberal perspectives, concepts of power and domination, as they pertain to people subject to racial domination in descriptively different institutions, for example, settler colonialism, colonial administration, antebellum slavery, Jim Crow, apartheid, all reside outside of democracy or are seen as failures or lessons for its experimental nature. The key point is that the institutions that both the structural Marxists (as well as some Marxist writing in the derivationist tradition) and Foucault study as accumulative and distributive centers of power make these "other" institutions. As Williams (1977) describes it, these "institutions" become separated and racial institutions fall away. This directly affects the institutional production of ideology and practices, whereby abstract liberalism and colorblind ideology are rooted in a "deeper blindness" or a historical absence pertaining to the partial institutional presence of institutions that govern all of us.

Foucault's (1978) governmentality helps to describe the institutional transmission of symbolic and real racist violence. Governmentality contains both a "periodization" of organizational models that guide forms of conduct and the incorporation of these models into modes of self-conduct. In other words, it is historical and sociological. More significantly, governmentality implies biopolitics, biopower, and power—concepts that depend on the disciplining (and imagining) of (certain) bodies so that they may be, simultaneously, both docile (to authority) and strong (effective at their task and maximally productive) (Foucault 1975; Rehmann 2013: 302; Smith 2012). It implies a subject in, first, the Althusserian sense and then, later—and with micro-relational modifications—in the Foucaultian sense. But, most importantly it implies a subject.

For these same institutions, the black body was and, in so many instances, remains an object. When it is productive it is a machine. When it is disciplined it is punished—its corporeality is as a thing and not a subject. The hidden history of these bodies—working both beyond Foucault's disciplinary regimes and, also, capital—is directly and precisely linked to the state, forms of governance, case law, policing practices, and the specific fractions of capital accumulation extant at the time (e.g., agro-industrial accumulation).[6]

These fragments of governmentality disseminated through institutions and exercised upon nonsubjects do not, then, add up to a subject that takes in discipline and is both controlled and rewarded (Foucault 1975), despite being produced through institutions that constitute subjects, individuals, laborers, among others. The black body, in these historical and institutional instances, is broken down into a multitude of aggregate objects-parts that are to be used, observed—as nature, phenomena, or event—hidden, immobilized, dominated, or destroyed but neither governed nor subjected to forces that affirm its docility through the *ideology* and *institutional practices* of abstract liberalism. In short, to be black is to not be coded for the purposes of docility (Smith 2012). It is to be exempted from both the ideology of abstract liberalism and the institutional practices that make *white* individualism available in a multitude of forms. There, then, is a persistent institutional and historical blindness to the black body that is, as the structural Marxists correctly maintain, reproduced through the liberal ideologies of state and civil society.

Aporetic governmentality, then, is the puzzle of structural racism; it is *the accumulation of the absences of racialized groups from an institutional gaze (in the Althusserian and Foucauldian sense of the subject) that subtends the institutional and structural array of persistent absences reproduced by repeated historical-institutional instantiations of state and civil society.* This, in short, is why abstract liberalism fails to see color through every imaginable prismatic angle. The ideology of colorblind racism is a lens grounded in concrete institutions that produced, and then hid, the governance and laws pertaining to settler colonialism and slavery in the United States while attempting to produce, simultaneously, new agro-industrial and industrial laboring subjects and new, often separate, ideologies of citizenship and moral conduct (see also, Kansas–Nebraska Act of 1854, Dred Scott [1857], Jim Crow, Black Codes [especially in South Carolina], and laws [labor, especially sharecropping] [see also Haney-López 1996]). As the synthesis of structural Marxism and colorblind racism is concerned, aporetic governmentality posits that as the conditions for the relations of production are reproduced, so are racist practices.

To elaborate, I will go on to review structural Marxist approaches that discuss the interrelation of ideology and state power, especially as it pertains to maintaining the domination of capital (profit) through techniques for renewing, broadly disseminating, and increasing labor exploitation.[7] My goal is to demonstrate the various structural strategies that comprise the interrelation between the state and private industry. The discussion of particular aspects of these Marxist approaches will help to frame my focus on the concept of colorblind racism in Bonilla-Silva's (2013) work, specifically, how the four frames of colorblind racism might be reorganized to facilitate our understanding of the reproduction of structural racism through state power alongside its concealment through ideology. However, the role that ideology (and the individuated expressions of colorblindness) plays in reproducing racial domination in its various forms needs to be explained. To do that, I turn to my theory of aporetic governmentality as a way to understand the intersection of class exploitation and racial domination through colorblind ideology. Specifically, I will link colorblindness to subjectivity to argue that institutional practices do not render black bodies docile but, rather, convert bodies to objects through "dismemberment" or destruction.

Marxist Approaches to Ideology

Antonio Gramsci

A substantial contribution from the structural Marxist tradition is the theorization of ideology as dependent upon practices. Practices represent concrete or real acts or instances, in both the spheres of private (civil) and public (state) organizations and institutions, *demonstrating* and in some cases *determining the reality of* expressions of political rhetoric from government. In the framework of structural Marxism, ideology is neither merely a system of values or beliefs nor is it a pure instrument of the ruling group. Rather, ideology implants itself with varying degrees of subtlety through concrete or real examples of the state acting in the most affirmative aspects of its expressed values and beliefs. It relies on necessary, functional, formal, and informal alliances between both public and private institutions and organizations (e.g., crafting of legislation, appointing of experts from industry to regulatory panels and advisory positions, dependence on lobbyists, political action committees, etc.). Ideology is a system of values that exist alongside its demonstrations to the public through institutionally based, socially, and economically affirmative forms of action; actions that require the application of political as well as economic power to affirm that, as a system of values, an ideology can be extended beyond its expression in the capitalist class (e.g., abstract liberalism) or a class fraction (e.g., neoliberalism or libertarianism) (Gramsci 1971, 1995a; Poulantzas 1973a, 1973b).

As Omi and Winant argue, *the consolidation of rulership* is neither given nor guaranteed, rather it requires that ideas be realized through a nexus of institutions, practices, and traditions. It is present concretely—geographically and visually—as Gramsci notes, "The press is the most dynamic part of the ideological structure, but not the only one. Everything that directly or indirectly influences or could influence public opinion belongs to it: libraries, schools, associations and clubs of various kinds, even architecture, the layout of streets and their names" (1971: 332–333). This points to a certain degree of concreteness and, also, ubiquity. Importantly, Gramsci's theoretical contributions to *the consolidation of rulership* inaugurate a trajectory in Marxist thought that gets picked up, most strongly, by structural Marxists (in France). Structural Marxists provide important theoretical insights into abstract liberalism. In short, they specify how rulership is consolidated through ideology as a set of institutionally supported and structured practices that link the state and capitalist society together. Structural Marxism provides the framework for this theoretical perspective and specifies aspects of the linkage between state and civil society or the public and private aspects of social life through social policy and other means of state intervention. But, more importantly, structural Marxism gives specific instances or examples of how ideology consolidates rule in specific contexts and circumstances.

As it pertains to the consolidation of power, Gramsci provides the most salient concept of the essential relationship between ideologies and organizations (of all kinds). Gramsci makes a distinction between the concept of ideology as a set of ideas and what he describes as "historically organic ideologies." He defines historically organic ideologies as "necessary to a given structure.... To the extent that ideologies are historically necessary ... they 'organize' human masses, and create the terrain on which men move, acquire consciousness of their position, struggle, etc." (Notebook 7, §19, §21; Gramsci 1971: 376–377). According to Gramsci, organizations require description but, more to the point, legitimation. In short, any organization creates, alongside itself, staff and a sense of the organization's purpose.

Though analytically distinct from one another, these elements are essential parts of any organization, whether public or private. Staffs are specialized in various ways. Gramsci describes how "intellectuals" comprise merely a functional role in an organization, but over time, they work to legitimate the social and political role of an organization and become an essential part of any organization connecting its role more broadly to society and to politics. All intellectuals have, or have at one time had, a specific function and a social role in an organization. But, intellectuals necessarily go beyond their specialized function, and must do so, in order to explain their own and their organizations' role. In short, they produce ideology only in relation to some aspect of the social structure.

Gramsci discerns two specific categories of intellectuals: organic and traditional. Although, at a given moment in time, all intellectuals are "organic," they do not remain so. The progression of history and the changes to a society—upon the terrain of economics and politics—change the intellectual's function (Morton 2007). In short: to the extent that an intellectual is involved in the development of society, he or she is organic. However, if an intellectual is not directly involved, but allied with the process of societal development, he or she is traditional. Gramsci, then, conceives of the intellectual as forming an empirical link to specific fractions of society. An intellectual is organic to the extent that "[e]very social group, coming into existence on the original terrain of an essential function in the world of economic production, creates together with itself, organically, one or more strata of intellectuals which give it homogeneity and an awareness of its own function not only in the economic but also in the social and political fields" (Notebook 12, §1; Gramsci 1971: 5). Whether this social group is a political one (not, however, a political party), a part of a private organization, or a part of the state bureaucracy makes no difference. The category of intellectual contains a specific conceptualization of the function that an intellectual fulfills. For example, when speaking of a specific type of intellectual and their role, say the role that an entrepreneur plays in civil society, Gramsci states:

> It should be noted that the entrepreneur himself represents a higher level of social elaboration, already characterized by a certain directive [*dirigente*] and technical (i.e. intellectual) capacity: he must have a certain technical capacity, not only in the limited sphere of his activity and initiative but in other spheres as well, at least in those which are closest to economic production. He must be an organizer of masses of men; he must be an

organizer of the "confidence" of investors in his business, of the customers for his product, etc. . . . It can be observed that the "organic" intellectuals, which every new class creates alongside itself and elaborates in the course of its development, are for the most part "specializations" of partial aspects of the primitive activity of the new social type which the new class has brought into prominence. (Notebook 12, §1; Gramsci 1971: 5–6)

The intellectual as the bearer of a specific kind of technical knowledge seeks to achieve—within the existing society—an end for the class or the group to which he or she is attached. The intellectual can only achieve this end by organizing and directing others—in other words, by becoming involved in politics.

Gramsci connects politics and political power to specific instances whereby fractions of the capitalist class (civil society) assert power by helping to consolidate the rulership of the state. In this arrangement, politics represents the mutual benefit of elite actors in the state and in private industry. Gramsci makes two important points in this regard. The first pertains to his theory of hegemony and the second to the dissemination of liberalism through both state and civil society (as bedrock to both individualism and the consolidation of rule through institutional forms). Structural Marxism expands upon the theme of institutions curtailing social and political energies alongside a fundamentally individualist ideology of political and economic practice. Ideologies are tied to institutions and institutions are tied to the dissemination of liberalism as an expressive freedom but, also, a political limit (for the working class).

The Connection between Abstract Liberalism, Organizational Structure, and Power

Liberalism is organic to the capitalist state. It serves two strong purposes. First, as the state encounters economic contradictions, liberalism explains those contradictions economically (with the promise of future equilibrium being achieved); next, it puts the onus on each of us, as individuals, to do our part for the health of the economy; and finally, it credits the emergence from crisis to economic elites who are represented through individual entrepreneurs, executive officers, leaders of industry—all specifically organic to sectors of production in civil society (also, for example, the "American Worker" is credited but through a synecdochal framework).

The atomization and prefigurative representation of working people requires the dissemination of abstract liberalism at any and all institutional nodal points. Political society works to consolidate rule through "traditional intellectual" modes. Gramsci's discussion of Benedetto Croce's triumphalism of abstract liberalism provides important insight into the dissemination of ideology through institutions (including institutional nexuses that promote culture—tradition, tastes, etc.) as a broad spatial and concrete network linked to the state. In Notebook 10, §59, Gramsci discusses how Benedetto Croce—the only Italian intellectual at the time who was internationally regarded—worked both through and above a party structure. For Croce,

> [t]he party [w]as general ideology, superior to the various more immediate groupings. In actual fact, the liberal party's mode of being in Italy after 1876 was that of presenting itself before the country as an "extended battle order" of fractions and national and regional groups. All were fractions of political liberalism—the liberal Catholicism represented by the *popolari* as much as the nationalists (Croce was a collaborator on A. Rocco and F. Coppola's *Politica*), the monarchist unions as much as the republican party and a large part of the socialist area, the radical democrats as much as the conservatives, Sonnino-Salandra as much as Giolitti, Orlando, Nitti and Co. Croce was the theoretician of what all these groups and grouplets, cliques and mafias had in common, the head of a central propaganda office which all these groups benefited from and made use of, the national leader of the cultural movements which sprang up to breathe new life into old political forms. (Gramsci 1995a: 463; Notebook 10II, §59i)

Culture as a site of spontaneity, creativity, and, potentially, transformation was countermanded through Croce and the dissemination of his, and others', "official" position on culture, which served to legitimate and delegitimate movements. Liberalism was the order of the day. Its (substantive) presence as a set of cultural practices contained within institutions—politics, mentioned here, and Gentile and education, mentioned elsewhere, was almost total. However, the process by which a liberal ideology came to dominate the perspective of people in society depended precisely on an active consolidation of new movements. Gramsci goes on:

> Croce shared with Giustino Fortunato this office of national leader of liberal democratic culture. From 1900 to 1914 and even after (but as its

resolution) Croce and Fortunato appeared as the inspirers (as the leaven) of every serious new movement among the young that aimed at renewing the overall political "conduct" and life of the bourgeois parties.... [T]he concept of liberty in the traditional terms of the individual personality. (Gramsci 1995a: 464; Notebook 10II, §59i)

Gramsci notes that Fortunato, relying on Croce as a national celebrity and international figure, "appears" as the launching pad for ideas pertaining to political and civil *conduct*. The parties become the institutional frame through which the idea of abstract liberalism is concretized as both sacrosanct and innovative—the domain of young and old ideas alike. More importantly, Gramsci explains how ideologies, like abstract liberalism, are grounded strongly in institutions as well as cultural and political practices. We see now that forces and practices produce and reproduce ideologies and their "proofs" via practice; we see how colorblindness can be reproduced both socially and historically.

Louis Althusser and Nicos Poulantzas

Poulantzas discusses the prefigurative aspects of politics. He describes the political *positioning* of classes through constitutive organizations: specifically, trade unions and political parties. These organizational forms organize workers' collective discontent, interest, and erstwhile acts into the polity so that the stolid aspects of politics—negotiation, compromise, cooperation—become the means by which gains are made and lost. At best, political groups become and stay class corporate—aware of collective interest without the hope of ever realizing them fully or hegemonically (Poulantzas 1978).

If we consider Gramsci's point about the prefiguration of culture not only in party practices but, also, in the sphere of education, two other important points must be made. Poulantzas discusses how ideology produces an "isolation effect." The individuation of political action (e.g., electoral politics) across various levels of practice (voting as a member of a trade union, in caucuses and primaries, in general elections) promotes the "power" of individualism and individual decision-making while, simultaneously, denying the power of collective social action. Self-interest becomes the guiding principle of political power (not collective interest), and where collective interest is promoted, politically (i.e., trade unions), the practices often involve voting and responding to calls for mobilization. Self-interest even in the framework of a political organization that is organized around promoting the collective good is predicated fundamentally on the idea that we are individuals first (and foremost) and, more to the point, nobody's fool (other rank-and-file members or the executive members of the union). The individual is isolated from the most effective forms of political practice and, through their "self-interest," from other workers and the power of collective participation.

In Althusser's view, individualism is a fiction that makes life in society (as productive relations) bearable. *It is, in short, abstract liberalism.* More than mere fiction, the individuation of "subjects," a category borrowed from Lacan's theory of self-development in infancy (Lacan [1949] 2006), allows a single person to bear a narrative that is consonant with abstract liberalism, on the one hand, while subjecting them—legally—to both private industry, as labor power, and also the violence of the repressive state apparatus on the other. Althusser demonstrates how ideology has a real hold over each of us precisely because we are subjected to both ideology as the narrative of individuality—believing in our radical individuation, which occurs and is reinforced through the same exact array of institutions and concomitant practices (with some variation, e.g., religions, secularism)—and, also, to capital (as labor power) and state power (as a collective legal entity). Abstract liberalism as an ideology binds political and civil-societal power together, blinding us to the relations of exploitation through which society experiences its economic continuity. Poulantzas, Althusser, and Lacan's theories illustrate how the dynamic interplay between institutions and practices manifests ideologically and enfolds each of us in a narrative as agents—as contributors to our own destiny in the world. It becomes impossible to imagine, then, that, or how, being black might exclude a person from the narrative. Blindness to race, then, is not only ideological but also institutional. You cannot have ideology without institutions and vice versa. If institutions have "reformed" to address inequalities such as race, and if individual behavior is more enlightened, how might it be the case that racism is reproduced even in its most vicious aspects?

Bonilla-Silva, Race, and Colorblind Ideology

Rhetorical and Discursive Categories/Strategies

Categorizing the four frames of colorblind racism, for the purposes of analysis, would require distinguishing between a "superstructure" of racist practices that one is confronted with and, then, the introduction of a deeper and more recursive racism that manifests as a rule. I wish to claim that the frames of "minimization" and "culture" belong to the former—the "representational/rhetorical" category—whereas "naturalization" and "abstract liberalism" belong to the latter, or the "recursive/rule-based" category.

Organizing the frames into categories will allow me to address the materialist basis for colorblindness as well as the representational aspects (in greater detail later), specifically, the ways that colorblindness is connected to institutional logic and organizational frameworks and, at the same time, the analytical aspects pertaining to how colorblindness works for and against individuals in specific contexts. I think that the synthesis between colorblind ideology, structural Marxism, and the result, aporetic governmentality, will help to demonstrate why colorblindness not only persists but predominates despite the availability of other discursive frameworks both affirmative and negative. The predominance of "colorblindness" and (as I theorize) its materialist basis extend our understanding, specifically, of the interrelation between ideology and contemporary racism, whereby ideology has a materialist basis.

Abstract liberalism falls into the category of "recursive/rule-based." It uses ideas associated with political liberalism and economic liberalism to explain racial matters. The economic and state-based shift over to liberalism persists through to today. Neoliberalism brings its own "specifications" or "intensifications" of liberalism, but it would certainly be safe to claim that the "staying power" of liberalism has something to do with the way it is both embedded in the common sense of economic and social life (e.g., increases in quality of life, primarily, through education and occupational advancement) as well as its institutional supports through both state and civil society. Bonilla-Silva states, "Equal opportunity is part of abstract liberalism—or—regarding each person as an individual with choices.... This claim requires *ignoring the multiple institutional and state-sponsored practices behind segregation, and being unconcerned about these practices' negative consequences*" (2013: 28, emphasis mine). Part of the reason that abstract liberalism works as an orienting frame is, precisely, that it conceals the state's investment in racist practices. Facts would weaken the value system that propounds individuality and choices as the great leveler of difference in contemporary society. Therefore, more rules are required to support the abstract liberalist ideology.

Naturalization allows whites to explain away racial phenomena by suggesting they are "natural occurrences." To be specific, ideology is often propped up by recourse to a human nature (Haney-López 1996). Naturalization adds support or legitimacy to an ideology by suggesting that the values of a particular moment were, somehow, always timeless and were waiting to be selected by historical and economic processes. They rely on a common sense that is linked to "popular scientific concepts" or scientific language that links itself well to commonsense platitudes—both lend an immediate and strong legitimacy and authority. The rhetorical linkage to science makes this category recursive and rule-based. Bonilla-Silva states:

> Naturalization is a frame that allows whites to explain away racial phenomena by suggesting they are natural occurrences. For example—whites can claim "segregation" is natural because people from all backgrounds gravitate toward likeness. Although, the above statements can be interpreted as "racist" and as contradicting the colorblind logic—they are used to reinforce the myth of nonracialism. How? By suggesting these preferences are almost biologically driven and typical of all groups in society, preferences for primary associations with members of one's race are rationalized as nonracial because "they (racial minorities) do it too." (2013: 28)

Although naturalization often works to demonstrate a "human nature" shared, in kind, by "all races," it is always the case with racism that nature is used to support present-day *cultural values* as immutable and transhistorical. In this way, cultural racism serves an important representational and rhetorical function. The "flexibility" of culture as a concept (which may signify something communal, shared, and learned and, also, something generational, traditional, and ingrained) is mirrored or matched by a rhetorical flexibility. Resultantly, cultural racism serves an important function in the framing schema in that it can link itself and support or, if the situation calls for it, uncouple itself—by differentiating itself—from the naturalization frame.

The minimization of racism suggests discrimination is no longer a central factor affecting minorities' life choices. In this way, it comes the closest to colorblindness in that it serves as a justification for blindness in that it presumes the waning or absence of racism from social life or, conversely, that social progress is as inevitable as time. As Bonilla-Silva notes, "Minimization of racism is a frame that suggests discrimination is no longer a central factor affecting minorities' life chances ('It's better now than in the past' or 'There is discrimination, but there are plenty of jobs out there.') This frame allows whites to accept facts such as the racially motivated murder of

James Byrd Jr. in Jasper, TX" (2013: 29). The transition from "minimization" to an individual's colorblindness is a simple rhetorical move. Minimization of racism is "double-edged" in that it views events as singularities, consonant with abstract liberalism and the weighting of choices and personal responsibility in civil society, and never sees racist patterns, focusing, intensively, on the details of a single case. Denise Ferreira da Silva refers to these phenomena as "strategies of particularization" and ascribes them to the sciences of man and society as a way to categorize human beings. Da Silva also, in this regard, demonstrates how institutions that emerge alongside the modern nation-state order race and theories of race. Individual choices (to neither back down nor back away from abjection and dehumanization) and civil responsibility become "rules" of "racial behaviors"—that is, aggressiveness, antiauthoritarianism, and lawlessness—and are ascribed to everyone (da Silva 2007).

Individuation, then, comes down to responsibility and choice—making choices and living with the consequences. One chooses to respond to circumstances in myriad ways. In some cases, falling outside of society and becoming its target becomes a repercussion of a litany of poor choices; in other cases, it is a product of being in the wrong place at the wrong time. Regardless, abstract liberalism constitutes a lens in a larger schema of frames that reduces all other aspects of the frame to individual instances, thoughts, and choices. Once removed from institutional context—the instance, the choice—both the exercises or the practices of liberalism are dependent upon state and civil society. The former (state) is organized to promote the practice of the latter (civil society) as structural Marxists have demonstrated. If Bonilla-Silva gives us the contemporary framework through which racism connects to predominant ideologies and if the structural Marxist tradition connects Bonilla-Silva's work to a reproductive and consolidating schema, then Foucault demonstrates how power works to produce across individual bodies results that favor the social structure. Read against his own theories, he also explains why some bodies are used yet discarded, as I will discuss further in this chapter.

A Negative Approach: From Governmentality to Aporetic Governmentality

Between the publication, in French, of the first volume of *The History of Sexuality* (*La Volonté de Savoir* [1976]) and the lectures published under the title *Security, Territory, Population (1978)* and *The Birth of Biopolitics (1979)*, a shift in language from Foucault's "power" concepts (docility and discipline and, later, biopolitics) to "governmentality" occurs. This shift marks the work of the late Foucault, what Jan Rehmann refers to as the late Foucault and Foucauldian "governmentality-studies" (2013, see also [Lemke 2002] for a similar perspective). The continuity of the concept of power in Foucault's work and how and why it changes over the course of his research is of interest, in part, because Foucault's project is firmly situated within a broad modernism consonant with sociology's interest (as an entire discipline) in explaining and describing society. It is also interesting because Foucault arguably demonstrates that power is grounded in collective social sites *for certain kinds of people only*—whether formal-institutional or quasi-institutional but informal. Foucault's paradigm (both archaeologically and genealogically) manifests both *historically* and *institutionally*; it manifests through identities, occupations, roles, substantive lived practices, and so forth (even in antiquity, for example: the Catholic Church and the confessional in Foucault's discussion of sexuality, and his discussion of the "pastoral" as it pertains to both Christianity and Islamic and Arabic cultures in the framework of governmentality). It never manifests in an explicitly racial way.

As both Rehmann (2013) and Lemke (2002) note, Foucault's concept of governmentality is positioned through a genealogical method or "periodized" beginning with Ancient Greece and moving through the Christian and "Oriental" concept of the pastorate into the sixteenth century, the Reformation, and Counter-Reformation, then to the process of moving away from sovereignty toward the nation-state in the eighteenth century and to Foucault's present: early neoliberalism.[8] In every case, Foucault seeks to demonstrate that in antiquity, the antecedents for governmentality were prevalent, understood as forms of leadership, guidance, and as relational, individuating, and invasive (Foucault 1997; Rehmann 2014: 305–307). The antecedents to political governance in the framework of modernity (e.g., nation-states, rationalized forms of industrial labor) included either a shared concept of conduct or an explicit institutional framework linked to a church (that exercised pastoral forms of power). Rehmann describes this work as " 'a line of force' that traverses the history of the West and leads to the preeminence of 'government' over all other types of power" (2014: 306).

Governmentality, however, enjoys some level of complicity, presumptively, with both liberalism and neoliberalism. Recently, it has been discovered that Foucault was more than merely fascinated with neoliberalism;

he believed, strongly, in its potential for a less-qualified human freedom. Zamora states:

> Foucault was highly attracted to economic liberalism: he saw in it the possibility of a form of governmentality that was much less normative and authoritarian than the socialist and communist left, which he saw as totally obsolete. He especially saw in neoliberalism a "much less bureaucratic" and "much less disciplinarian" form of politics than that offered by the postwar welfare state. He seemed to imagine a neoliberalism that wouldn't project its anthropological models on the individual, that would offer individuals greater autonomy vis-à-vis the state. (Zamora 2014)

A significant effect of this new attempt at imagining the mechanics of power resulted in two moves. The first was away from techniques of applying power to the body "retail" to guiding forms of conduct, in society, such that power coordinated and directed a range of already existing and intelligible conducts (the conduct of conduct) while, potentially, opening itself up to new forms of conduct for the sake of extending (while not having to directly manage) the range of governmentality (Foucault 1975). Lemke notes:

> Governmentality is introduced by Foucault to study the "autonomous" individual's capacity for self-control and how this is linked to forms of political rule and economic exploitation. In this regard, Foucault's interest in processes of subjectivation does not signal that he abandons the problematics of power but, on the contrary, displays a continuation and correction of his older work. . . . The concept of power is not abandoned but the object of a radical "theoretical shift." Foucault corrects the findings of the earlier studies in which he investigated subjectivity primarily with a view to "docile bodies" and had too strongly stressed processes of discipline. Now the notion of government is used to investigate the relations between technologies of the self and technologies of domination. (Lemke 2002: 52)

In other words, governmentality depended more staunchly on the subject's autonomy. "Technologies" (derived from techne) parallel the craft of the self in relationship to statecraft. According to Foucault, the practice of self-conduct appears across history and has a vast functional range. In so many ways, institutions and practices—the arrangement put forward in structural Marxism (which allows for a more robust degree of analytical specification—see Rehmann [2014] for a critique) is collapsed in governmentality—institutions and practices are internalized in such a way that individual conduct is immediately subject to strategies for conducting the conduct of others. Consonant with neoliberalism, institutional interventions, whether public or private, become internalized as pathways to a better self. Self-improvement (techne) is linked to technologies of domination. New forms of autonomy are prey to technologies of domination such that the recognition of new conduct is, at the same time, its incorporation into governmentality. It is here that Foucault's definition of domination allows for the introduction of aporetic governmentality. Foucault states, "We must distinguish the relationships of power as strategic games between liberties—... that some people try to determine the conduct of others—and ... domination, which ... we ordinarily call power. And ... between the games of power and the states of domination, you have governmental technologies" (1987: 30).

This definition indicates a limit to Foucault's understanding of domination. Domination cannot reside outside of either traditional Western practices that were transmitted through (simultaneous and differentiated) institutional sites, customs and traditions, and practices that were indispensable and functional (the vast array of practices that constitute pastoralism across traditions) or modern institutional frameworks, which constituted and constructed the modern subject and extended their grasp through the governmental coordination of forms of private conduct. For Foucault, domination is the limitation of the space of freedom in a severely narrow way. The following example is telling. Foucault describes domination thusly:

> If there are relations of power throughout every social field it is because there is freedom everywhere. *Now there are effectively states of domination.* In many cases the relations of power are fixed in such a way that they are perpetually asymmetrical and *the margin of liberty is extremely limited. To take an example, very paradigmatic to be sure: in the traditional conjugal relation in the society of the eighteenth and nineteenth centuries,* we cannot say that there was only male power; the woman herself could do a lot of things: be unfaithful to him, extract money from him, refuse him sexually. She was, however, subject to a state of domination. (Foucault 1984: 123, my emphasis)

The example matters, and it is not referring to the Atlantic slave trade. How might one describe those subjected to settler colonialism, colonial administration, antebellum slavery, Jim Crow, or apartheid—all dependent upon interlocking institutional arrangements and all absent entirely from the paradigm of power and domination? Practices of racial domination, "the crude ones," were often focused on bodies, but not on subjects. Racial domination was conducted wholesale and not retail on bodies that contained no distinction in the humanist tradition because they were a mass—they were not human and, thusly, distinct from one another in no way. These institutional arrangements did not seek to develop a subject that might experience autonomy through power but, in fact, experienced domination in its most direct, destructive, and widespread facets. These institutional arrangements and practices are invisible to the West, to its institutional arrangements and to its practices of governance, even when domination was the predominant practice. Slavery, to be sure, was present in and beyond the antebellum period in the Southern United States; *it was coexistent with traditional conjugal relations in the eighteenth and nineteenth centuries,* but it is absent from Foucault's reduction of freedom to domination to marginal autonomy. It was not visible. The "legal subjects" of slavery were slaves and not people—laborers, wives, and citizens. Neither property nor rights were at issue. What then do we call racial domination? Where does it reside in the institutional history of the West? How does racial domination and its inverted or absent institutional history—when we speak of and theorize power and domination—relate to contemporary ideologies of colorblindness?

Conclusion

Grounding colorblind ideology in institutions raises exclusive difficulties. It is my contention that the concept of aporetic governmentality exposes and addresses these difficulties, making sense of the constellation of contemporary racism. As it concerns race in the United States, there simply is "no ground" to go to. New forms of "racial talk" and the ideology of abstract liberalism are meant to ensure this lack of ground. However, Marxism demonstrates a broad variety of theories of ideology from the instrumental to the historically organic. In each instance, institutions intensively shape values, behaviors, relationships, and roles through the connection between ideas and social action. The affirmative presence of race as values, behaviors, practices, and relationships is absent. This valorizes colorblindness, but the institutional absence has a deeper and far more nefarious historical and theoretical basis. The inversion of institutional histories and content—whereby black people and others (either persistently or at different points and periods across history) are racialized as an aporetic, if abject, aspect of institutional practices that persist today.

Today, education—the most affirmative of state institutions—has become an aporetic and abject space for black children, especially girls.

> The disproportionate arrest rate for black students in Delaware is consistent with the proportion of black-student involvement in suspensions and expulsions: black students in Delaware composed 52 percent of those suspended and 51 percent of those expelled during the 2009–2010 school year. This finding is also consistent with the proportion of black youth in the juvenile justice system generally. Black youth accounted for 58 percent of juveniles arrested in Delaware between September 2010 and June 2011, while only making up 25 percent of the juvenile population. Just as in schools, black juveniles across the state were three-and-a-half times more likely to be arrested than white juveniles. (Wolf 2013: 77)

And, specifically, regarding black girls:

> Black females were *more than twice as likely* to face arrest for fighting in school than their white male counterparts. This was the case even though black females and white males reported fighting in school at similar rates.... The school arrests data from Delaware not only confirms concerns that *harsh disciplinary practices disproportionately affect minority youth*, it indicates that female students (and black female students in particular) receive *differential treatment under strict disciplinary regimes*. (Wolf 2013: 79, emphasis mine)

The view toward abjection is rendered visible, here, if not entirely clear. How difficult would it be to imagine the pipeline from school to prison simply, in such a way, that a young black girl goes to school, defends herself, and winds up, shortly thereafter, in solitary confinement? How did she go to a state of qualified freedom to unfreedom so rapidly? Is she a "subject"? What is her margin of freedom like? What is her historical and institutional relationship to her ancestors like? And, finally, how have our theories of power and domination entirely occluded the possibility—rendered it entirely aporetic—to imagine the blindness toward race beyond the conduct of others, beyond framing meanings, but, most significantly, beyond state-based institutions that purport a logic of means, rights, protections, and—eventually—equality, liberty, and justice for everyone?

Finally, here, we can locate a piece of the puzzle to see the aporetic operations of racism and governmentality. Today, when the highest representatives of the US government remain silent as fascists and white supremacists march on Charlottesville, Virginia, bearing torches, inciting violence, killing demonstrators, chanting, "Jews will not replace us! You will not replace us!," *The most ancient and violent forms of racist practice can manifest with tacit governmental sanction just like acts of public collective violence prior to the civil rights movement.* Institutional silences in the face of the most base and collective forms of racist practice (that borrow from a historical moment we, supposedly, all believed was a part of the past and best left forgotten) actually work to ally these racist practices with the state. When we literally see police kill black people and watch the juridical justification of their actions, when we hear a discourse around protocol and police procedures serve as the means for these justifications, the state directly and officially sanctions the most base and violent racist practices. These silences and discourses of racial violence framed through police proceduralism and the reification of proper practices persistently mask a deep repressive pit of racial violence that more than merely threatens to return. In short, practices and institutions become aligned in new ways that the emergence of the concept of institutionality has begun to map out through its investigation into the rearrangement of the intersections of neoliberalism, structural racism, history, and subjectivity, which occur through new forms of administration, new procedures, and moralizing practices (Melamed 2011, 2016). Institutionality has begun to demonstrate how the incorporation of rhetorical tropes and discursive frameworks, like colorblindness, reproduces racism at structural levels with broader ramifications for specifying and distinguishing the administration of racist practices in contemporary contexts (Aho 2017).

Culture and Tactics represents a theoretical inquiry into the tactical practices pointed toward the economic, social, cultural, and racial self-determination of people represented through the struggles of social and political movements. I have focused on antisystemic movements that have tried to configure, imagine, and establish—through their political communities, their praxiological focus on developing consciousness and subjectivity, their organization building, their theorizing about movement activity in relation to the broader society, their strategies, and, most importantly, tactics—a fundamentally more just world. A world of economic justice and social justice consisting of a vast terrain of expressive cultures and communities, in short, a world reordered. Tactics represent courageous and collective points of intervention into a world that we already participate in, a world that could make good on delivering its democratic promises since it is we who can and must make those deliveries and we who receive the goods. We deliver this world unto ourselves. This is the promise of democracy and it need not be an idealism. Tactics transform our orientation toward this world and make another one possible. Struggles to eradicate the class structure and stamp out every vestige of racial domination, however hopeless this may seem to some at times, lead us toward a better horizon no matter how difficult, hazardous, and, at times, disconsolate the trajectory may seem. In fact, these public struggles against what often seem to be insurmountable odds demonstrate that the persistent presence of groups of committed activists is the only thing that changes the world and, indeed, is the only thing that ever will.

NOTES

Introduction

1. In the introduction to a recently published book of Hall's work *The Fateful Triangle: Race, Ethnicity, and Nation* (2017), which includes published portions of talks drawn from the W. E. B. Du Bois lectures that Hall gave at Harvard University in 1994, Kobena Mercer points out that the concept of articulation—which remains central to "the relational mode in which Hall has always conceptualized race, ethnicity, and nation" (to which I would also add class) is actually an approach that comes from his earlier sociological texts (Hall 2017: 8). So what I, here, and others have identified as an important cultural studies approach to race was, for Hall, the introduction of a concept into the sociological study, particularly a theory that captured the dynamics of race.

2. Tellingly, Sherry B. Ortner (1984) reintroduces the concept of cultural practices into the lexicon of anthropological and cultural theory as a realm of collective action that, at a minimum, expresses the desire for activities that escape the orbit of structuration. Consonant with more contemporary insights into the role of practice in contemporary cultural theory, expressly the "impulses to move these disciplines beyond current problematic dualisms and ways of thinking," where "practices at once underlie subjects and objects . . . and illuminate the conditions of intelligibility" (Schatzki 2001: 10). Ortner explicitly takes up the role of tactics in the framework of cultural practices when she states: "From a tactical point of view, actors seek particular gains whereas from a developmental point of view, actors are seen as involved in relatively far-reaching transformations of their states of being— of their relationships with things, persons, and self. We may say, in the spirit

of Gramsci that action in a developmental or 'projects' perspective is more a matter of 'becoming' than of 'getting' (1957). Intrinsic to this latter perspective is the sense of motive and action as shaped not only by problems being solved and gains being sought, but by images and ideals of what constitutes goodness—in people, in relationships, and in conditions of life" (Ortner 1984: 152). *Culture and Tactics* takes a different perspective on Gramsci; it marries, in Ortner's theoretical framework, the tactical and the cultural-developmental through the concept of tactical practices as both expressions of free activity and attempts to solve problems and seek gains by *implanting or concretizing* the images and ideals that constitute goodness—in people, in relationships, and in conditions of life—into society through political struggle. In short, culture, through tactical action, brings, in Ortner's words: the images and ideals of what constitutes goodness into society by making images and ideals concrete with the frameworks of democratic institutions and processes or, in short, politics. The chapters that follow demonstrate that for Gramsci, tactics are the means of any "developmental" point of view that concerns "far-reaching transformations."

3. The concept of articulation is both central to the foundation of contemporary cultural studies and continues to be so largely due to Stuart Hall's development of the concept across his work. In "Race, Articulation, and Societies Structured in Dominance" (1980), an article I use extensively across the beginning of the fourth chapter of this book, Hall intimates the efforts that go into establishing a structure within which to produce articulation. He states: The unity formed by this combination or articulation is always, necessarily, a 'complex structure': a structure in which things are related, as much through their differences as through their similarities. This requires that the mechanisms which connect dissimilar features must be shown—since no 'necessary correspondence' or expressive homology can be assumed as given. It also means—since the combination is a structure (an articulated combination) and not a random association—that there will be structured relations between its parts . . ." (Hall 1980: 325). Compare with note 5 in this chapter on Edward Said's interpretation of Gramsci's concept of elaboration.

4. In "On Postmodernism and Articulation: An Interview with Stuart Hall" (1986b), Hall makes a point that is central to the concept of articulation and that can be interpreted as the strategic reliance on context to produce relationships. The point also might be interpreted to suggest that politics and tactical action drives the possibility to produce mobilizations where they may not have existed in prior contexts. He states that "the form of the connection . . . can make a unity of two different elements, under certain

conditions. It is a linkage which is not necessary, determined, absolute and essential for all time. You have to ask, under what circumstances can a connection be forged or made? The so-called 'unity' ... is really the articulation of different, distinct elements which can be rearticulated in different ways because they have no necessary 'belongingness.' The 'unity' which matters is a linkage between the articulated discourse and the social forces with which it can, under certain historical conditions, but need not necessarily, be connected" (Hall 1986b: 53). For the purposes of the argument in this book, to understand the unity that matters, in Hall's words, is to pursue the substantive and political aspects of the historical conditions that give rise, precisely, to the necessary instances where the connection between articulated discourse and social forces produce the bases for transformation in the framework of class exploitation and racial oppression and domination, a political reading of the concept of articulation that drives the project of subaltern groups' seizure of social power. Said, in note 5, in this chapter, provides a more acute political reading of this linkage.

5. Where the concept of articulation can be interpreted in strategic and political contexts, Edward Said reads Gramsci's use of the word "elaboration" as the means by which culture is deployed in the political field and, also, the prefigurative possibilities of culture as politics. Or, rather, Said views the role of politics in producing trajectories for culture where the latter remains a distinctive yet relational sphere of human activity. In *The World, the Text, and the Critic* (1983) Said defines elaboration, from Gramsci's work, as both the process of establishing a perspective and, also, the process of "working" a perspective "into" a vehicle for political mobilization. Said states: "By elaboration Gramsci means two seemingly contradictory things. First, to elaborate means to refine, to work out (*e-laborare*) some prior or more powerful idea, to perpetuate a world view. Second, to elaborate means something more qualitatively positive, the proposition that culture itself or thought or art is a highly complex and quasi-autonomous extension of political reality and, given the extraordinary importance attached by Gramsci to intellectuals, culture, and philosophy, it has a density, complexity, and historical-semantic value that is so strong as to make politics possible. Elaboration is the ensemble of patterns making it feasible for society to maintain itself" (Said 1983: 170–171). The two notes on articulation immediately preceding this one lend a substantive critical-cultural dimension to the perspective taken on tactics in this book.

1. Jameson's deeper point, which follows, is consonant with my larger point about Gramsci, knowledge, and tactics. In footnote 74 on page 97 of *The Political Unconscious*, Jameson discusses Ernst Bloch's analysis of Marx's dialectical method as "nonsychronism." In this description, Jameson indicates what is distinct in Marxist epistemologies: from particularities to abstraction and the transcendence of abstraction by using thought to intervene in capitalism; the instances of contradiction originating in the capitalist mode of production. This note should be compared to Buci-Glucksmann's "gnoseology of politics," which is discussed later in this chapter and, also, Peter Thomas's insights about Gramsci's thought. The comparison between the levels of reality, also discussed later in the chapter, and this footnote from *The Political Unconscious* is quite clear.

2. The term "articulation" should be compared with Stuart Hall's use of the term. See chapter 4 "Agile Materialisms."

3. These fields also contain radical expressions of these positions and are self-critical. Most recently, Coulthard (2014) argues that in the framework of the history of indigenous relations to the Canadian state, demands for mutual recognition fail as a decolonial strategy. Bracey (2015) similarly argues that black movements in the United States face extraordinary roadblocks when it comes to access to the state and polity and that liberalist and pluralist strategies have run their course. Also, the "standpoint epistemology" strategy in feminist theory (see note 4 in this chapter) and some early radical feminist approaches from the "second wave" stretch the bounds of identitarian approaches.

4. The "standpoint epistemology" tradition in feminist thought demonstrates this argument well. The question of liberation (specifically from scientific practice and scientific justifications of forms of patriarchal domination) requires an opposing standpoint: thought and approach. It requires an "oppositional consciousness," communal expression of political subjectivity, a decisive narrowing of the political field, and directing the political field toward specific challenges or approaches. The internal critique is significant, too, whereby internal challenges to "knowing" radicalized women's subjectivities into different standpoint epistemologies, sometimes stark with an expressed focus on the relationship between structures and knowledge as it pertained to ethnicity, sexuality, disability, class, religion, and age. See, especially, Hartsock (1983), Haraway (1983), Harding (1993), Hennessey (1993), Stacey (1997), Collins (1997).

5. Timothy Brennan's contribution goes beyond the framework of the argument in this chapter. Brennan is an astute Gramsci scholar in his own right. His article, "Antonio Gramsci and Postcolonial Theory: 'Southernism' " (2001) is an early and important intervention in postcolonial theory and subaltern studies interpretations of Gramsci (along with Green [2002]). In *Wars of Position* Brennan introduces a concept he calls "The Organizational Imagination." Briefly, and in the context of his appearance here, Brennan states: "Partaking of this imaginary means 'finding a rational solution in human practice and in the comprehension of this practice.' To invoke organization is to do more than talk about a division between the abstract and the concrete, or between theory and practice as we are typically used to hearing about it. Entailed by the division is rather a series of binary conflicts in which binarism itself is resituated centrally in logic and in action" (Brennan 2006: 150). Brennan points out that the framework of an organizational imaginary requires that tactical interventions, political acts, and their relevance depend upon recognizing that political activity is not always easily or comfortably reconcilable with theoretically developed truths or broadly pluralistic principles. To avoid what he calls a logic of "sophistry" or "left barbarism," Brennan states that "being involved in politics means taking responsibility, assuming the conviction that running from power does not absolve one from power's outcomes. . . . *The collective subject of politics is never all-inclusive.* One fights on behalf of some, not all—even at the expense of others. One's principles are always unevenly applied which is all the more reason to *pick them carefully and argue them openly*" (2006: 151, emphasis mine). Brennan's position on politics finds its prerequisite in dissensus, debate, and, fundamentally, the need to approach politics tactically. Not merely consonant with my argument here, but Brennan's position is similar to Jodi Dean's (2015) injunction that politics requires a division.

6. Egan's concern with regard to tactics, and the distinction between strategy and tactics, diverge from my analysis in *Culture and Tactics.* Regardless, it is important to mention that in this passage from *The Dialectic of Position and Maneuver: Understanding Gramsci's Military Metaphor* (2018), Egan is actually making a larger point about how this very contemporary dynamic lacks a "political agent" that can unify "specific struggles in an operational way over time and space into a viable strategic challenge" (88). He further notes that theorizing this contemporary dynamic marks the limit to Gramsci's insights as it pertains to his military metaphor for the strategy and tactics of revolutionary political organizations. I explore a similar claim made by Adam David Morton in his book *Unravelling Gramsci: Hegemony and*

Passive Revolution in the Global Political Economy (2007) in chapter 3 of this book. Egan's concern here also echoes a broad contemporary problematic that has come to the attention of left-revolutionary intellectuals in the contemporary strategic conjuncture.

7. See also Bracey (2016) for a critique of the approach to social movement analysis of black movements.

8. On important contemporary insights about the role of political subjectivity in the framework of contemporary protest events and movements, see Dean (2016). For insights pertaining to the history of political subjectivity in Marxist thought, Rehmann (2013) is incomparable.

9. Gramsci addresses this issue, albeit more abstractly, in Notebook 13, §17 (1971: 181) in "the relations of political forces."

10. This model of subjection/subjectivization becomes more complex in Gramsci's work and in contemporary political thought as I demonstrate later. Hardt and Negri's "multitude" and Negri's reading of Spinoza allow for a model of "becoming subject" that is similar, in some ways, to the construction I am leading into. The power of the multitude, in Hardt and Negri, is a becoming through power. See Rehmann (2013): "When Michael Hardt and Antonio Negri describe the 'power of the multitude' in terms of its 'becoming subject,' they refer to the Latin verb *posse*—'power as a verb, as activity,' part of the Renaissance triad 'esse-nosse-posse,' being-knowing-having power, and expressing 'what a body and what a mind can do' " (242).

11. See Notebook 11, §12 (Gramsci 1971: 340–341) for a discussion of the relationship between thought, will, collectivity, and constraint.

12. The complexity of this type of theoretical work that deals with dynamics that uncover and assemble dynamics of racial power has stretch the boundaries of theories of race. Most recently, Christina Sharpe's (2016) and Denise Ferreira da Silva's (2007) work represent powerful analyses that materialize and imagine the dynamic constellations of material constraints and what lies beyond them. Sharpe unifies materiality and theory through a figuration of wake, ship, and hold to determine a framework of extraordinary constraint from which possibilities for subjectivities and conscious expression of important experience emerge. Da Silva captures the logic of that figuration in a broad and sustained theory of the interrelation of racialization and space at the global level; in this context new inquiry and racial articulations become possible. Both redirect while strengthening and deepening our understanding of the materiality of the reality and the limitations of real and symbolic expressions of racial violence. These issues are explored through my concept of aporetic governmentality in the last chapter of this book.

13. See, especially the introduction; "Edward Said Talks to Jacqueline Rose," and "Edward W. Said and the American Public Sphere: Speaking Truth to Power," by Rashid I. Khalidi.

14. This point is repeated in chapter 2, "Ideological Contention."

15. For an explicit discussion of democratic and organic centralism, see chapter 3.

16. This detached authoritarian dynamic is dramatized somewhat in the style of Franz Kafka's *The Castle* in the work of Victor Serge. See especially *Midnight in the Century* ([1933] 2014) for an example of the party operating through authoritarian closure upon its rank and file, and intellectuals, in the expressive contexts of morality, culture, and conduct. In this same context, *What Everyone Should Know About State Repression* ([1926] 1979) identifies, empirically, a part of the mechanisms required to produce authoritarian closure.

17. Translated as "command structure" in *Selections from the Prison Notebooks*, the following note is included: "*Organica* has no exact equivalent in English—it means the organization of armed forces, their division into different arms and corps, their system of ranks, etc." (Notebook 13, §2; Gramsci 1971: 176, note 76). I define the term differently or more closely to what the translators describe as its full meaning since it is significant in this context.

18. The war of position is most closely associated with the issue of strategy and tactics in Gramsci's work. I have chosen to focus more broadly on political organization, external and internal forces that affect that organization, the "sorting out" of forces through analytical frames pointing to different passages from different notebooks. It is important to notice that recent work on Gramsci begun in Thomas (2009, 2013) and taken up by Egan (2014, 2015, 2016) has zeroed in on the importance of the concept "war of position" in Gramsci's work. The war of position is most closely associated with political strategy in the late nineteenth and, especially, early twentieth century where civil society is more strongly developed (the trench/fortification metaphor signaling the difficulty of revolution). Egan (2014) points out that as the relationship between war of position/maneuver becomes collapsed (in Gramsci), the logic of the metaphor (important conceptual and logical distinctions) is better specified in the work of "contemporaries": Engels, Lenin, and Trotsky. He describes the relationship between strategy and tactics in the framework of the war of position/maneuver thusly: "In the past, strategy was defined by the war of movement, with war of position relegated to tactical uses such as siege warfare. By the late nineteenth century,

however, the relative status of these had switched; war of position had become strategic, and war of movement had become more tactical" (2014: 523).

19. Ben Fontana's work on Gramsci is authoritative, especially in political science and political theory—(including comparative and international approaches) but, most importantly, his work on Gramsci and Machiavelli is incomparable. Criticisms of his work are limited. Mansfield (1995–1996) and Blair (1995) come down on different sides with regard to Fontana's engagement with broader issues in political theory. Blair argues that an effective reading of the relationship between Gramsci and Machiavelli allows for an intervention into normative political theory where Mansfield argues that Fontana effectively counters Golding's (1992) claim that Gramsci's positioning of the working class is essentialist and teleological (an old "orthodox" or "vulgar" anti-Marxist materialist charge) in multiple ways. According to Mansfield, however, Fontana misses the opportunity to point out the differences in Gramsci's and Machiavelli's projects, whereby the former was concerned with advancing a historical materialist analysis and revolutionary socialism and, of course, the latter was concerned with the role of "the prince" in a world that was modernizing the framework through which power and authority are exercised. In my view (and Mansfield agrees) these issues are outside the scope of the book. More fundamentally, I think that Fontana's goal of intervening in normative political theory is most laudable.

20. Gramsci defines the "organic intellectual" thusly: "Every social group, coming into existence on the original terrain of an essential function in the world of economic production, creates together with itself, organically, one or more strata of intellectuals" (Notebook 12, §1; 1971: 5). This includes workers whose level of technical development, general intellect, experience with labor rationalization, and discipline are a part of the essential function in the world of economic production. The issue of elaborating a group of intellectuals within these occupational strata linked, fundamentally and organically, to the economic-organizational structure is political and societal within the framework of the hegemonic group (class).

21. One of the limitations of the factory councils was that they attempted to maneuver via the factory system, which is connected, most closely, to refractory reality and is affected by the variables that Gramsci notes, in detail, in Notebook 13. For details on the theory of the councils in the framework of "industrial democracy" and the potentials and pitfalls that Gramsci perceived at the conjuncture under discussion in this chapter, see Darrow Schecter, *Gramsci and the Theory of Industrial Democracy*.

22. Althusser's footnote in *For Marx* (1969), in part 3, "Contradiction and Overdetermination," where Althusser discusses praxis, the development of political consciousness, and the role of economic determinism in over-determination from Gramsci's work, which signals a complex dynamic of fatalism/faith in opposition to the development of praxis.

23. For an important discussion of the relationship between tactics, ethics, and the role of revolutionary political activity in the framework of a robust legal-national framework (where the notion of "ethics" takes on a very specific meaning), see Georg Lukács, "Tactics and Ethics" and " 'Intellectual Workers' and the Problem of Intellectual Leadership,' " in *Tactics and Ethics: Political Essays, 1919–1929.*

24. This passage is where Thomas establishes the departure point for the inquiry that frames his book; one of the most important books on Gramsci in decades. Thomas's inquiry has a strong relationship to what Buci-Glucksmann is posing as a "gnosis."

25. Alessandro Carlucci's book provides an example that helps anchor the argument posed in this chapter. The significance of Carlucci's contri-bution cannot be understated: Carlucci's original contribution to Gramsci goes beyond language; it is an incomparable contemporary work on Gramsci; it will be of continued importance to Gramsci scholars and, also, will serve to change Gramsci's reception within the general theoretical frameworks where his work had been adopted.

Chapter 2

1. As described in my introduction, the case study that focuses on the strategic conjuncture in and around a specific organizational and mobili-zation effort is a "limited-depth case study" (Mills, Durepos, and Wiebe 2010). It was carefully selected to illustrate the historical context within which I develop a new theory, ideological contention, and it is strengthened by the critical review of several other theoretical perspectives on ideology in social movements (Eckstein 1992). The case study consists of Antonio Gramsci's (1995b) 1926 essay, "Some Aspects of the Southern Question," and secondary literature on Gramsci's essay. It includes other historical material on race and pseudoscience in Europe, the development of race as a category in Italy in relationship to Italian political ideology to demon-strate both the scope of the theoretical perspective of ideological contention and the variables that both this theoretical perspective, and the book as a

whole, are attempting to work through (Brennan 2001; Carley 2013; Foot 1997; Ghosh 2001; Gould 1993; Gramsci [1926] 1995b; Gramsci 1971, 1977; Green 2002; Green 2011; Green 2013; Green and Ives 2009; Haas 2008; Hall 1986a; Heatherington 2010; Sassoon 1987; Lombroso 1876; Moe 2002; Niceforo 1897; Pick 1989; Portelli 2003; Reiter and Mitchell 2010; Rosengarten 2009; Schneider 1998; Stauder 1993; Urbinati 1998a; Verdicchio 1995; Zene 2011. The case study in this chapter, based off of a primary document, is theoretically directed, uses multiple secondary sources, and is broadly situated with other research to provide a depth of context consistent with the framework of a limited-depth case study approach. Mills, Durepos, and Wiebe note that limited-depth cases "draw upon existing analytical accounts of key social processes to illuminate key features of the case even when . . . not directly accessible using limited-depth methods. On these bases it is possible to envisage that limited-depth but theoretically directed case studies could sometimes meet the criteria for effective case study research" (2010: 531–532). Also consistent with other examples of limited-depth cases, this study "present(s) documentation of events, quotes, samples and artifacts" (Wilson 1979: 448) "to illustrate an idea, to explain the process of development over time . . . to explore uncharted issues . . . and to pose provocative questions" (Reinharz 1992: 167). An obvious problem with the limited-depth case study approach is that it "makes it more difficult . . . to declare the results applicable to . . . similar cases" (Verschuren and Doorewaard 2005: 170).

2. I explore the political and ideological heterogeneity of peasants and workers in the south of Italy and Gramsci's specific positions on this further in the fourth chapter, "Agile Materialisms."

3. Snow et al. 1986; Snow and Benford 1988; Snow and Benford 1992; Benford 1997; Benford and Snow 2000; Benford and Snow 2000; Snow and Corrigall-Brown 2005; Snow and Byrd 2007; Snow 2004, 2008.

4. Platt and Williams 1997; Williams 1999; Oliver and Johnston 2000a, 2000b; Zald 2000a, 2000b; Platt and Williams 2002.

5. Westby 2002; Snow 2004; Snow and Byrd 2007.

6. Entman 2003; Carragee and Roefs 2004; Reese 2007.

7. Williams and Blackburn 1996; Zald 2000a, 2000b; Westby 2002.

8. Freeman 1972; Williams and Blackburn 1996; Miller 1999; Platt and Williams 1999; Williams 1999; Zald 2000a, 2000b; Platt and Williams 2002.

9. For example, Mooney and Hunt 1994; Johnston 1995; Mooney 1995; Carroll and Ratner 1996; Noonan 1997; Westby 2002.

10. For example, see also Williams and Blackburn (1996) and Platt and Williams (1999), where they distinguish between "operative ideology" and higher-order ideology, which is more abstract, formulaic, and recursive.

11. Hosseini (2010) uses the phrase "field of ideological contention." He relates it to collective action in a movement organization. Hosseini distinguishes between deliberative and strategic actions. He defines "field of ideological contention" as "a constellation of relatively autonomous 'open spaces' constructed through 'intersubjective' actions among different movement actors with diverse and even contending orientations in confronting commonly experienced structural changes" (2010: 46). In my conception, ideological contention is neither based upon a field construction nor, more fundamentally, can it be autonomous but, rather, is integrated into a persistent process where political action, political community, political subjectivity (also, collective memory), organizational structure, and ideology are interrelated and reproduced in a context of political and social forces.

12. Brennan 2001: 158; Green 2002, 2011: 395, 2013; Zene 2010; Carley 2013; Carley 2016.

13. Patriarca 1996, 1998; Schneider 1998; Moe 2002; Rosengarten 2009; Green 2013.

14. For more on frame alignment, see Snow et al. 1986; Snow and Benford 1988; Gamson, Fireman, and Rytina 1982; and Westby 2002.

15. Coles 2001; Van den Brink, Kuipers, and Lagendijk 2005; Myers 2008; Tombari 2010.

Chapter 3

1. Oliver and Johnston 2000a, 2000b; Zald 2000a, 2000b; Westby 2002; Gillan 2008; Carley 2016.

2. The discussion of the relationship between the concept of ideology and frames—which mobilize ideas—in the social movement studies literature is vast. In part, it encompasses the relationship between culture and political organization (Freeman 1972; Miller 1999; Platt and Williams 1997; Platt and Williams 2002; Williams 1999; Williams and Blackburn 1996; Zald 2000a, 2000b); the interrelation of ideas, beliefs, and values (Oliver and Johnston 2000a, 2000b); the elaboration of movement strategies (Westby 2002); and how standpoints have different empirical effects on movement messages, strategies, and organization (e.g., Carroll and Ratner 1997; Johnston 1995; Mooney 1995; Mooney and Hunt 1994; Noonan 1997; Westby 2002). One

important note should also be made here. In a debate between Pamela Oliver, Hank Johnston, David Snow, and Robert Benford in the pages of the journal *Mobilization*, Oliver and Johnston (2000a, 2000b) point out that key analytical categories in the frame perspective are derived from Wilson's decomposition of ideology. This detail about Wilson is also noted in Gillan (2008). In the service of the debate, Oliver and Johnston make this point to affirm their supposition that framing masquerades as a theory of social movement ideology. What I would like to point out is that one way of viewing the issue of ideology in social movement studies is that it gets revisited repeatedly and addressed repeatedly through the literature on framing and not through literatures on ideology that fall outside of this subdisciplinary area of inquiry.

3. PIT is, in German, *Projekt Ideologietheorie* or "Project Ideology Theory."

4. Very recently, Marxist theorists have drawn upon robust analytical perspectives that are specifically focused upon concepts that complicate the constraints and possibilities that exist between "structure" and "agency" in the framework of social movement studies (Feenberg 2015).

5. The approach that Rehmann develops in *Theories of Ideology* is reflected in combination with and through other theoretical schools that have little relationship to Marx's thought. Rehmann also works to combine Michel Foucault's later work on "governmentality" and "biopolitics" with his Marxist lens on ideology theory, influenced most substantively by Wolfgang Fritz Haug and the PIT group. Briefly, *Theories of Ideology* (2013) provides a critical discussion of the approaches that have been developed by Marx and Engels and extended by Lenin, Lukács, members of the Frankfurt School (to Habermas), Gramsci, Althusser and the Althusser School (especially Pêcheux), the Post-Marxists (especially, Stuart Hall, Ernesto Laclau, and Chantal Mouffe), Foucault, Bourdieu, and—most importantly in this context—W. F. Haug and PIT.

6. Snow et al. 1986; Snow and Benford 1988; Snow and Benford 1992; Benford 1997; Benford and Snow 2000; Snow and Corrigall-Brown 2005; Snow and Byrd 2007; Snow 2004, 2008.

7. Johnston and Klandermans 1995; Swidler 1995; Johnston 1995; Foran 1997.

8. Tarrow 1992; Zald 1996; Oliver and Johnston 2000a, 2000b; Platt and Williams 2002. For Platt and Williams (2002) ideologies are operative, or operate culturally, as both a structural as well as a structuring component of a SMO. In a context where the authors describe segregation's "moral reality" as a posture of sorts that needed to be represented in and related to

forms of conduct, and reflected in the organizational frameworks through which segregation was both maintained and communicated, they draw a distinction between an "operative ideology" and higher-order ideology, reflective of their moral reality, that is more abstract, formulaic, and recursive—this latter category is closer to the notion that ideology is a repository of cultural resources.

9. Entman 2003; Carragee and Roefs 2004; Reese 2007.

10. Williams and Blackburn 1996; Zald 2000a, 2000b; Westby 2002.

11. Freeman 1972; Williams and Blackburn 1996; Miller 1999; Platt and Williams 1997; Williams 1999; Zald 2000a, 2000b; Platt and Williams 2002.

12. See also, for example, Mooney and Hunt 1994; Johnston 1995; Mooney 1995; Carroll and Ratner 1997; Noonan 1997; Westby 2002.

13. For example, Mark Zuckerberg and the advent of the social network application (which has both an organizational and functional basis and catalyzed technologies, techniques, and products into a societal context) is organic to combined conditional aspects—civil and social, technological and cultural, educative and occupational, and so forth—that add up to the quality and expectations of life in the present. These categories raise issues for industry and governance that Zuckerberg and others of his ilk are uniquely suited to solve as organic intellectuals. Zuckerberg is necessary and sufficient to the contexts in and to which they "contributed" to the state and to civil society.

14. Cammett 1967; Williams 1975; Karabel 1976. See also Gramsci's "The Revolution against Capital," "Worker's Democracy," "First: Renew the Party," "The Factory Council," "Unions and Councils," and "The Turin Factory Councils Movement" (Gramsci 1977).

15. This might also suggest that the variable that requires theoretical explanation is ideology itself. Such a theory would require the belief that ideology and organizations are intertwined, such that they affect one another as well as the belief that SMOs are sui generis and require theorization (that as an organizational type something can be learned about organizations in general by theorizing SMO ideology specifically). It is possible to both adjust the role of ideology in the framing perspective and theorize social movement ideology because, in the latter case, as a dependent variable it can add something to our understanding of social movements.

1. A review of Stuart Hall's work shows a concerted focus on excavating theories and methodological guidelines from Marx and Marxism. After an extensive view of Hall's early work, I contend that his volume with Peter Walton, *Situating Marx* (Walton and Hall 1972), is the first collective attempt to work out, specifically, the insights in Marx's *Grundrisse*. In 1974 Hall writes his first essay about using the *Grundrisse* as a methodological tool for cultural studies. I think that Stuart Hall's conception of historical materialism includes Gramsci's theory of hegemony and Marx's categories of abstract and concrete, as well as his notion of *differentia specifica*. In all, I would say that the most significant impact Marxism has on Hall's work is between the early 1970s (possibly earlier than 1972) through to the early 1990s in "Cultural Studies and Its Theoretical Legacies" (1992a). It is arguable, however, that the Marxist materialist focus begins to wane in the mid to late 1980s. See also, Rojek (2003).

2. To the extent that "The Southern Question" is the first Marxist document in the modern era that specifically deals with race as a political issue, this was one of the significant political problems of Gramsci's time and, specifically, a strategic problem for the Communist Party.

3. As McKee (1993) points out, there are the possible exceptions to certain anthropological conceptions of race.

4. See Walton and Hall (1972). This book demonstrates that Hall's involvement with Marx's *Grundrisse* in the early 1970s was across multiple scholarly communities that raised different questions. It reflects more the sociological aspects of the cultural and structural Marxist positions of the time than it does British cultural studies in particular.

5. Hall's perspective here can be connected to the discussion of Buci-Glucksmann's "gnoseology of politics" in the first chapter.

6. For support of this claim, see John Holloway and Sol Picciotto's *State and Capital: A Marxist Debate* (1978); for the original source, see Evgeny Pashukanis's *The General Theory of Law and Marxism* ([1924] 2003).

7. Susan Thistle made a similar point in her historical study of the gendered division of labor in the United States as it intersects with race, specifically that of white and black women: "While in urban areas a far greater percentage of African American married women of color worked for pay than white women, it is important to recognize this was not a turn to 'free wage labor' as in the present but a stalled straddling of two economies" (Thistle 2000: 278). In point of fact, gendered and racialized urban labor in the

United States and in the North depended, at least until World War II, and possibly afterward, on this "informal" labor market that was fundamentally rooted in the US antebellum period.

8. Secondary sources on racial and criminological discourses issuing from the positivist school in Italy provide needed historical context to establish the extent to which Gramsci's contemporaneous claims regarding race are both counterdiscursive and a precursor to cultural and constructivist perspectives on race and difference.

9. The method of selection required an investigation of Gramsci's published essays and personal correspondences. I selected excerpts that help illuminate the relationship between the first and second parts of this chapter. There are other linkages that can be drawn depending on the question posed. For example, one could link Frantz Fanon's work on race, colonialism, and national culture ("On National Culture") in *The Wretched of the Earth* (1964) to the section "The Intellectuals: The Formation of the Intellectuals" in *Selections from the Prison Notebooks* (1971). A comparative analysis of these texts could result in a richer theory of the relationship between the formation of intellectuals in the context of shifting social forces (expressly the shift from industrialization to modernization, during the cold war period, in the "third" or "underdeveloped" world) across the early part of the twentieth century. This, however, exceeds the scope of this chapter.

10. Gramsci was charged under article 184 of the newly enacted Single Text of Laws on Public Security, and he was sentenced to five years of internment (see Gramsci 2010a: 86).

11. In his correspondences with Tania, Gramsci refers to himself as of Albanian origin. To him, there is a discrete national-cultural mapping exceeding the Italian discourse of race and criminology.

12. A study of the Concordance Tables (compiled in Gramsci 1995a: 476–506) demonstrates how extensively Gramsci dealt with the topic of Catholicism. I am interested first in the position that "Catholicism" occupies in the discourse under discussion as well as Gramsci's discussion of Catholicism and its conception of "modernization" through politics, which I will discuss further in this chapter. Also, the editors of the 1971 edition of Gramsci's notebooks state that the section I quote later in this chapter is the most "editorially manipulated" by the original Einaudi editorial group. I have tried to compare the occurrence of these passages to the 1995 edition, *Antonio Gramsci: Further Selections from the Prison Notebooks* (Gramsci 1995a), and also to Joseph A. Buttigieg's new three-volume edition (Gramsci 2010a).

13. See, for example, Giuseppe Mazzini's "To the Italian Working Man" in his *The Duties of Man*, where Mazzini's explains what it means to participate in a unified Italian democratic nation-state. It follows the logic that I describe here.

14. Gramsci anticipates many of the most successful arguments that link oppression, identity, and political economy to modernity—in the case of gender and feminism, see Susan Thistle (2000).

15. "The Socialist Party gave its blessing to all the 'southernist' literature of the clique of writers of the so-called positivist school, such as Ferri, Sergi, Niceforo, Orano" (Gramsci [1926] 1995b: 20–21). The sentence that this footnote is connected to describes Gramsci's awareness of the ramifications of the work of the Positivist school. In fact, it was very possible that Gramsci was all too aware. Alfredo Niceforo, student of Enrico Ferri, wrote a book, *Crime in Sardinia*, which was published when Gramsci was six years old. It refuted an older study in which Cesare Lombroso, the prolific leader of this school of thought, stated that Sardinia was the only part of the South free of violent crime. Niceforo stated that Sardinia was the most violent and he listed statistical evidence. What is worse, this school popularly believed that a (male) criminal was arrested in his evolutionary development. The outward signs of this took the form of "atavisms" or physical deformities, dark skin being an "atavism" of sorts. Gramsci was a dark-skinned (he speaks of his complexion in his letters) Sardinian, extremely short, and hunchbacked.

16. Not much of consequence has been published on Gramsci's youth. Much of the work that discusses Gramsci's youth is either conducted through journalistic research and describes details of a physically painful childhood experienced in a context of poverty, or it poses careful speculation about the relationship between Gramsci's childhood and his life in journalism and politics (see Fiori [1971] and Cammett [1967], respectively). Some work attempts to interpret the relationship between Gramsci's childhood, youth, and politics based through his own perspective: a totalizing or hermeneutic-style approach (Urbinati 1998a, 1998b).

17. For an interesting catalog of this ideology and its intellectuals, see Gibson (1998). Gramsci, in a passage directly following the preceding quotation, names all of the intellectuals featured in this article.

18. Gramsci's discussion of the Brigata Sassari includes an encounter between an industrial worker from Sardinia and a member of the Sassari Brigade. This encounter dramatizes, in some detail, the type of interaction I refer to here (Gramsci [1926] 1995b: 26).

19. For data on the composition of the strikers and a history of the strike, see Spriano (1975, 1979), Procacci (1989), and Corner and Procacci (1997).

Chapter 5

1. Indigenous people in the United States experience higher rates of police death. According to the Lakota People's Law Project "Native Lives Matter" report (2015), although Native Americans represent 0.8 percent of the population, they constitute 1.9 percent of all police killings. I think that aporetic governmentality may apply in the case of indigenous peoples and settler colonialism.

2. William's encounters with Gramsci as well as his ongoing dialogue with E. P. Thompson on class assisted in producing the perspective quoted earlier. See, also, Painter (2010), especially chapter 6, for an apt illustration of Williams's concept in the context of pseudoscientific practice.

3. For a cultural theory that describes the phenomena of old practices repeating or becoming refashioned for "new times" as well as the emergence of "new practices," see Williams's categories of "residual, dominant, and emergent" (1977).

4. Césaire [1955] 2000; Fanon 1964; Cabral [1970] 1992; Rodney 1976.

5. Gramsci 1971, 1995a; Althusser 1971; Poulantzas 1973a, 1973b, 1975, 1978; Jessop 1982.

6. Darren Wilson's grand jury testimony in Ferguson, Missouri, actually renders Michael Brown a demon—to the point of death. Brown is possessed with demonic strength. When Wilson kills him, Wilson gives no indication that he felt he killed another human person. Rather, what leaves Michael Brown is aggression (not life). Wilson recounts the following events thusly. First, after a shot rang out, not hitting Michael Brown, rather than surrender, Brown turned into a monster: "The only way I can describe it, it looks like a demon, that's how angry he looked." Wilson states that while he was firing bullets into Michael Brown's body, "it looked like he was almost bulking up to run through the shots, like it was making him mad that I'm shooting at him. And the face that he had was looking straight through me, like I wasn't even there, I wasn't even anything in his way. . . . I saw the last one go into him. And then when it went into him, the demeanor on his face went blank, the aggression was gone, it was gone" (Cave 2014). Michael Brown is not described as human—this goes toward Wilson's legitimation for his actions.

Consider, in this context, how civil and state institutions in the United States organized African people. Slaves were, categorically, beyond exploitation (not variable capital). *At best*, they were reduced to a "start-up cost" and lived lives of "overhead." They didn't enjoy participation in the category of "historically variable minimum" and, when acquired like a machine part and replaceable like one, even a "rate of exploitation" is not available to the slave. They may not be exploited but, rather, worked to death. Slavery, as a practice, was both fundamentally modern and antihuman. However, slavery broke human bodies down and it legally defined them as property, as *alienable* from rights.

7. Gramsci 1971; Althusser 1971; Poulantzas 1973a, 1973b, 1975, 1978; Jessop 1982.

8. Foucault 1997: 67; Lemke 2002: 50; Rehmann 2014: 306–307; Zamora and Behrent 2015.

REFERENCES

Adamson, Walter L. 1983. *Hegemony and Revolution: A Study of Antonio Gramsci's Political and Cultural Theory*. Berkeley: University of California Press.

Aho, Tanja. 2017. "Neoliberalism, Racial Capitalism, and Liberal Democracy: Challenging an Emergent Critical Analytic." *Lateral* 6.1: http://csalateral.org/issue/6-1/forum-alt-humanities-institutionality-neoliberalism-racial-capitalism-aho/.

Althusser, Louis. 1969. "Contradiction and Overdetermination." Pp. 117–128 in *For Marx*. New York: Pantheon Books.

Althusser, Louis. 1971. "Ideology and Ideological State Apparatuses." Pp. 127–186 in *Lenin and Philosophy and Other Essays*. New York: Monthly Review Press.

Andersen, Rick. 1999. "Violence Works: The Thrashers Set the Tone, the City Follows." *Seattle Weekly*, December 2. Retrieved December 9, 2017 (http://www.seattleweekly.com).

Augelli, Enrico, and Murphy, Craig. 1988. *America's Quest for Supremacy and the Third World: A Gramscian Analysis*. London: Pinter.

Bacchi, Umberto, Ludovica Iaccino, and Gianluca Mezzofiore. 2015. "Milan Expo 2015: Violent May Day Protests at No Expo Anti-Capitalist Demonstration." *International Business Times*, May 1. Retrieved November 15, 2018 (http://www.ibtimes.co.uk/milan-expo-2015-violent-may-day-protests-no-expo-anti-capitalist-demonstration-1499334).

Barker, Chris, and Emma A. Jane. 2016. *Cultural Studies: Theory and Practice*. 5th edition. Los Angeles: Sage.

Benford, Robert D. 1997 "An Insider's Critique of the Social Movement Framing Perspective." *Sociological Inquiry* 67:409-430.

Benford, Robert D., and David A. Snow. 2000. "Framing Processes and Social Movements: An Overview and Assessment." *Annual Review of Sociology* 26: 611–639.

Biebricher, Thomas, and Robin Celikates. 2012. "Saying 'We' Again: A Conversation with Jodi Dean on Democracy, Occupy and Communism." *Krisis 2*. Accessed online July 1, 2016 (http://criticall egalthinking.com/2012/11/06/saying-we-again-a-conversation-with-j odi-dean-on-democracy-occupy-and-communism/).

Boggs, Carl. 1984. *The Two Revolutions: Antonio Gramsci and the Dilemmas of Western Marxism*. Boston: South End Press.

Bonilla-Silva, Eduardo. 2013. *Racism without Racists: Color-Blind Racism and the Persistence of Racial Inequality in the United States*. 4th edition. Lanham: Rowman & Littlefield.

Bonilla-Silva, Eduardo, and Tyrone Forman. 2000. " 'I'm Not a Racist but …' Mapping White College Students' Racial Ideology in the U.S.A." *Discourse and Society* 11: 53–85. Borg, Carmel, Joseph A. Buttigieg, and Peter Mayo (eds.). 2002. *Gramsci and Education*. Lanham: Rowman & Littlefield.

Bourdieu, Pierre. 1989. "Social Space and Symbolic Power." *Sociological Theory* 7: 14–25.

Bové, Paul A. (ed.) 2000. *Edward Said and the Work of the Critic: Speaking Truth to Power*. Durham: Duke University Press.

Bracey, Glenn E., II. 2015. "Toward a Critical Race Theory of State." *Critical Sociology* 41: 553–572.

Bracey, Glenn E., II. 2016. "Black Movements Need Black Theorizing: Exposing Implicit Whiteness in Political Process Theory." *Sociological Focus* 49: 11–25.

Brennan, Timothy. 2001. "Antonio Gramsci and Postcolonial Theory: 'Southernism.' " *Diaspora* 10: 143–87.

Brennan, Timothy. 2006. *Wars of Position: The Cultural Politics of Left and Right*. New York: Columbia University Press.

Blair, Brook M. 1995. "Hegemony and Power: On the Relation between Gramsci and Machiavelli by Benedetto Fontana (Review)." *Millennium: Journal of International Studies* 24: 145–146.

Buci-Glucksmann, Christine. 1980. *Gramsci and the State*. Translated by David Fernbach. London: Lawrence and Wishart.

Burawoy, Michael. 1989. "Two Methods in Search of Science: Skocpol versus Trotsky." *Theory and Society* 18: 759–805.

Buttigieg, Joseph A. 1990. "Gramsci's Method." *boundary 2* 17: 60–81.

Buttigieg, Joseph A. 2010. Introduction. Pp. 1–64 in Antonio Gramsci, *Prison Notebooks*, 3 vols., edited by Joseph A. Buttigieg. New York: Columbia University Press.

Byrne, Ciara. 2010. "G20 Police Move Aggressively against Protests, One Day after Chaos in Toronto." *The Canadian Press*, AM 1150. June 27. Retrieved December 9, 2017 (https://www.metro.us/news/g20-p olice-move-aggressively-against-protests-one-day-after-chaos-in-toronto/ tmWjfB—25PtulzXhaUtw).

Cabral, Amilcar. [1970] 1992. "National Liberation Culture." Pp. 53–65 in *Colonial Discourse and Postcolonial Theory: A Reader*, edited by Patrick Williams and Laura Chrisman. New York: Columbia University Press.

Caceres, Mario. 1986. "The Organic Functions of Factory Councils According to the Gramscian Conception and Their Homology with the Historical Block Theory." *Recherches sociologiques* 17: 247–264.

Cammett, John McKay. 1967. *Antonio Gramsci and the Origins of Italian Communism*. Stanford: Stanford University Press.

Carley, Robert. 2013. "Agile Materialisms: Antonio Gramsci, Stuart Hall, Racialization, and Modernity." *Journal of Historical Sociology* 26: 413–441.

Carley, Robert F. 2016. "Ideological Contention: Antonio Gramsci and the Connection between Race and Social Movement Mobilization in Early Twentieth-Century Italy." *Sociological Focus* 49: 28–43.

Carley, Robert F. 2019a. "A Materialist and Standpoint Critique of Social Movements' Theoretical Presumptions." *Theory in Action* 12: 86–111.

Carley, Robert F. 2019b. *Autonomy, Refusal, and the Black Bloc: Positioning Class Analysis in Critical and Radical Theory*. London: Rowman & Littlefield International.

Carlucci, Alessandro. 2015. *Gramsci and Languages: Unification, Diversity, Hegemony*. Chicago: Haymarket.

Carragee, Kevin M., and Winn Roefs. 2004. "The Neglect of Power in Recent Framing Research." *Journal of Communication* 54: 214–233.

Carroll, William K., and Robert S. Ratner. 1996. "Master Frames and Counter-Hegemony: Political Sensibilities in Contemporary Social Movements." *The Canadian Review of Sociology and Anthropology* 33: 407–435.

Cave, Damien. 2014. "Officer Darren Wilson's Grand Jury Testimony in Ferguson, Mo., Shooting." *nytimes.com*, November 25. Retrieved April

26, 2016 (http://www.nytimes.com/interactive/2014/11/25/us/da rren-wilson-testimony-ferguson-shooting.html).

Césaire, Aimé. [1955] 2000. *Discourse on Colonialism.* Translated by Joan Pinkham. New York: Monthly Review Press.

Chibber, Vivek. 2006. *Locked in Place: State Building and Late Industrialization in India.* Princeton: Princeton University Press.

Cimino, Guido, and Renato Foschi. 2014. "Northerners versus Southerners: Italian Anthropology and Psychology Faced with the 'Southern Question.'" *History of Psychology* 17: 282–295.

Coles, Roberta L. 2001. "Building the Clinton Legacy through Frame Alignment." *Cultural Studies/Critical Methodologies* 1: 459–448.

Collins, Patricia Hill. 1997. "Comment on Hekman's 'Truth and Method: Feminist Standpoint Theory Revisited': Where's the Power?" *Signs* 22: 375–381.

Corner, Paul, and Giovanna Procacci. 1997. "The Italian Experience of 'Total' Mobilization, 1915–1920." Pp. 223–240 in *State, Society, and Mobilization during the First World War,* edited by John Horne. Cambridge: Cambridge University Press.

Cotta, Maurizio, and Luca Verzichelli. 2007. *Political Institutions in Italy.* Cambridge: Oxford University Press.

Coulthard, Glen Sean. 2014. *Red Skin, White Masks: Critiquing the Colonial Politics of Recognition.* Minneapolis: University of Minnesota Press.

Crehan, Kate. 2016. *Gramsci's Common Sense: Inequality and Its Narratives.* Durham: Duke University Press.

Cress, Daniel M., and David Snow. 2000. "The Outcomes of Homeless Mobilization: The Influence of Organization, Disruption, Political Mediation, and Framing." *The American Journal of Sociology* 105: 1063–1104.

da Silva, Denise Ferreira. 2007. *Toward a Global Idea of Race.* Minneapolis: University of Minnesota Press.

Dahbour, Omar, and Micheline R. Ishay. 1995. *The Nationalism Reader.* Atlantic Highlands: Humanities Press.

Davidson, Alistair. 1977. *Antonio Gramsci: Towards an Intellectual Biography.* London: Merlin Press.

Dean, Jodi. 2014. "Response: The Question of Organization." *South Atlantic Quarterly* 113: 821–835.

Dean, Jodi. 2015. "The Party and Communist Solidarity." *Rethinking Marxism* 27: 332–342.

Dean, Jodi. 2016. *Crowds and Parties.* New York: Verso.

Derrida, Jacques. 1976. *Of Grammatology*. Translated by Gayatri Chakravorty Spivak. Baltimore: Johns Hopkins University Press.

Derrida, Jacques, 1980. *The Post Card: From Socrates to Freud and Beyond*. Translated by Alan Bass. Chicago: University of Chicago Press.

Derrida, Jacques. 1982. "Différance." Pp. 1–28 in *Margins of Philosophy*, translated by Alan Bass. Chicago: University of Chicago Press.

Diani, Mario. 2000. "The Relational Deficit of Ideologically Structured Action." *Mobilization* 5: 17–24.

Douglas-Bowers, Devon. 2014. Unmasking the Black Bloc: Who They Are, What They Do, How They Work." *Occupy.com*, December 18. Retrieved December 7, 2017 (http://www.occupy.com/article/unmasking-black-bloc-who-they-are-what-they-do-how-they-work#sthash.J6MnX2Ei.dpbs).

Dupuis-Déri, Francis. 2013. *Who's Afraid of the Black Blocs? Anarchy in Action Around the World*. Toronto: Between the Lines.

Durr, Marlese. 2015. "What Is the Difference between Slave Patrols and Modern Day Policing? Institutional Violence in a Community of Color." *Critical Sociology* 41: 873–879.

Dussel, Enrique. 1998. "Beyond Eurocentrism." Pp. 3–31 in *The Cultures of Globalization*, edited by Fredric Jameson and Masao Miyoshi. Durham: Duke University Press.

Eckstein, Harry. 1992. *Regarding Politics: Essays on Political Theory, Stability, and Change*. Berkeley: University of California Press.

Egan, Daniel. 2014. "Rethinking War of Maneuver / War of Position: Gramsci and the Military Metaphor." *Critical Sociology* 40: 521–538.

Egan, Daniel. 2015. "Insurrection and Gramsci's 'War of Position.' " *Socialism & Democracy* 29: 102–124.

Egan, Daniel. 2016. "Gramsci's War of Position as Siege Warfare: Some Lessons from History." *Critique: Journal of Socialist Theory* 44: 435–450.

Egan, Daniel. 2018. *The Dialectic of Position and Maneuver: Understanding Gramsci's Military Metaphor*. Chicago: Haymarket Books.

Engels, Frederick. [1845] 1996. *Ludwig Feuerbach and the Outcome of Classical German Philosophy*. New York: International Publishers.

Ennis, James G. 1987. "Fields of Action: Structure in Movements' Tactical Repertoires." *Sociological Forum* 2: 520–533.

Entman, Robert. 2003. "Cascading Activation: Contesting the White House's Frame after 9/11." *Political Communication* 20: 415–432.

Escobar, Arturo. 1994. *Encountering Development: The Making and Unmaking of the Third World*. Princeton: Princeton University Press.

Evans, Peter. 1995. *Embedded Autonomy: States and Industrial Transformation*. Princeton: Princeton University Press.

Fanon, Frantz. 1964. *The Wretched of the Earth*. Translated by Constance Farrington. Middlesex: Penguin.

Feenberg, Andrew. 2015. "Lukács's Theory of Reification and Contemporary Social Movements." *Rethinking Marxism* 27: 490–507.

Felice, Franco de. 1982. "The Factory Councils." Pp. 200–210 in *Approaches to Gramsci*, edited by Anne Showstack Sassoon. London: Writers and Readers.

Ferguson, Roderick A. 2012. *The Reorder of Things: The University and Its Pedagogies of Minority Difference*. Minneapolis: University of Minnesota Press.

Fernandez, Luis A. 2008. *Policing Dissent: Social Control and the Anti-Globalization Movement*. New Brunswick: Rutgers University Press.

Fiori, Giuseppe. 1971. *Antonio Gramsci: Life of a Revolutionary*. New York: Dutton.

Fontana, Benedetto. 1993. *Hegemony and Power: On the Relation between Gramsci and Machiavelli*. Minneapolis: University of Minnesota Press.

Foot, John M. 1996. "Socialist-Catholic Alliances and Gender: Work, War, and the Family in Milan and Lombardy, 1914–1921." *Social History* 21: 37–53.

Foot, John M. 1997. " 'White Bolsheviks?' The Catholic Left and the Socialists in Italy, 1919–1920." *The Historical Journal* 40: 415–433.

Foran, John. 1997. "Discourses and Social Forces: The Role of Culture and Cultural Studies in Understanding Revolutions." Pp. 203–226 in *Theorizing Revolutions*, edited by John Foran. London: Routledge.

Foucault, Michel. 1975. *Discipline and Punish: The Birth of the Prison*. New York: Vintage Books.

Foucault, Michel. 1978. *The Birth of Biopolitics: Lectures at the College de France 1977–1978*. London: Palgrave Macmillan.

Foucault, Michel. 1987. "The Ethic of Care for the Self as a Practice of Freedom: An Interview with Michel Foucault on January 20, 1984." *Philosophy and Social Criticism* 12: 112–131.

Foucault, Michel. [1976] 1990. *The History of Sexuality, Vol. 1: An Introduction*. Translated by Robert Hurley. New York: Vintage.

Foucault, Michel. 1997. "Security, Territory, and Population." Pp. 67–71 in *Michel Foucault, Ethics: Subjectivity, and Truth*, edited by Paul Rabinow. New York: The New Press.

Foucault, Michel. [1979] 2000. "Governmentality." Pp. 201–222 in *Power: Essential Works of Foucault, 1954–1984*, edited by James D. Faubion. New York: The New Press.

Freeman, Jo. 1972. "The Tyranny of Structurelessness." *Berkeley Journal of Sociology* 17: 151–165.

Galanaki, Maria. 1986. Gramsci's Concept of Proletarian Hegemony: Political and Philosophical Roots (Graduate Thesis). McGill University, Montreal, Quebec.

Gamson, William A. 1975. *The Strategy of Social Protest*. Homewood: Dorsey.

Gamson, William A., Bruce Fireman, and Steven Rytina. 1982. *Encounters with Unjust Authority*. Homewood: Dorsey.

Geertz, Clifford. 1973. "The Impact of the Concept of Culture on the Concept of Man." Pp. 33–54 in *The Interpretation of Cultures*. New York: Basic Books.

Ghosh, Peter. 2001. "Gramscian Hegemony: An Absolutely Historicist Approach." *History of European Ideas* 27: 1–43.

Gibson, Mary. 1998. "Biology or Environment? Race and Southern 'Deviancy' in the Writings of Italian Criminologists, 1880–1920." Pp. 99–116 in *Italy's "Southern Question": Orientalism in One Country*, edited by Jane Schneider. Oxford: Berg.

Gillan, Kevin. 2008. "Understanding Meaning in Movements: A Hermeneutic Approach to Frames and Ideologies." *Social Movement Studies* 7: 247–263.

Goffman, Erving. 1974. *Frame Analysis: An Essay on the Organization of Experience*. London: Harper & Row.

Goldberg, David Theo 2002. "Racial States." Pp. 233–258 in David Theo Goldberg and John Solomos, *A Companion to Racial and Ethnic Studies*. Oxford: Blackwell.

Golding, Sue. 1992. *Gramsci's Democratic Theory*. Toronto: University of Toronto Press.

Gould, Stephen Jay. 1993. "American Polygeny and Craniometry before Darwin: Blacks and Indians as Separate, Inferior Species." Pp. 84–115 in *The "Racial" Economy of Science*, edited by Sandra Harding. Bloomington: Indiana University Press.

Gramsci, Antonio. 1949. *Note sul Machiavelli sulla Politica e sullo Stato Moderno*. Turin: Einaudi.

Gramsci, Antonio. 1951 "Passato e Presente." In *Opere di Antonio Gramsci*, Volume 7. Turin: Einaudi.

Gramsci, Antonio. 1971. *Selections from the Prison Notebooks*. Edited by

David Forgacs and Geoffrey Nowell Smith. London: Lawrence and Wishart.

Gramsci, Antonio. 1975. *Letters from Prison: Antonio Gramsci*. Translated by Lynne Lawner. New York: Harper & Row.

Gramsci, Antonio. 1977. *Selections from the Political Writings 1910–1920*. Edited by Quintin Hoare and Geoffrey Nowell Smith, translated by John Matthews. London, UK: Lawrence and Wishart.

Gramsci, Antonio. 1978. *Selections from the Political Writings 1921–1926*. Edited by Quintin Hoare and Geoffrey Nowell Smith, translated by John Matthews. London: Lawrence and Wishart.

Gramsci, Antonio. 1985. *Selections from Cultural Writings*. Edited by David Forgacs and Geoffrey Nowell Smith. Cambridge: Harvard University Press.

Gramsci, Antonio. 1995a. *Antonio Gramsci: Further Selections from the Prison Notebooks*. Translated and edited by Derek Boothman. Minneapolis: University of Minnesota Press.

Gramsci, Antonio. [1926] 1995b. *The Southern Question*. Translated by Pasquale Verdicchio. West Lafayette: Bordighera.

Gramsci, Antonio. 2010a. *Prison Notebooks, Volume 1*. Edited by Joseph A. Buttigieg. New York: Columbia University Press.

Gramsci, Antonio. 2010b. *Prison Notebooks, Volume 2*. Edited by Joseph A. Buttigieg. New York: Columbia University Press.

Gramsci, Antonio. 2010c. *Prison Notebooks, Volume 3*. Edited by Joseph A. Buttigieg. New York: Columbia University Press.

Green, Marcus. 2002. "Gramsci Cannot Speak: Presentations and Interpretations of Gramsci's Concept of the Subaltern." *Rethinking Marxism* 14: 1–24.

Green, Marcus E. 2011. "Rethinking the Subaltern and the Question of Censorship in Gramsci's Prison Notebooks." *Postcolonial Studies* 14: 387–404.

Green, Marcus E. 2013. "Race, Class, and Religion: Gramsci's Conception of Subalternity." Pp. 116–28 in *The Political Philosophies of Antonio Gramsci and B. R. Ambedkar: Itineraries of Dalits and Subalterns*, edited by Cosimo Zene. New York: Routledge.

Green, Marcus, and Peter Ives. 2009. "Subalternity and Language: Overcoming the Fragmentation of Common Sense." *Historical Materialism* 17: 3–30.

Haas, François. 2008. "German Science and Black Racism: Roots of the Nazi Holocaust." *The FASEB Journal* 22: 332–337.

Hallgrímsdóttir, Helga K. 2003. "Ideology and Frame: Understanding the Discursive Choices of the Knights of Labor and the Woman's Christian Temperance Union." Paper presented at the annual meeting of the American Sociological Association, Atlanta Hilton Hotel, Atlanta, GA.

Hall, Stuart. 1971. "Deviancy, Politics and the Media." *Stencilled Occasional Paper: Media Series* 11. University of Birmingham, UK: Centre for Contemporary Cultural Studies.

Hall, Stuart. 1978. "Pluralism, Race and Class in the Caribbean." Pp. 150–182 in *Race and Class in Postcolonial Society*, edited by UNESCO. Paris: UNESCO.

Hall, Stuart. 1980. "Race, Articulation, and Societies Structured in Dominance." Pp. 305–345 in *Sociological Theories: Race and Colonialism*, edited by UNESCO. Paris: UNESCO.

Hall, Stuart. 1986a. "Gramsci's Relevance for the Study of Race and Ethnicity." *Journal of Communication Inquiry* 10: 5–27.

Hall, Stuart. 1986b. "On Postmodernism and Articulation: An Interview with Stuart Hall," edited by Lawrence Grossberg. *Journal of Communication Inquiry* 10: 45–60.

Hall, Stuart. 1987. "Minimal Selves." Pp. 44–46 in *The Real Me: Post-Modernism and the Question of Identity (ICA Documents 6)*, edited by Lisa Appignanesi. London: Institute of Contemporary Arts.

Hall, Stuart. 1990. "The Emergence of Cultural Studies and the Crisis of the Humanities." *October* 53: 11–24.

Hall, Stuart. 1992a. "Cultural Studies and Its Theoretical Legacies." Pp. 277–294 in *Cultural Studies*, edited by Lawrence Grossberg, Cary Nelson, and Paula Treichler. New York: Routledge.

Hall, Stuart. 1992b. "New Ethnicities." Pp. 252–259 in *"Race," Culture, and Difference*, edited by James Donald and Ali Rattansi. London: Sage.

Hall, Stuart. [1974] 2003. "Marx's Notes on Method: A 'Reading' of the '1857 Introduction.'" *Cultural Studies* 17: 105–149.

Hall, Stuart. 2016. *Cultural Studies 1983: A Theoretical History*. Edited by Jennifer Daryl Slack and Lawrence Grossberg. Durham: Duke University Press.

Hall, Stuart. 2017. *The Fateful Triangle: Race, Ethnicity, Nation (the W. E. B. Du Bois Lectures)*. Edited by Kobena Mercer. Cambridge: Harvard University Press.

Hall, Stuart, and Les Back. 2009. "At Home and Not at Home: Stuart Hall in Conversation with Les Back." *Cultural Studies* 23: 658–687.

Hall, Stuart, Chas Critcher, Tony Jefferson, John Clarke, and Brian Roberts. 1978. *Policing the Crisis: Mugging, the State and Law and Order.* London: Macmillan.

Hamed, Hosseini, S. A. 2010. *Alternative Globalizations: An Integrative Approach to Studying Dissident Knowledge in the Global Justice Movement.* New York: Routledge.

Haney López, Ian. 1996. *White by Law: The Legal Construction of Race.* New York: New York University Press.

Haraway, Donna. 1983. "The Ironic Dream of a Common Language for Women in the Integrated Circuit: Science, Technology, and Socialist Feminism in the 1980s or a Socialist Feminist Manifesto for Cyborgs." *Das Argument,* Orwell 1984 (October). Retrieved March 21, 2017 (http://www.egs.edu/faculty/donna-haraway/articles/donna-haraway-the-ironic-dream-of-a-common-language-for-women-in-the-integrated-circuit/).

Harding, Sandra. 1993. "Rethinking Standpoint Epistemology: 'What Is Strong Objectivity'?" Pp. 49–82 in *Feminist Epistemologies*, edited by Linda Alcoff and Elizabeth Potter. New York: Routledge.

Hartsock, Nancy. 1983. "The Feminist Standpoint: Developing the Ground for a Specifically Feminist Historical Materialism." Pp. 283–310 in *Discovering Reality: Feminist Perspectives on Epistemology, Methodology, Metaphysics, and Philosophy of Science*, edited by Sandra Harding and Merrill B. Hintikka. Boston: D. Reidel.

Haug, Wolfgang Fritz. 1987. *Commodity Aesthetics, Ideology, and Culture.* New York: International General.

Heatherington, Tracey. 2010. *Wild Sardinia: Indigeneity and the Global Dream-Times of Environmentalism.* Seattle: University of Washington Press.

Hennessey, Rosemary. 1993. "Women's Lives/Feminist Knowledge: Feminist Standpoint as Ideology Critique." *Hypatia* 8: 14–34. Holloway, John, and Sol Picciotto (eds.). 1978. *State and Capital: A Marxist Debate.* London: Edward Arnold.

Horn, David. 1994. *Social Bodies: Science, Reproduction, and Italian Modernity.* Princeton: Princeton University Press.

Hosseini, S. A. Hamed. 2010. *Alternative Globalizations: An Integrative Approach to Studying Dissident Knowledge in the Global Justice Movement.* New York: Routledge.

Jackson, Shona. 2012. *Creole Indigeneity: Between Myth and Nation in the Caribbean.* Minneapolis: University of Minnesota Press.

Jameson, Fredric. 1971. "Metacommentary." *Publications of the Modern Language Association* 86: 9–18.

Jameson, Fredric. 1972. *The Prison-House of Language: A Critical Account of Structuralism and Russian Formalism.* Princeton: Princeton University Press.

Jameson, Fredric. 1974. *Marxism and Form.* Princeton: Princeton University Press.

Jameson, Fredric. 1981. *The Political Unconscious: Narrative as a Socially Symbolic Act.* Ithaca: Cornell University Press.

Jessop, Bob. 1980. "The Gramsci Debate." *Marxism Today.* February: 23–25.

Jessop, Bob. 1982. *The Capitalist State.* Oxford: Blackwell.

Johnston, Hank. 1995. "A Methodology for Frame Analysis: From Discourse to Cognitive Schema." Pp. 217–246 in *Social Movements and Culture,* edited by Hank Johnston and Bert Klandermans. Minneapolis: University of Minnesota Press.

Johnston, Hank. 2001. "Verification and Proof in Frame and Discourse Analysis." Pp. 62–91 in *Methods in Social Movement Research,* edited by Suzanne Staggengborg and Bert Klandermans. Minnesota: University of Minnesota Press.

Johnston, Hank, and Bert Klandermans. 1995. "The Cultural Analysis of Social Movements." Pp. 3–24 in *Social Movements and Culture,* edited by Hank Johnston and Bert Klandermans. Minneapolis: University of Minnesota Press.

Jung, Moon-Kie, João Costa Vargas, and Eduardo Bonilla-Silva. 2011. *State of White Supremacy: Racism, Governance, and the United States.* Stanford: Stanford University Press.

Karabel, Jerome. 1976. "Revolutionary Contradictions: Antonio Gramsci and the Problem of Intellectuals." *Politics and Society* 6: 123–172.

Katznelson, Ira. 2005. *When Affirmative Action Was White.* New York: W.W. Norton.

Kautsky, Karl. [1907] 2009. "Nationality and Internationality," translated by Ben Lewis. *Critique* 37: 371–389.Kendall, Diana. 2006. *Sociology in Our Times.* Belmont: Thomson Wadsworth.

Kettley, Sebastian. 2017. "Hamburg G20 Protests: What Is Antifa? Who Are the 'Welcome to Hell' Protestors?" *Daily Express,* July 9. Retrieved December 7, 2017 (https://www.express.co.uk/news/world/826336/Hamburg-g20-protests-what-is-Antifa-demonstrations-protestors-Welcome-to-Hell).

Klandermans, Bert. 2000. "Must We Redefine Social Movements as Ideologically Structured Action?" *Mobilization* 5: 25–30.

Koivisto, Juha, and Veikko Pietilä. 1996. "Ideological Powers and Resistance:

W. F. Haug and *Projekt Ideologie-Theorie.*" *Rethinking Marxism* 9: 40–59.

Lacan, Jacques. [1949] 2006. "The Mirror Stage as Formative of the Function of the I as Revealed in Psychoanalytic Experience." Pp. 75–81 in *Écrits*, translated by Bruce Fink, Heloise Fink, and Russell Grigg. London: W. W. Norton.

LaCapra, Dominick. 1982. ""The Political Unconscious: Narrative as a Socially Symbolic Act. by Fredric Jameson." *History and Theory* 21: 83–106.

Lakota People's Law Project. 2015. Native Lives Matter. Retrieved July 30, 2016 (http://lakotalaw.org/special-report/native-lives-matter).

Legaré, Anne. 1980. "Heures et Promesses d'un Debat: Les Analyses de Classes au Quebec (1960–1980)." *Cahiers du Socialisme* 5: 60–84.

Lemke, Thomas. 2002. "Foucault, Governmentality, and Critique." *Rethinking Marxism* 14: 49–64.

Lenin, Vladimir I. 1902. *What Is to Be Done? Burning Questions of Our Movement.* Retrieved July 20, 2015 (https://www.marxists.org/archive/lenin/works/1901/witbd/).

Lenin, Vladimir I. [1914] 1927. *The Right of Nations to Self-Determination.* Pp. 393–454 in *Collected Works of V. I. Lenin.* Vol. 20. New York: International Press.

Lenin, Vladimir I. 1964. "Revolutionary Adventurism." Pp. 186–207 in *Lenin Collected Works.* Vol. 6. Moscow: Progress Publishers.

Lombroso, C. 1876. *L'uomo delinquente (The Criminal Man).* Milan: Hoepli.

Lukács, George. 1972. *Tactics and Ethics: Political Essays, 1919–1929.* New York: Harper & Row.

Luxemburg, Rosa. 1909. "The Right of Nations to Self-Determination." *The National Question and Autonomy.* Retrieved December 7, 2015 (http://www.marxists.org/archive/luxemburg/1909/national-question/ch01.htm).

Mackey, Robert, Sergio Peçanha, Taylor Barnes, and Nadia Sussman. 2013. "Video of Clashes in Brazil Appears to Show Police Infiltrators among Protesters." *New York Times*, July 24. Retrieved December 2, 2017 (http://thelede.blogs.nytimes.com/2013/07/24/video-of-clashes-in-brazil-appears-to-show-police-infiltrators-among-the-protesters/).

Mannheim, Karl. [1926] 1997. *Ideology and Utopia: An Introduction to the Sociology of Knowledge.* New York: Routledge.

Mansfield, Steven R. 1995–1996. "Hegemony and Power: On the Relation

between Gramsci and Machiavelli by Benedetto Fontana (Review)."
Science and Society 59: 572–574.

Marcuse, Herbert. 1965. "Repressive Tolerance." Pp. 81–123 in *A Critique of Pure Tolerance*, edited by Robert Paul Wolff, Barrington Moore, and Herbert Marcuse. Boston: Beacon Press.

Marcuse, Herbert. 1970. *Five Lectures*. Translated by Jeremy Shapiro and Shierry Weber. Boston: Beacon Press.

Marcuse, Peter. 2016. "Occupying and Refusing Radically: The Deprived and the Dissatisfied Transforming the World." Pp. 66–82 in *The Great Refusal: Herbert Marcuse and Contemporary Social Movements*, edited by Peter N. Funke, Andy Lamas, Todd Wolfson. Philadelphia: Temple University Press.

Marx, Anthony. 1998. *Making Race and Nation: A Comparison of the United States, South Africa, and Brazil*. New York: Cambridge University Press.

Marx, Karl. 1859. "Preface to a Contribution to a Critique of Political Economy." Pp. 3–6 in *The Marx-Engels Reader*, edited by Robert C. Tucker. New York: W. W. Norton.

Marx, Karl. [1894] 1959. *Capital: A Critique of Political Economy: Volume 3– The Process of Capitalist Production as a Whole*. New York: International Publishers.

Marx, Karl. [1844] 1971. *The Economic and Philosophic Manuscripts of 1844*. New York: International Publishers.

Marx, Karl [1857] 1973. *Grundrisse: Foundations of the Critique of Political Economy (Rough Draft)*. Translated by M. Nicolaus. Harmondsworth: Penguin.

Marx, Karl. [1843] 1975. "Contribution to the Critique of Hegel's Philosophy of Law." Pp. 175–187 in *Karl Marx, Frederick Engels: Collected Works*. Vol. 3. New York: International Publishers.

Marx, Karl. [1846] 1975. "Letter from Marx to Pavel Vasilyevich Annenkov." P. 95 in Karl *Marx, Frederick Engels: Collected Works*. Vol. 38. New York: International Publishers.

Marx, Karl, and Friedrich Engels. [1845] 1960. *The German Ideology*. New York: International Publishers.

Mason, Paul. 2012. *Why It's Kicking Off Everywhere: The New Global Revolutions*. London: Verso.

Mazzini, Giuseppe. 1912. "The Duties of Man." Pp. 7–124 in *The Duties of Man and Other Essays*. London: J. P. Dent.

McAdam, Doug. 1982. *Political Process and the Development of Black Insurgency*. Chicago: University of Chicago Press.

McAdam, Doug. 1983. "Tactical Innovation and the Pace of Insurgency." *American Sociological Review* 48: 735–754.

McCarthy, John D., and Mayer N. Zald. 1977. "Resource Mobilization and Social Movements: A Partial Theory." *American Journal of Sociology* 82: 1212–1241.

McKee, James B. 1993. *Sociology and the Race Problem: The Failure of a Perspective.* Chicago: University of Illinois Press.

Melamed, Jodi. 2011. *Represent and Destroy: Rationalizing Violence in the New Racial Capitalism.* Minneapolis: University of Minnesota Press.

Melamed, Jodi. 2016. "Proceduralism, Predisposing, Poesis: Forms of Institutionality, in the Making." *Lateral* 5.1: http://csalateral.org/issue/5-1/forum-alt-humanities-institutionality-making-melamed/.

Miliband, Ralph. 1969. *The State in Capitalist Society: An Analysis of the Western System of Power.* New York: Basic Books.

Miller, Frederick D. 1999. "The End of SDS and the Emergence of Weatherman: Demise Through Success." Pp. 303–324 in *Waves of Protest Social Movements since the Sixties*, edited by Jo Freeman and Victoria Johnson. New York: Longman.Mills, Albert J., Gabrielle Durepos, and Elden Wiebe. 2010. *Encyclopedia of Case Study Research: L–Z.* Thousand Oaks: Sage.

Mills, Charles W. 1997. *The Racial Contract.* Ithaca: Cornell University Press.

Mills, Charles. 2011. "Liberalism and the Racial State." Pp. 27–46 in *State of White Supremacy: Racism, Governance, and the United States*, edited by Moon-Kie Jung, João H. Costa Vargas, and Eduardo Bonilla-Silva. Stanford: Stanford University Press.

Moe, Nelson. 2002. *The View from Vesuvius: Italian Culture and the Southern Question.* Berkeley: University of California Press.

Mooney, Patrick. 1995. *Farmers' and Farm Workers' Movements: Social Protest in American Agriculture.* New York: Twayne.

Mooney, Patrick H., and Scott A. Hunt. 1994. "A Repertoire of Interpretations: Master Frames Ideological Continuity in U.S. Agrarian Mobilization." *The Sociological Quarterly* 37: 177–197.

Morris, Aldon. 1981. "Black Southern Student Sit-In Movement: An Analysis of Internal Organization." *American Sociological Review* 46: 755–767.

Morton, Adam David. 2007. *Unravelling Gramsci: Hegemony and Passive Revolution in the Global Political Economy.* London: Pluto Press.

Moynihan, Colin. 2013. "A Black Bloc Emerges in Egypt." *New York Times*, January 25. Retrieved December 2, 2017 (https://thelede.blogs.nytimes.com/2013/01/25/a-black-bloc-emerges-in-egypt/).

Myers, Daniel. 2008. "Ally Identity: The Politically Gay." Pp. 167–189 in *Identity Work in Social Movements*, edited by Jo Reger, Daniel Myers and Rachel Einwohner. Minneapolis: University of Minnesota Press.

Niceforo, Alfredo. 1897. *La Delinquenza in Sardegna* (Crime in Sardinia). Palermo: Remo Sandron Editore.

Noonan, Rita K. 1997. "Women against the State: Political Opportunities and Collective Action Frames in Chile's Transition to Democracy." Pp. 252–267 in *Social Movements: Readings on Their Emergence, Mobilization, and Dynamics*, edited by Doug McAdam and David A. Snow. Los Angeles: Roxbury.

Oliver, Pamela, and Hank Johnston. 2000a. "What a Good Idea! Frames and Ideologies in Social Movement Research." *Mobilization* 5: 37–54.

Oliver, Pamela, and Hank Johnston. 2000b. "Reply to Snow and Benford: Breaking the Frame." *Mobilization* 5: 61–64.

Omi, Michael, and Howard Winant. 1994. *Racial Formation in the United States: From the 1960s to the 1990s*. New York: Routledge.

Ortner, Sherry B. 1984. "Theory in Anthropology since the Sixties." *Comparative Study in Society and History* 16: 126–166.

Painter, Nell Irvin. 2010. *The History of White People*. New York: W.W. Norton.

Pashukanis, Evgeny B. [1924] 2003. *The General Theory of Law and Marxism*. Translated by Barbara Einhorn. New Brunswick: Transaction.

Patriarca, Silvana. 1996. *Numbers and Nationhood: Writing Statistics in Nineteenth-Century Italy*. Cambridge: Cambridge University Press.

Patriarca, Silvana. 1998. "How Many Italies? Representing the South in Official Statistics." Pp. 77–98 in *Italy's "Southern Question": Orientalism in One Country*, edited by Jane Schneider. Oxford: Berg.

Pick, Daniel. 1989. *Faces of Degeneration: A European Disorder*. Cambridge: Cambridge University Press.

Pizza, Giovanna. 2012. "Second Nature: On Gramsci's Anthropology." *Anthropology and Medicine* 19: 95–106.

Platt, G. M., and R. H. Williams. 1997. "Religion, Ideology, and Electoral Politics." Pp. 221–236 in *Cultural Wars in American Politics*, edited by R. H. Williams. New York: Aldine de Gruyter.

Platt, G. M., and R. H. Williams. 2002. "Ideological Language and Social Movement Mobilization: A Sociolinguistic Analysis of Segregationists' Ideologies." *Sociological Theory* 20: 328–359.

Portelli, Alessandro. 2003. *The Order Has Been Carried Out: History, Memory, and Meaning of a Nazi Massacre in Rome*. New York: Palgrave.

Poster, Mark. 1981. "The Political Unconscious: Narrative as a Socially Symbolic Act by Fredric Jameson." *Nineteenth-Century Fiction* 36: 252–256.

Poulantzas, Nicos. 1973a. *Political Power and Social Classes*. London: Sheed and Ward.

Poulantzas, Nicos 1973b. "On Social Classes." *New Left Review* 78: 37–54.

Poulantzas, Nicos. 1975. *Classes in Contemporary Capitalism*. London: New Left Books.

Poulantzas, Nicos. 1978. *State, Power, Socialism*. London: Verso.

Pozzolini, Alberto. 1970. *Antonio Gramsci: An Introduction to His Thought*. Translated by Anne Showstack. London: Pluto.

Procacci, Giovanna. 1989. "Popular Protest and Labor Conflict in Italy 1915–1919." *Social History* 14: 31–58.

Public Broadcasting System (PBS). 1997. "Frontline: Interview with Kathleen Cleaver." Retrieved January 18, 2018 (https://www.pbs.org/wgbh/pages/frontline/shows/race/interviews/kcleaver.html).

Punter, David. 2001. "Review of *The Political Unconscious*." Pp. 362–364 in *Contemporary Literary Criticism Volume 142*, edited by Jeffrey W. Hunter. Farmington Hills: Gale.

Raboy, Marc. 1984. *Movements and Messages: Media and Radical Politics in Quebec*. Toronto: Between the Lines.

Reese, Stephen D. 2007. "The Framing Project: A Bridging Model for Media Research Revisited." *Journal of Communication* 57: 148–154.

Rehmann, Jan. 2013. *Theories of Ideology: The Powers of Alienation and Subjection*. Chicago: Haymarket.

Reinharz, Shulamit. 1992. *Feminist Methods in Social Research*. Oxford: Oxford University Press.

Reiter, Bernd, and Gladys L. Mitchell. 2010. "The New Politics of Race in Brazil." Pp. 1–33 in *Brazil's New Racial Politics*, edited by Bernd Reiter and Gladys L. Mitchell. London: Lynne Rienner.

Rodney, Walter. [1976] 2007. "The Angolan Question." Pp. 139–141 in *No Easy Victories: African Liberation and American Activists over a Half*

Century, 1950–2000, edited by William Minter, Gail Hovey, and Charles Cobb Jr. Trenton: Africa World Press.

Rodríguez, Dylan. 2011. "White Supremacy as Substructure: Toward a Genealogy of a Racial Animus, from 'Reconstruction' to 'Pacification.'" Pp. 47–76 in *State of White Supremacy*, edited by Moon-Kie Jung, João Costa Vargas, and Eduardo Bonilla-Silva. Stanford: Stanford University Press.

Rohlinger, Deana A., and David A. Snow. 2003. "Social Psychological Perspectives on Crowds and Social Movements." Pp. 503–527 in *Handbook of Social Psychology: Sociological Perspectives*, edited by John DeLamater. New York: Kluwer-Plenum.

Rojek, Chris. 2003. *Stuart Hall.* Cambridge: Polity Press.

Rosengarten, Frank. 2009. "The Contemporary Relevance of Gramsci's Views on Italy's 'Southern Question.'" Pp. 134–144 in *Perspectives on Gramsci: Politics, Culture and Social Theory*, edited by Joseph Francese. London: Routledge.

Rouse, Joseph. 2001. "Two Concepts of Practices." Pp. 198–208 in *The Practice Turn in Contemporary Theory*, edited by Theodore R. Schatzki, Karin Knorr Cetina, and Eike Von Savigny. London: Routledge.

Rucht, Dieter, and Friedhelm Neidhardt. 1999. "Methodological Issues in Collecting Protest Event Data: Units of Analysis, Sources and Sampling, Coding Problems. Pp. 65–89 in *Acts of Dissent*, edited by Dieter Rucht, Ruud Koopmans, and Friedhelm Neidhardt. New York: Rowman & Littlefield.

Rucht, Dieter, and Friedhelm Neidhardt. 2002. "Towards a 'Movement Society'? On the Possibilities of Institutionalizing Social Movements." *Social Movement Studies* 1: 7–30.

Said, Edward W. 1978. *Orientalism.* New York: Pantheon Books.

Said, Edward W. 1979. "Reflections on Recent American 'Left' Literary Criticism." *boundary 2* 8: 11–30.

Said, Edward. 1983. *The World, the Text, and the Critic.* Cambridge: Harvard University Press.

Said, Edward W. 1993. *Culture and Imperialism.* New York: Vintage Books.

Sassoon, Anne Showstack. 1987. *Gramsci's Politics.* 2nd ed. Minneapolis: University of Minnesota Press.

Schatzki, Theodore R. 2001. "Introduction: Practice Theory." Pp. 10–23 in *The Practice Turn in Contemporary Theory*, edited by Theodore R. Schatzki, Karin Knorr Cetina, and Eike Von Savigny. London: Routledge.

Schecter, Darrow. 1991. *Gramsci and the Theory of Industrial Democracy.* Brookfield: Gower.

Serge, Victor. [1926] 1979. *What Everyone Should Know about State Repression.* Translated by Judith White. London: New Park Publications.

Serge, Victor. [1933] 2014. *Midnight in the Century.* New York: New York Review of Books.

Sharpe, Christina. 2016. *In the Wake: On Blackness and Being.* Durham: Duke University Press.

Sitrin, Martina. 2006. *Horizontalism: Voices of Popular Power in Argentina.* Oakland: AK Press.

Skocpol, Theda. 1979. *States and Social Revolutions.* Cambridge: Cambridge University Press.

Smith, David Livingstone. 2012. *Less Than Human: Why We Demean, Enslave, and Exterminate Others.* New York: St. Martin's Griffin.

Snow, David A. 2004 "Framing Processes, Ideology, and Discursive Fields." Pp. 380–412 in *The Blackwell Companion to Social Movements*, edited by David A. Snow, Sarah A. Soule, and Hanspeter Kriesi. Oxford: Blackwell.

Snow, David A. 2008. "Elaborating the Discursive Contexts of Framing: Discursive Fields and Spaces." *Studies in Symbolic Interaction* 30: 3–28.

Snow, David, and Robert Benford. 1988. "Ideology, Frame Resonance, and Participant Mobilization." *International Social Movement Research* 1: 197–217.

Snow, David A., and Robert D. Benford. 1992. "Master Frames and Cycles of Protest." Pp. 133–155 in *Frontiers in Social Movement Theory*, edited by Aldon D. Morris and Carol McClurg Mueller. New Haven: Yale University Press.

Snow, David, and Robert Benford. 2000. "Clarifying the Relationship between Framing and Ideology in the Study of Social Movements: A Comment on Oliver and Johnston." *Mobilization* 5: 37–54.

Snow, David, and Catherine Corrigall-Brown. 2005. "Falling on Deaf Ears: Confronting the Prospect of Nonresonant Frames." Pp. 222–238 in *Rhyming Hope and History: Activists, Academics, and Social Movement Scholarship*, edited by David Croteau, William Hoynes, and Charlotte Ryan. Minneapolis: University of Minnesota Press.

Snow, David, and Scott C. Byrd. 2007. "Ideology, Framing Processes, and Islamic Terrorist Movements." *Mobilization* 12: 119–136.

Snow, David A., E. Burke Rochford Jr., Steven K. Worden, and Robert D. Benford. 1986. "Frame Alignment Processes, Micromobilization, and Movement Participation." *American Sociological Review* 51: 464–481.

Spivak, Gayatri Chakravorty. 1988. "Can the Subaltern Speak?" Pp. 271–313 in *Marxism and the Interpretation of Culture*, edited by Cary Nelson and Lawrence Grossberg. Urbana: University of Illinois Press.

Spriano, Paolo. 1975. *The Occupation of the Factories: Italy 1920*. London: Lawrence and Wishart.

Spriano, Paolo. 1979. *Antonio Gramsci and the Party: The Prison Years*. London: Lawrence and Wishart.

Stacey, Judith. 1997. "Disloyal to the Disciplines: A Feminist Trajectory in the Borderlands." Pp. 126–150 in *Feminist Sociology: Life Histories of a Movement*, edited by Barbara Laslett and Barry Thorne. New Brunswick: Rutgers University Press.

Staggenborg, Suzanne. 1989. "Stability and Innovation in the Women's Movement: A Comparison of Two Movement Organizations." *Social Problems* 36: 75–92.

Stauder, Jack. 1993. "The 'Relevance' of Anthropology to Colonialism and Imperialism." Pp. 408–427 in *The "Racial" Economy of Science*, edited by Sandra Harding. Bloomington: Indiana University Press.

Swidler, Ann. 1995. "Cultural Power and Social Movements." Pp. 25–40 in *Social Movements and Culture*, edited by Hank Johnston and Bert Klandermans. Minneapolis: University of Minnesota Press.

Tarrow, Sydney. 1992. "Mentalities, Political Cultures and Collective Action Frames: Constructing Meanings through Action." Pp. 174–202 in *Frontiers in Social Movement Theory*, edited by Aldon Morris and Carol McClurg Mueller. New Haven: Yale University Press.

Taylor, Verta. 1989. "Social Movement Continuity: The Women's Movement in Abeyance." *American Sociological Review* 54: 761–775.

Texier, Jacques. 1979. "Gramsci, Theoretician of the Superstructures." Pp. 48–79 in *Gramsci and Marxist Theory*, edited by Chantal Mouffe. London: Routledge and Kegan Paul.

Therborn, Goran. 1985. *Science, Class and Society: On the Formation of Sociology and Historical Materialism*. London: Routledge.

Thistle, Susan. 2000. "The Trouble with Modernity: Gender and the Remaking of Social Theory." *Sociological Theory* 18: 275–289.

Thomas, Peter D. 2009. *The Gramscian Moment: Philosophy, Hegemony and Marxism*. Leiden: Brill Academic.

Thomas, Peter D. 2013. "Hegemony, Passive Revolution, and the Modern Prince." *Thesis Eleven* 117: 20–39.

Thomas, Peter D. 2014. "Historical Materialism at Sixteen: An Interview with Peter D. Thomas." *Jacobin*, May 10. Retrieved April 27, 2017

(https://www.jacobinmag.com/2014/05/historical-materia
lism-at-sixteen/).

Thompson, A. K. 2017. "The Work of Violence in the Age of Repressive
Desublimation." Pp. 159–175 in *The Great Refusal: Herbert Marcuse
and Contemporary Social Movements*, edited by Andrew T. Lamas, Todd
Wolfson, and Peter N. Funke. Philadelphia: Temple University Press.

Tombari, Stephanie L. 2010. "Click if You Care: Frame Alignment Processes
in Anti-Poverty Movement Websites." *Canadian Journal of Applied
Research* 1: 48–67.

Urbinati, Nadia. 1998a. "The Souths of Antonio Gramsci and the Concept of
Hegemony." Pp. 135–156 in *Italy's "Southern Question": Orientalism in
One Country*, edited by Jane Schneider. Oxford: Berg.

Urbinati, Nadia. 1998b. "From Periphery to Modernity: Antonio Gramsci's
Theory of Subordination and Hegemony." *Political Theory* 26: 370–391.

Van den Brink, Margo, Kirsten Kuipers, and Arnoud Lagendijk. 2005.
"Framing Regionalisation: How a Dutch Environmental Organization
Puts the Concept of Sustainability into Practice through Frame
Alignment." Pp. 100–101 in *Sustainable Regions: Making Regions
Work*, edited by Sally Hardy, Lisa Bibby-Larsen, and Frankie Freeland.
Seaford: Regional Studies Association.

Van Deusen, David, and Xavier Massot. 2010. *The Black Bloc Papers: An
Anthology of Primary Texts from the North American Anarchist Black Bloc,
1988–2005*. Shawnee Mission: Breaking Glass Press.

Verdicchio, Pasquale. 1995. "Introduction." Pp. 7–26 in *The Southern
Question*, translated by Pasquale Verdicchio. West Lafayette: Bordighera.

Verschuren, Piet, and Hans Doorewaard. 2005. *Designing a Research Project*.
Utrecht: LEMMA.

Waldram, Hannah. 2013. "Brazil Protests Continue as Story Develops over
Social Media." *The Guardian*, June 21, accessed July 6, 2018 (https://
www.theguardian.com/world/2013/jun/21/brazil-protest-social-media).

Walton, Peter, and Stuart Hall (eds.). 1972. *Situating Marx*. London: Human
Context Books.

West, Cornel. 1993. "Race and Social Theory." Pp. 251–270 in *Keeping Faith:
Philosophy and Race in America*. New York: Routledge.

Westby, David L. 2002. "Strategic Imperative, Ideology, and Frame."
Mobilization 7: 287–304.

Williams, Gwyn. 1975. *Proletarian Order: Antonio Gramsci, Factory Councils
and the Origins of Italian Communism, 1911–1921*. London: Pluto
Press.

Williams, Raymond 1963. *Culture and Society 1780–1950*. Harmondsworth: Pelican.

Williams, Raymond. 1977. *Marxism and Literature*. Oxford: Oxford University Press.

Williams, Rhys H. 1999. "Ideology, Culture, and the Dynamics of Collective Action." *Quarterly Journal of Ideology* 22: 31–41.

Williams, Rhys H., and Jeffery Neal Blackburn. 1996. "Many Are Called but Few Obey: Ideological Commitment and Activism in Operation Rescue." Pp. 167–85 in *Disruptive Religions: The Forces of Faith in Social Movement Activism*, edited by Christian Smith. London: Routledge.

Wilson, S. 1979. "Exploration of the Usefulness of Case Study Evaluations." *Evaluation Quarterly* 3: 446–459.

Wolf, Kerrin C. 2013. "Booking Students: An Analysis of School Arrests and Court Outcomes." *Northwestern Journal of Law and Social Policy* 9: 58–86.

Zald, Mayer N. 1996. "Culture, Ideology, and Strategic Framing." Pp. 261–274 in *Comparative Perspectives on Social Movements*, edited by Doug McAdam, John D. McCarthy, and Mayer N. Zald. Cambridge: Cambridge University Press.

Zald, Mayer N. 2000a. "Ideologically Structured Action." *Mobilization* 5: 1–16.

Zald, Mayer N. 2000b. "New Paradigm? Nah! New Agenda? I Hope So." *Mobilization* 5: 31–36.

Zamora, Daniel. 2014. "Can We Criticize Foucault?" *Jacobin*, December 14. Retrieved April 21, 2016 (https://www.jacobinmag.com/2014/12/foucault-interview/).

Zamora, Daniel, and Michael C. Behrent (eds.). 2015. *Foucault and Neoliberalism*. London: Polity.

Zene, Cosimo. 2011. "Self-Consciousness of the Dalits as 'Subalterns': Reflections on Gramsci in South Asia." *Rethinking Marxism* 23: 83–99.

Zuckert, Catherine H. 2011. *Political Philosophy in the Twenty-First Century*. Cambridge: Cambridge University Press.

INDEX

alter-globalization movement, 13
Althusser, Louis, 31, 43, 72, 103, 166, 175, 176, 182, 203
Articulation, 26, 28, 31, 48, 97, 127, 140, 141, 143, 160, 161, 183, 196, 197
Autonomen (German), 13
Autonomia (Italian), 13
Autonomy, 6, 116, 120, 122, 123, 188–190
Avanti!, 65

Bakhtin, Mikhail, 31
Benford, Robert, 110, 206
Bettoni, Camilla, 64
Biennio Rosso, 59, 60, 69, 126, 133, 147, 152–155, 158
Black Panther Party, 114
Bloch, Ernst, 198
Bobbio, Norberto, 119
Bonilla-Silva, Eduardo, 151, 161, 163, 164, 170, 173, 177, 183–186
Bordiga, Amadeo, 81, 115
Bracey, Glenn E., 168, 200
Brennan, Timothy, 31–33, 43, 83, 199
Buchez, Philippe, 72
Buci-Glucksmann, Christine, 42, 44, 48, 50, 55, 58, 198
Bundy, Ammon, 163
Bundy, Cliven, 163
Byrd, James Jr., 186

Cammett, John M., 152, 157
Carlucci, Alessandro, 58, 59, 62, 64, 203
Catholicism, 146, 209
Catholic humanism, 20, 147, 149, 151, 152, 154
Catholic modernization movement, 9, 130, 147, 152, 154, 209
centralism, 36, 46
  bureaucratic, 46
  democratic, 36, 46
Certeau, Michel de, 32
Charlottesville, VA, 192
Christian Democratic Party, 152
class, 2, 8, 10, 19, 22, 25, 26, 29, 31–33, 37, 40, 43, 47, 48, 52, 53, 62, 64, 65, 66, 84, 90, 95, 96, 99, 116, 118, 120, 126, 131, 132, 135–137, 140, 141, 143, 158, 160, 170, 178, 180, 182, 193
Clausewitz, Carl von, 35
Cleaver, Kathleen, 114, 117
collective memory, 2, 20, 28, 74, 90, 101, 105, 113, 122, 124, 126
collective will, 48, 55
colorblind racism, 9, 22, 140, 151, 163–171, 173–177, 182–184, 190
commune, 63, 64
conjuncture, 26, 30, 31, 45, 51, 52,

www.ingramcontent.com/pod-product-compliance
Lightning Source LLC
Chambersburg PA
CBHW030402270326
41926CB00009B/1232